Days of Infamy

Contents

Copyright © 1999 A&E Television Networks and Disney Enterprises, Inc.

Days of Infamy: Military Blunders of the 20th Century is largely based on the TV series, *Military Blunders*, copyright © *1999* Nugus/Martin Productions Limited.

The photographs reproduced in this book were supplied by The Imperial War Museum—London, and Hulton Getty Images to Nugus/Martin Productions Limited for their TV series, *Military Blunders*. In addition the producers gratefully acknowledge the assistance afforded them by The National Archives in Washington, D.C.

Library of Congress Cataloging-in-Publication Data

Coffey, Michael
    Days of infamy : military blunders of the 20th century / by
Michael Coffey ; introduction by Mike Wallace. — 1st ed.
        p.   cm.
    ISBN 0-7868-6556-3
    1. Military history, Modern—20th century.   2. Errors.   I. Title.
D431.C57   1999
355'.009'04—dc21   99-30839
                                                                        CIP

Book design by Richard Oriolo

FIRST EDITION

1   3   5   7   9   10   8   6   4   2

DAYS OF INFAMY

Military Blunders of the 20th Century

MICHAEL COFFEY

Introduction by Mike Wallace

HYPERION

New York

Part V

SENDING HITLER HOME, AND TOJO, TOO— BRINGING WORLD WAR II TO AN END

Part VI

OF COLD WARS AND HOLY WARS— SUPERPOWER STANDOFFS AND DESERT STORMS

Acknowledgments

I MUST FIRST AND FOREMOST ACKNOWLEDGE the talented producers of the documentary television program *Military Blunders*, to which this book is a humble companion. Producers Philip Nugus and Jonathan Martin conceived of the shape and scope of just how the blunders of this century, small and large, should be presented. Though this book's shape and scope is quite independent of their program's, I did rely to a considerable extent upon the story lines and draft scripts they provided for many of the episodes covered herein. The writer on the film project, Charles Messenger, provided expert narratives and the fruits of dogged research, and I am much indebted to him. I must also thank Jonathan Paisner, manager of consumer product development at the History Channel, for his assistance throughout the writing of this book.

In researching the many historical and military events in the pages that follow, I relied upon a few major texts, each of which proved masterful at summarizing, analyzing, and bringing fresh light to these magnificent stories of our century. Specifically, I am referring to Martin Gilbert's brilliant work *The First World War: A Complete History* (New York: Henry Holt, 1994); John Keegan's stirring *The Second World War* (New York: Viking Penguin, 1990), and Martin Walker's extraordinary *The Cold War* (New York:

Henry Holt, 1993). For the connections between the French experience at Dien Bien Phu and the Americans' experience at Khesanh and throughout the Tet Offensive, I relied upon Stanley Karnow's analyis in his lucid *Vietnam: A History* (New York: Penguin, 1983). For background on much of the seagoing exploits mentioned in the text, I relied upon Lincoln Paine's exhaustive *Ships of the World: An Historical Encyclopedia* (Boston: Houghton Mifflin, 1997). And for ciphering out exact dates and movements of troops in the many conflicts detailed herein, I am indebted to the monumental *Harper Encyclopedia of Military History: From 3500 B.C. to the Present*, 4th ed., by R. Ernest Dupuy and Trevor N. Dupuy (New York: HarperCollins, 1993). I must thank them all for the grand achievements of their works, and their example of how exhaustive one must be to get things right, which, when writing about war, is no easy task. I hasten to add that any errors of fact or interpretation in this volume I claim as my own.

I must also thank my editor at Hyperion, Maureen O'Brien, who had sufficient faith in both the project and me to bring *Days of Infamy* to fruition. Last, I thank my wife and partner, Jenny Doctorow, who once again has proven that no book is written alone.

Introduction

ALONG WITH MILLIONS OF YOU around the world I am, plain and simple, a sucker for war stories. So from the moment I began reading Michael Coffey's *Days of Infamy: Military Blunders of the 20th Century*, I was fascinated. How can you fail to be caught up in tales entitled "Disaster at Jutland," "Mutiny in the Trenches," and "German Hesitation at Dunkirk"?

As to my bona fides to write about this, I'm afraid my military background is lamentably limited, but I take vicarious consolation in the trials and tribulations of others who have actually come under fire in the heat of the battle or have suffered at the hands of incompetent or misguided commanders. During the Second World War, I served as a communications officer lieutenant junior grade in the submarine force of the Seventh Fleet, but only infrequently did I submerge. Instead, I pushed back and forth what we called encoding strips, and I operated top-secret ECM machines in encoding and decoding rooms, ashore at SUBPAC headquarters in Pearl Harbor and later aboard the submarine tender USS *Anthedon* in Fremantle, West Australia, and later at Subic Bay in the Philippines. Yearning for action but effectively out of harm's way, we communicators sent top secret messages, dictated by the submarine fleet's commanders to their "boats," as the subs were called, out on war patrol, and we got encoded messages back, telling us how many Japanese MARUs our comrades had come upon and sent to the bottom, or how many of their own torpedoes had gone astray. Occasionally, seasick or not, we got to ride one of these subs that had been tied up alongside our USS *Anthedon* for repair and refit after a war patrol, so that the resourceful technicians and mechanics aboard our tender could make them properly seaworthy again; we "stay behinders" also got to be submarine sailors for a day or two at a time when we took the refurbished vessels to sea to make sure everything aboard was working properly.

Communications gear was my alleged specialty, actually taken charge of by my chief warrant officer who—unlike me—knew what he was doing; then we gave the subs back to the guys who braved the South China Sea and environs in search of anything big and Japanese afloat.

Since then, a half century ago, I've devoted myself—in things military—mainly to reporting disasters and defaults, scandals and scurrility. An occasional victory, too, of course, although I confess it's somehow more satisfying for a reporter to dig down and find out where things went wrong and why.

Example: Vietnam. Back in 1984 at *CBS Reports* we came across a story alleging that General William Westmoreland, Supreme Commander of United States troops in Vietnam, had "cooked the books" in 1967–68; he had purposefully underestimated the number of enemy troops the U.S. was facing in the field. Why? Because Americans at home were tiring finally of a war that was taking too many American lives, too much American treasure, a war many Americans felt we shouldn't have gotten bogged down in to begin with.

Now, if ordinarily a combat general might be tempted to inflate the huge hordes of enemy he and his troops had to confront, Westy simply read tens and tens of thousands out of the enemy order of battle. He altered it in order to reassure Americans that we'd achieved the "crossover point," which meant our troops were finally killing more of the enemy than could be sent down the Ho Chi Minh trail as replacements. But it was a fiction. A CIA man by the name of Sam Adams went out to Vietnam from Washington to find the truth. He studied captured enemy documents, talked to U.S. Army intelligence officers in the combat areas, and came to the conclusion that our U.S. troops were facing not the mere 300,000 enemy listed officially in reports out of the MACV Command, but instead a number closer to 600,000. That estimate took into account North Vietnamese regulars, Vietcong, guerrilla fighters, and villagers who possessed all manner of means to kill Americans. And so Sam Adams reported that, far from perceiving "the light at the end of the tunnel" that General Westmoreland had begun to see, he was certain we were heading into even deeper trouble.

Then along came Tet in January 1968, and an enemy offensive the fury and determination of which shocked the U.S. Embassy in Saigon and Americans at home. There is still controversy about who did what to whom in that series of battles, in which over 100 South Vietnamese cities were attacked, but there is no doubt whatsoever about its impact on American reporters, surprised by the number of enemy troops in action across the length and breadth of the country. About that time Walter Cronkite went out to Vietnam to take a look and came to the conclusion that we were involved in an endless stalemate, and he said as much to Americans on his *CBS Evening News*, suggesting we should cut the best deal we could and get out of Vietnam. Lyndon Johnson heard Walter, and told folks close to him that if he had lost Cronkite, he'd probably lost the support of the country. And that, of course, was the beginning of the long journey to the end of our Vietnam adventure.

It was a huge blunder to begin with because our leaders in the United States—beginning with JFK—failed to understand the Vietnamese revolution, sparked by the determined and single-minded Ho Chi Minh and led by the brilliant General Giap. They'd beaten the French, and now they and their cohorts took the superpower USA and cut them down to size.

The U.S. blunder, of course, was hardly Westmoreland's or Johnson's alone. From John F. Kennedy to Lyndon Johnson to Richard Nixon to almost all of their aides and advisers, civilian and military, in the 1960s and 1970s there was insufficient understanding of what they had gotten America into. Americans were told that if we were to lose to communism in Southeast Asia, Vietnam's neighbors, too, would fall like "dominoes" before the communist onslaught. South Korea, Thailand, Malaysia would go, and who knows what other countries would follow.

Well, America lost the war, but those "dominoes" are now bastions of capitalism in Southeast Asia. Vietnam's communists won the war, but that country's economy is still struggling, trying to climb out of poverty and despair, aiming to mimic the success of the "dominoes" that didn't fall after all.

Following our broadcast of the *CBS Reports* in 1982, General Westmoreland sued CBS for libel, another blunder. He named me in his suit along with Sam Adams and various others. But after five long months in a federal courtroom, the general withdrew his lawsuit, paid his own legal tab (aided by his supporters), and CBS News didn't have to retract a single word of our broadcast.

Another blunder to which I was eyewitness: the Six Day War in the Middle East. In June 1967, Egypt, Syria, and Iraq decided to take on the upstart Israelis, who they believed had been getting too big for their britches. The Arab leaders felt something had to be done, and they wanted the King of Jordan to help. Perhaps, they thought, the Arabs could drive the Israelis into the sea.

Of course, King Hussein had none of the wealth and surely not the force of arms possessed by his Arab big brothers. He couldn't make up his mind as to what to do, so Egyptian leader Gamel Abdel Nasser made up his mind for him. After the Israelis had loosed their lightning air strike on the unsuspecting Egyptians on the first day of the war, stunning their air force and putting countless planes out of action, Nasser got on the wire with King Hussein.

Of course, this was before the days of satellite pictures and live reporting from the battlefield, so Hussein had no way of knowing for sure how much damage the Egyptians had incurred. And Nasser was not about to tell him the truth. Instead, he persuaded Jordan's king that stories of Egyptian losses had been fabricated by the Israelis, and that Hussein should get on the bandwagon and share in the victory and the spoils that were to come. The king bought Nasser's line and sent his crack tanks into action on the West Bank, moving in the direction of Israel.

But the Israeli air force still had enough planes to go after Hussein's tanks, which turned out to be sitting ducks. I'll never forget the pictures I saw in Israel at the time: strategically placed cannon salvoes sent down the back of innumerable Jordanian tank turrets with stunning precision. It was a slaughter. King Hussein had made a huge bet at Nasser's urging, and he lost hugely. He lost the West Bank, lost the part of Jerusalem that was his seat of government. It took him and his small legions years to recover.

Of course, kings and presidents, dictators and prime ministers, warlords and bureaucrats, have stumbled and miscalculated from the beginning of time and have fallen from power as a consequence. But the men—and now the women—under their command have done more than forfeit power, they've lost their lives.

War, bloody war, can sometimes give a nation and its people a sense of purpose; acts of courage committed in battle can be ennobling; troops can bond in their common cause, sometimes in common sacrifice. And for some, beyond the blood and bone and gristle and horror, comes a kind of glamour, a test of will, a commitment felt by few of us in our lifetimes.

But all that can quickly turn to ashes when we learn, as you will as you read on, what blunders by fallible commanders, military and civilian, can do to turn victory's promise into defeat's reality. And so, get ready to embark on some riveting cautionary tales.

—MIKE WALLACE

Part I

Europe Loses Its Way—

The First World War from

Sarajevo to Versailles

Can a war be started by a driver taking a wrong turn? It seems a facetious question, even if more than a few marriages have edged toward disaster for no grander reason. More seriously, though, historians and philosophers have long been fascinated by the mysterious chain links of causality, wondering just how large an outcome can be triggered by how small a cause. The First World War, perhaps, was inevitable. It could claim a thousand causes; and for every possible cause that didn't survive historical scrutiny, there would be another willing volunteer.

As the nineteenth century became the twentieth, Europe was a roily community dominated by monarchies and growing increasingly unstable. The industrializing economies were looking increasingly abroad to find natural resources. Such a situation encourages opportunism and military adventurism. But still, the event that started the world's first world war, the assassination of an Austrian prince, seems so small in comparison to the five horrid years of conflict that followed, that one naturally prefers to see it as a blunder, in order to maintain the fantasy that war is not inevitable, that it requires a spark. After all, the refusal to see war as inevitable once we'd entered the nuclear age proved to be the key to the world's survival.

World War I took an enormous toll on mankind. Nearly eight million soldiers were killed, and as many civilians. Three very old monarchies—Imperial Russia, the Ottoman Empire, and the dual monarchy of Austria-Hungary—would disappear. The war was filled with heroism and courage and insanity, like all wars, and marked by many, many mistakes that would cost men their lives. From the killing of the archduke by 19-year-old Gavrilo Princip to the disastrous campaign by Allied forces in Gallipoli to the sinking of the *Lusitania*, with all those civilians on board, and on to the ill-conceived naval engagements at Jutland to the senseless slaughter of men in the trenches of France, and through so many stories too countless to detail in a book of this size, this Great War left its mark on what Man thinks of himself. It became, for a time, a dark and defining moment for world culture, or did so for at least the vast part of the world that was touched by its brutal demands. But in the end, when peace had been achieved, an irrepressible belligerence and dearth of contrition combined to make of the treaty that ended the war grounds for another conflict, a war that would reduce what had been known, with quaint optimism, as the Great War, into just the first in a series that as yet has not ended.

The Assassination of the Archduke

STANDING AT THE VERY LIP of the new century, a young Winston Churchill looked ahead and saw a violent future. "The wars of peoples," he predicted, "will be more terrible than those of kings." At the time—May 1901—Churchill was a Conservative member of Parliament serving in the House of Commons, and no stranger to war: he had experienced fighting on the British side in India, in the Sudan and in South Africa during the Boer War just a few years back.

As always, tensions between traditional rivals threatened to erupt into conflict. France was still smarting over its surrender of its eastern provinces of Alsace and Lorraine to Germany after their war of 1870. Germany, amassing a large navy while building up its army as well, scowled disapprovingly at the expansionist ambitions of Imperial Russia. The Hapsburg empire of Austria and Hungary was trembling with its own internal convulsions, as the Slavs to the south, mostly Serbian, agitated for more direct access to the Adriatic, while Germany promised to support the dual monarchy of Austria-Hungary in whatever it did and Russia intimated it would unite behind the various Slavic peoples, whether independent states like Serbia or parts of the Hapsburg empire. And the Ottoman Empire had long-standing designs of its own to push northward, strategizing with Germany, agitating Russia.

Such tensions were commonplace. Ancient, time-honored disputes marked the very character of nations and their people. What Churchill foresaw, however, was that in the new century an escalation of diplomatic disputes into military conflicts promised death and destruction on an unprecedented scale. The wars of horses and wagons and pikes would give way to a war of incendiary devices, chemical weapons, heavy cannon, air raids, and men floating perilously in engagements at sea. The threat to human life that these territorial and racial differences now posed was enormous. How right he would be.

Still, the very forces that could escalate the level of warfare and enormously raise the stakes—economic might and industrial capacity—were the very forces that an optimist might hope would mitigate against warmongering. In much of Europe, and certainly in Britain, France, Germany, Austria, as well as in Russia, prosperity and profits seemed to counsel peace. What full-scale war might do to both corporate interests and government interests was hard to predict with any precision, but surely the effects would be dire.

As the century moved on, war by no means seemed inevitable. There was always the hope that "family ties" would find a way to sort out differences. Would Queen Victoria's grandson, the German Kaiser Wilhelm II, risk war with Britain, or with his cousin by marriage, Tsar Nicholas of Russia? Would the Kaiser allow his sister's husband, the King of Greece, to endanger himself by getting into a petty dispute with the Serbians?

As Tolstoy wrote in *Anna Karenina*, "Happy families are all alike, [but] every unhappy family is unhappy in its own way." And this unhappy European family of related royalty was unhappy in its own very complicated ways. Although in hindsight it appears that the tension that held Europe in its grip necessarily would have to have found some violent resolution, we can also look back at the very start of the First World War, in August 1914, and wonder what would have happened if a driver had just asked for directions to the hospital in Sarajevo. We will never know.

A long-standing dispute concerned access to the Adriatic coastline. In fact, so long-standing is that dispute that at century's end, 85 years later, the NATO alliance of nations is sending bombing sorties across the Adriatic, from Italy, into what is now Yugoslavia, in an attempt to bring resolution to an ethnic conflict between Serbs and Albanians. Back in 1912, the players were somewhat different, but the atmosphere eerily familiar. Italy had defeated Turkey in the Italo-Turkish War, a struggle for borders and regional domination. Italy's more specific ambition was to conquer Libya in order to get a colonial presence in Africa. After all, France had a formidable colonial empire there, in Algeria and Tunisia. The Italians bombed Tripoli and then invaded it against only token Turkish resistance. Italy also seized the Dodacanese Islands in the Mediterranean. At the Treaty of Ouchy in October 1912, Turkey ceded Libya and the islands to Italy.

With Turkey reeling from the disgrace and the defeat, the Balkan Wars began. The "Balkan League," consisting of Greece, Bulgaria, and Serbia, sought to eliminate Turkish power in the Balkans and increase their own territories. Eight months of skirmishing later, the Treaty of London took all of Turkey's European possessions but two peninsulas (one of them being Gallipoli). The victorious combatants squabbled over the disposition of the spoils, so much so that they had to have a Second Balkan War among themselves to try to get it right. Serbia got what it wanted—Albania, on the Adriatic coast. But not for long.

Unfortunately for the Serbs, Austria-Hungary looked on the Serbian annexing of Albania as an occupation, and one that must be repulsed. In October 1913 the Austrians issued an ultimatum, demanding that the Serbs evacuate Albania within eight days. The Triple Entente powers—that is, France, Britain, and Russia—were not happy that Austria had seen fit to get involved. As one British diplomat, Eyre Crowe, put it: "Austria has broken loose from the concert of Powers in order to seek a solution single-handed of a question hitherto treated as concerning all Powers." Crowe's remark is inaccurate in one respect: Austria did not act alone. Kaiser Wilhelm had promised his support of the Austrian action. The Serbs complied. And, it might be said, a fuse had been lit.

Or, it might be also be said that a lightbulb went on, at least for the Germans. They sensed that the continuing Serbian-Austrian conflict might very well bring Russia onto the scene, for the Russians maintained (and do to this day) a concern for Slavic peoples, including the Serbs. If Russia could be drawn in, and drawn in quickly, the Germans, backing Austria, could deliver punishing blows to its age-old eastern nemesis, first cousins be damned. Behind the scenes, during the spring and summer of 1914, the Kaiser worked on Austrian Emperor Franz Josef, then 83 years old, and on Franz Josef's heir apparent, his 50-year-old grand-nephew, the Archduke Franz Ferdinand, to precipitate a conflict.

The Kaiser congratulated them for their triumph in forcing the Serbians to back down; he gave them diplomatic assurances that no "restraining advice" would be forthcoming on the part of Germany. After all, Franz Josef had been on the throne for 72 years, longer than any previous European sovereign had held royal authority. And the Kaiser was pleased to hear that Franz Josef and the Archduke both were annoyed by "the continuing Russification of Galicia," an eastern Austrian province.

In June 1914, the Kaiser spent a weekend with the Archduke, just outside Prague. They hunted and dined, but also cleverly pressed their agendas. The Kaiser found occasion to express his admiration of the Hungarian prime minister, knowing that this would rile, and perhaps threaten, the Archduke, who did not care for Hungarians at all, much less the prime minister. The Archduke had publicly stated his disapproval of what he felt was the excessive Hungarian influence in his kingdom. In fact, when and if Franz Ferdinand ascended to the throne, he planned on lessening Hungarian clout and strengthening that of the non-Hungarian minorities, meaning the Serbs, Croats, and Slovaks. For the time being, however, the Archduke was unhappy with the trouble being stirred up by the Serbs, still seething after having to withdraw from Albania. The Kaiser assured Franz Ferdinand that Germany would back him in whatever had to be done, and told him not to worry about the Russian army. They were not ready for war, he said. But of course, that was just the point for the clever Kaiser, who would like nothing more than to provoke into conflict an unready foe.

Two weeks later, on June 28, 1914, the Archduke and his wife were on a state visit to the Bosnian capital of Sarajevo. It was not a good day to visit.

In the streets of Sarajevo that day were six conspirators, all determined to free Bosnia from the Hapsburg Empire and to reunite with the cowed yet still independent Serbia. And for many in the streets of Sarajevo it was a day of solemn memories, since it was also Serbia's National Day, commemorating the countrymen lost at the Battle of Kosovo in the year 1389. That's a long time to remember, and it was surely a sign of arrogance on the part of the Archduke to have forgotten that there might be better days to tool around in his open car.

The Archduke and his wife were on their way to visit the

Bosnian governor at his residence, and right away things turned bad. A bomb was thrown at the elegant archducal car; it banged off the side door before exploding. When it did, it left the Archduke and wife unharmed but injured two officers in the next car. The Archduke saw to it that his officers were taken to the hospital and then ordered his driver to continue to city hall. Unfazed, Franz Ferdinand derided the assembled with "So you welcome your guests with bombs?" After a formal ceremony, he asked his driver, whose name was Franz Urban, to proceed to the hospital so that he could visit the two injured officers.

With this part of the state visit unscheduled, Franz Urban had no route mapped out to the hospital. Trusting that he could find his way based on a previous stay in Sarajevo, Urban set out from city hall with his royal passengers. The Archduke, rather impatient with the traffic and the warm weather, for which he was considerably overdressed, pressed Urban to hurry. A wrong turn down a narrow street irked him even more. When Urban realized his mistake, he was down a street so narrow that he had to back out slowly. Standing there in the small street, having visited a café to cheer his sunken spirits, was one of the six Serb conspirators, a 19-year-old named Gavrilo Princip. He had missed his chance earlier at sighting the Archduke, and he knew of the bomb that had missed its target. But there was the Archduke, in an open car, 30 feet away, moving slowly in reverse. And there was the gun in Princip's hand. He fired two shots.

Franz Urban finally got the car turned around. Now he had a more urgent reason to find his way to the hospital, not to visit the wounded, but to deliver them. But the Archduke and his wife bled to death in the car. There was to be much more bleeding.

· · ·

Austria-Hungary declared war against Serbia immediately. Within the next month, Russia ordered a mobilization, whereupon Germany declared war against Russia and, following an attack plan that had been finely honed, moved through Luxembourg and Belgium and into France and declared war there. Great Britain then declared war on Germany, and Austria-Hungary declared war on Russia. Italy waited to see which side would gain the upper hand, while the U.S. would not get involved for another three years. Europe, like Franz Urban, had clearly lost its way, and history took a wrong turn into world war.

Disaster in the
Dardanelles and Gallipoli

DURING THE LAST HALF OF 1914, after the flurry of declarations of war, there was no mistaking what was going on: it
was total war. Churchill's prediction that the wars of "peoples"
·would be more terrible than the wars of kings was proving prescient. Unprecedented levels of troop mobilization, the transition of a
churning industrial economy into a fierce wartime industry, and the
application of sophisticated attack and defense strategies brought
conflict to a new level. The Germans pursued their crafty Schlieffen
Plan, a war strategy evolved at the turn of the century by then chief
of the German General Staff Alfred von Schlieffen. Its aim was to
hold the plodding Russian army in check using as little force as
necessary, and to deploy 90 percent of German manpower in the
West with the immediate goal of crushing France. A variety of
diversions were planned to draw the French into mountainous terrain to battle for their beloved Alsace-Lorraine region on the eastern
border, and then drive around to the north and west and overrun
Paris.

There is no lack of blunders in any hour of any war. The
Germans improvised on von Schlieffen's plan in countless ways,
diluting its effectiveness. Still, the German army moved through
Belgium and Luxembourg into France; the resistance, as expected,

was fierce, with battles being fought that have come to define the First World War's grimmest features. The fighting at Ypres, the bombarding of Antwerp, and worst of all, the Battle of the Marne, the river extending eastward from Paris along which the Germans, the French, and the British Expeditionary forces fought heroically for six days, are forever burned into the landscape of twentieth-century history. At the Marne, though the battle was tactically inconclusive, it was an Allied strategic victory of sorts, thanks to the brilliant scheming of French General Joseph Joffre, who managed to build an effective counterattack upon the ruins of another failed plan. Casualties were heavy, with more than a million men killed, wounded, or captured.

On the Eastern front, at the other end of the Schlieffen Plan, there was carnage aplenty, too. And more blunders. The Germans repeatedly managed to encircle divisions of the Russian Army in August and on through September, as the Russians suffered from an appalling lack of preparedness, just as the Germans had figured.

Elsewhere, the Austrians were pursuing their revenge against the countrymen of Gavrilo Princip. They bombarded Belgrade, and 200,000 troops invaded Serbia, but did not have an easy go of it. In fact, the dogged Serbs repulsed the Austrian army in early December at the Battle of Kolubra, incurring casualties of more than 50 percent.

In Poland, both Austrian and German forces pounded the Russians in the eastern Polish province of Galicia. As the year 1914 drew to a close, it appeared that the results of the Schlieffen Plan were mixed. Fighting was still fierce and the outcome far from certain in France, but in Russia it seemed to be only a matter of time before there was a complete victory by the Austrian-German forces. With Turkey having declared war on the Allies, and sitting upon both shores along the only way to get support to the Russians from the Mediterranean to the Black Sea, things looked grim indeed. The Allies decided they must fight for that supply route for the sake of their comrades. They must fight for the Dardanelles Strait and the Gallipoli Peninsula. To do so would mean an amphibious invasion. And it would lead to one of the most indelible blunders of World War I.

In the war to come, the war that no one in "The Great War" of World War I thought *would* ever come, there would be widespread use of amphibious operations to land troops on hostile shores. It became a dominant feature of World War II in both Europe and the Pacific. But World War I would see only one such operation—now known as the Gallipoli campaign. From its outcome, it is hard to believe that another generation would ever have the courage to launch one.

When the Ottoman Empire entered the war on the side of Germany and Austria-Hungary in October 1914, Turkish troops were immediately deployed to attack across their common border with Russia in the Caucasus. The Russians were pushed back immediately. To relieve the Turkish pressure, they asked the Western Allies to make a "demonstration" against Turkey.

The British initially recommended a purely naval operation. The French agreed. The target was to be the forts in the Dardanelles which guarded the narrows separating the Aegean Sea from the Sea of Marmora. The operation was begun by the combined British and French Mediterranean fleets on February 18, 1915. After two days' bombardment, and having knocked out most of the forts, the ships withdrew. This in itself was a mistake, for any hope of using the element of surprise was lost, since an air attack by sea clearly signals that a larger effort is to come, and the Ottoman Army began to prepare for any eventuality, including invasion.

Back in Britain, government disappointment that decisive

victory had not been gained by the end of 1914 sparked a debate over what to do next. The Easterners in the cabinet, as they were called because of their concern about German ambitions on the Eastern Front, were led by Winston Churchill, who wanted to open a second front in the Mediterranean. Perhaps more important, Churchill felt that such a thrust might divert German firepower and manpower in France, and help break the deadlock there. The Westerners, on the other hand, felt that the major German threat was in the West, in France. The debate was about which front to defend first.

The Easterners, that is, Churchill, won out. The plan was for the Allies to make an amphibious landing in the Dardanelles, opening a way for the British Navy to move and capture Constantinople, and thereby force Turkey out of the war. They would then thrust northward up through the Balkans and invade Austria-Hungary. At the very least, the supply route to the beleaguered Russians would be protected. And just possibly, the German-Austrian forces would have to be redeployed from France, and the stalemate there would end, perhaps bringing a negotiated end to the war.

The camp in opposition to Churchill continued to dissent against the Gallipoli plan, arguing that the bulk of the German Army was already in France, and that was where the war would be won or lost. To draw troops away from there would merely prolong the conflict.

In spite of these objections, the Allies decided to deploy troops in the Dardanelles, but they would become an invading amphibious force only if the fleet found itself unable to force its way through the Narrows and capture Constantinople on its own.

In mid-March 1915, the first contingent of troops was sent from Britain and France to Egypt. Others, notably the Australian and New Zealand Army Corps—the Anzacs—were already protecting Egypt against Turkish attack. A few months earlier, so low was the British estimation of Turkish resistance that Lord Kitchener felt that the Anzacs alone would be sufficient to do the job. But General Sir Ian Hamilton, appointed to command the expedition, was a little more cautious. He was considered Britain's most intellectual soldier, with experience in numerous colonial campaigns. He arrived in Egypt on March 24.

Before assembling an Anglo-French ground attack force, the British and French navies, intent on forcing the Narrows on their own, had already returned there on March 18 to do more shelling and to try to run the Narrows, as planned. The shelling compounded the earlier Allied blunder of having signaled their intent with bombing. By now the Turks were dug in and ready. In fact, they had fortified the positions that had been bombed months before, and had laid sea mines. Three battleships were sunk. The Turks were now doubly aware of the Allied threat, having now twice suffered bombardment by air.

By twice committing their ships on their own too early, the Allies had lost strategic surprise. But these were only the first of many blunders that would dominate this disastrous campaign.

The German General Liman von Sanders was appointed to the prepare the Dardanelles against landings from the sea. He found that beach defenses were nonexistent, but he quickly organized the construction of trenches and beach obstacles.

The navies having failed, Hamilton set up a forward Allied base at Mudros, on the island of Lemnos, closer to the Dardanelles Strait, the waterway from the Mediterranean to the Black Sea. From there he planned his landings on the Gallipoli peninsula. A number of simultaneous landings were planned. A British division would land at Cape Helles at the southern tip. The Anzacs would assault at Gaba Tepe, 11 miles to the north, to cut off the neck of the peninsula. Two diversionary operations would be carried out—a landing by the French at Kum Kale on the Asiatic side of the Narrows and a false diversionary landing by the British at the extreme northern end of the peninsula, at Kuvla.

The landings were fixed for April 25. Hamilton wanted to land by night to gain some surprise, but the admirals argued that navigation in the dark would be too difficult. It was therefore agreed that the troops would go ashore at dawn.

Hamilton moved with his operations staff to Mudros on April 8, leaving his logistical staff back at his headquarters in Egypt, nearly 700 miles away. This was another blunder. The key logistics planning was left to the operations staff, which had no experience. So while Hamilton had close to hand what he needed for planning the attacks, he did not have the expertise to move supplies and support into the proper regions. The result was a severe shortage of ammunition and other necessities, from medicine to food. The troops involved in the operation had never carried out an amphibious landing. Now they had to do it under combat conditions. During the landings Hamilton chose to base himself aboard the battleship HMS *Queen Elizabeth*, flagship of the naval commander Admiral de Robeck. But he placed his operations people on a transport vessel. This was another blunder for two reasons. First, de Robeck had the fleet to command, and he would not necessarily position his flagship precisely where Hamilton needed to be. Also, by separating himself from his staff, Hamilton made communications very difficult.

The troops who were to carry out the landings, most facing combat for the first time, had high hopes and believed that their efforts would ultimately bring about a victorious end to the war. Their objectives were to take high, commanding positions inland on the peninsula, from which heights protection for a wider invasion could be maintained. But optimism soon bled away.

Still, the day at last had come. On April 25, 1915, the Gallipoli landings took place.

At Gaba Tepe the Australians and New Zealanders—the Anzacs—made a promising start, meeting only scattered rifle fire when they landed, incurring few casualties. Unfortunately, they came ashore largely on the wrong beach—at Ari Buni, a small beach a few miles to the north—and their units became intermingled. The Turks counterattacked later in the afternoon, but could not prevent 15,000 Anzacs from landing by the end of the day.

The Anzacs, despite the logistical problems in the landing, did have their chances. Their objective: the slopes of Chunuk Bair, a hill dominating the entire Gallipoli Peninsula, was almost within reach. A contingent moved ahead, and could see the high bluff was unoccupied. But Turkish commander, Mustafa Kemal, who would gain legendary status from his heroic leadership at Gallipoli, scaled the heights quickly with his division behind him and took the hill. It was back to the beach trenches for Anzac.

The British were aware that the Turks were girding for yet another assault, so to distract them a diversionary attack at Cape Helles was planned The British landed on five different beaches at Cape Helles amid a flurry of miscommunication and faulty planning.

But part of the attacking division made its way to the foot of its objective, Achi Baba, a dominant inland hill, the other side of which was the Dardanelles Strait. However, with General Hamilton far away on his command ship, the British troops lacked further direction. They stopped to brew tea before scaling the hill, which was still unoccupied. When they set out again, though, they found they had lost their advantage: the hill had been taken by the

Turks. Without these key positions the success of any subsequent landings seemed nil. It was not a good time for tea.

On the beaches, losses were very heavy. The Allied troops were trapped by heavy Turkish fire, not only on the beach but on the landing vessel, the collier *River Clyde*, which had been purposefully run aground as a sort of Trojan horse, with two Irish battalions and a British one inside. When they broke out at night to attack the beaches, they were cut down by machine-gun fire. Senior commanders became casualties up and down the beaches, and instead of linking up the various beaches and advancing inland again, the troops dug in because the junior commanders now in charge had not been properly briefed on the concept of the operation. This fundamental operational blunder meant that the chance of an early decisive success was missed.

During the next few days the Turks rushed reinforcements onto the Gallipoli Peninsula. Efforts by the Allies to enlarge their beachheads met with increasingly heavy casualties. Trench systems similar to those on the Western Front soon developed.

The Allies were able to get only a few guns ashore during the first days, and naval fire support proved largely ineffective due to poor communications. Hamilton had few reinforcements available. The fighting on the Western Front was beginning to intensify once more, so no more troops could be immediately spared from Britain.

Spring passed into the heat of summer on the Gallipoli Peninsula, and the stalemate continued. Repeated Allied attacks failed to break through the Turkish trenches. Sickness compounded Allied troubles. Flies were everywhere, and dysentery and other diseases became rife, adding considerably to the casualty lists. The British tried to break the deadlock by using armored cars, but the trenches severely restricted their mobility and they were later withdrawn.

In July 1915, Hamilton finally received significant reinforcements and evolved a new plan to break the deadlock. While the beachhead at Cape Helles could not be exploited, he believed that the Anzacs could still strike across the neck of the Gallipoli Peninsula. Yet their existing beachhead had no room for the necessary reinforcements.

Once more a deadlock ensued. The Allies on Gallipoli were like a whale stranded on a beach. There would be three more months of bitter fighting on the rocky slopes. Then Hamilton ordered a second landing in August.

The elderly General Sir Frederick Stopford was put in charge of the Suvla landings. The Anzacs bore the main brunt of the assault, taking heavy losses in a campaign by now spectacularly doomed. The Allies began to look for a way to save this blunder-filled campaign, or end it.

The overall failure of the Easterners' plan to take Gallipoli, combined with some reverses in the war with Germany in France, led to a shake-up in Britain, and the country writhed in the grip of a crisis of confidence. A disastrous shell shortage embarrassed the Liberal administration that had been in control of war policy. A coalition government was forced by the Conservatives, and one of the conditions was that Winston Churchill be removed from the Admiralty. Field Marshal Lord Kitchener remained in the War Office, not having to pay as dearly for his early underestimation of Turkish resistance. Now he was, understandably, deeply concerned by the stalemate on Gallipoli, which was tying down Allied troops that could be used to greater benefit elsewhere. He therefore sent out General Sir Charles Monro, who had already distinguished himself in France, to relieve Ian Hamilton. Monro recommended evacuation, and after Kitchener had visited the Dardanelles to see for himself, the Allied governments agreed. But before the evacuation could take place, the troops on Gallipoli had one final horror to face. This was a sudden sharp spell of wintry weather at the end of November, which began with heavy rain and biting winds and quickly turned into a blizzard. Two hundred and eighty men lost their lives, and a further 16,000 went down with frostbite. For troops who had already suffered so much, it was almost the final straw.

The evacuation from Gallipoli took place in two phases. The Anzac and Suvla withdrawals were carried out during three December nights just before Christmas 1915. The Cape Helles withdrawal was mounted on the night of January 8, 1916. The evacuations were the only successful part of the Gallipoli campaign. Thanks to elaborate deception measures, the Turks did not realize what was happening, and not a man was lost. But the operation's overall losses were staggering: Allied casualties amounted to more than 250,000 men. And the losses taken by the Anzacs were such that April 25, the date of the first landings, is painfully observed in Australia as Anzac Day.

Meanwhile, as the evacuation took place, Winston Churchill, pulled from the Admiralty for his advocacy of the failed Eastern operation, found himself spending his first days as a battalion commander on the Western Front.

Initially mounted to help Russia, the Gallipoli campaign did nothing to restore Russia's fortunes. Russian troops continued to suffer on all fronts. The reality is that even if the Dardanelles had been secured and Constantinople captured, it would have been almost impossible to sustain a major offensive in the region. The terrain was too difficult, and Allied forces would have had to be supported by very long lines of communication running the length of the Mediterranean.

German and Austrian submarines and U-boats were already preying on Allied shipping in the eastern Mediterranean. An American merchant ship, *Gulflight*, had been sunk by German subs near Sicily on May 1, 1915. The Germans were prowling the shipping lanes elsewhere as well, as in the Atlantic, where later in May a U-boat would sink a British passenger liner bound from New York, with many citizens aboard from a neutral country—the United States.

The Sinking of the *Lusitania*

N MAY, DURING THE INTERIM between the two landings on Gallipoli, prospects on both the Eastern and Western Fronts were grim for the Allies, and decidedly brighter for the Central Powers. The Austro-German forces were driving the Russians out of the Carpathians to the east. Russian fort after Russian fort, town after town, were falling to the advancing forces led by General August von Mackensen. The Austrian foreign minister even felt that the Russians might be ready to sign an agreement, giving up to Austria thousands of square miles, and millions of people. The Germans, though, felt that more was to be gained, including France's English Channel coastline and wide swaths of the Anglo-French colonial empire. In the end, it was decided that it was premature to push for a settlement just then, when so much more could be won.

On the Western Front, the long stalemate in France was evolving into a German advantage. Gas attacks were proving capable of driving British forces out of their entrenchments, as in Ypres, and Germany was avidly pursuing its policy of denying materiel supplies to British forces by policing the North Atlantic for Allied ships. It was not averse to sinking any ship flying the British flag.

On the day in May that the German sub sank the merchant

ship *Gulflight* in the Mediterranean, the German Embassy in Washington took out ads in New York newspapers, warning U.S. citizens away from any ships headed into British territorial waters. As quoted in Lincoln Paine's exhaustive *Ships of the World*, the warning said that such ships "are liable to destruction in those waters and that travelers sailing in the war zone do so at their own risk."

RMS *Lusitania* set sail from New York that very day, May 1, 1915, with 1,965 passenger and crew, under the command of Captain William Turner. With America still untouched by the European war, its wealthy citizens wanted to take a late spring Atlantic cruise; it would be the last innocent cruise for quite some time.

Although *Lusitania* had been built in 1907 in Clydebank, Scotland, as a speedy passenger ship, its origin was not completely innocent of the notions of war. In 1904, the American financier J. P. Morgan, alarmed at the demise of the U.S. merchant marine, began buying controlling interests in many major shipping companies, including Britain's White Star Line. Fearful that England would be hard pressed in the event of war to mount a significant auxiliary fleet, the British government loaned the Cunard Line 2.6 million pounds and subsidized the construction of two passenger liners—*Lusitania* and her sister ship, *Mauretania*. In 1907 these two were the largest and fastest and most luxurious liners in the world, and the pride of the British Cunard line.

At the outbreak of World War I there were strict rules on surface warships or submarines engaging unarmed merchant vessels. If in fact a merchant vessel flying an enemy flag was found in contested waters, a warning had to be given and the crew allowed to take to the lifeboats before the ship was sunk. It was a tough accommodation that merchant shipping had to make in the presence of war.

Neutral vessels, however, from non-warring countries, could not be attacked, although boarding them was permitted and certain specified cargoes that would help the enemy's war effort could be impounded. Such actions were to take place only in the territorial waters of the countries at war. But such activities quickly went beyond the realms of legality. The British, having a difficult time with its blockade of Germany, illegally declared areas of North Sea to be off limits to Germany-bound cargoes, at times even seizing American ships carrying cargo that might arguably be aiding the German war effort. Germany countered by making the area all around the British Isles and Ireland an area of war. And in January 1915 the Kaiser permitted a policy of unrestricted submarine warfare in the waters around the British Isles. This meant that any British vessel could be sunk. Neutral ships were warned that their safety within these seas could not be guaranteed, although every care would be taken not to sink them.

The war had not stopped the sailings of passenger vessels across the Atlantic, with Americans continuing to visit Europe. And, as envisioned in 1907, the *Lusitania* and the *Mauretania* were commandeered by the Admiralty with a view to converting them into armed merchant cruisers. However, the Admiralty changed its mind, although gun mountings were fitted, and the ships were handed back to Cunard. Nevertheless, the 1914 *Jane's Fighting Ships*, which was the bible for identifying ships, and used by all navies to do so, had them listed as armed cruisers.

Lusitania made two transatlantic crossings in October 1914 and then did a monthly round trip thereafter. In January 1915 the *Lusitania* achieved notoriety when Captain Dow, her captain at the time, decided to hoist the U.S. flag when sailing between Liverpool and the Irish port of Queenstown so as to reduce the threat of a U-boat attack. This was reported in the world press.

Yet most people did not believe that the Germans would stoop so low as to attack an unarmed passenger vessel even if it was flying the British flag, despite the German warnings. In fact, when *Lusitania* embarked from New York's Pier 54 on that fateful May 1, the ads in the newspapers scared off only one passenger. So she set sail with nearly 2,000 souls aboard and a mixed cargo, some of which would later contribute to the ship's fate.

Six days later, on May 7, the *Lusitania* was approaching Ireland, and Captain William Turner took precautions against an attack. The British Admiralty was aware that German submarines lurked in the waters off southern Ireland; the day before, two British merchant ships, the *Centurion* and the *Candidate*, had been sunk by torpedoes. That night Turner received a telegraph message that "Submarines were active off the south coast of Ireland." And although Captain Turner had been issued orders to sail a zigzag course, avoid headlands (where subs were most likely to be hiding in wait), and steer mid-channel, he steamed at only about 15–18 knots—*Lusitania* was capable of 25—followed a straight course, and veered to within 12 miles of Cork, about 25 miles north of mid-channel.

Were these blunders? Or was Turner under secret orders to make his ship vulnerable to German attack? Some have suggested as much, citing that Britain was anxious—as they would be a quarter century later—to get the United States officially involved in the war effort. With so many Americans on board, surely the public outcry in America would force President Wilson's hand.

In any event, at 2:15 P.M. one of the officers spotted a torpedo heading toward the ship. It was fired by U-20, whose skipper, Walther Schwieger, believed that he was engaging a troop ship, perhaps relying on the mistaken *Jane's Fighting Ships* registry. *Lusitania* sank in just 20 minutes, taking 1,198 passengers and crew with her, including 128 Americans. Only 764 people survived.

Although Schwieger's log indicated that only one torpedo was fired, and only one was seen, some of the survivors claimed there was a second explosion, followed by subsequent ones. Schwieger surmised that he had hit a boiler or a hold filled with coal powder, but the Lusitania's manifest showed there were over 50 tons of shrapnel and 10 tons of ammunition on board in the "mixed cargo."

Americans were indeed outraged. But although President Woodrow Wilson condemned the German actions, he held steadfastly to a position of neutrality. Former American president Teddy Roosevelt would not go so quietly, however. He argued persuasively against "professional pacifism" and urged for American rearmament. It did not sit well with Roosevelt that America "set a spiritual example" to the world "by sitting idle."

Despite such fiery rhetoric, America's will to enter the fray was difficult to rouse. There were more provocations, more sinkings of neutral ships. At the very end of 1915, in the eastern Mediterranean, well after the fiasco at Gallipoli had ended, the steamship liner *Persia* was torpedoed by a German submarine, drowning 334 passengers, including two Americans, one of whom was the United States consul in Aden. Three days later, an American diplomat, John Coolige, writing in his diary, predicted with disdain that there would be no American response. "Probably Mr. Lansing will buy a new box of note-paper and set to work," he wrote. Robert Lansing was the Secretary of State. Coolige was right: Lansing did nothing, and America did nothing. And yet these incidents could not help but accumulate. Germany was toying with a delicate balance in the world conflict.

As for the tragic events that befell RMS *Lusitania*, blame, motive, intentions remain a mystery to this day. Was such heavy loss of civilian life due to the blundering of Captain Turner? Did the British knowingly sacrifice innocent lives in order to coax the

U.S. into the war? Did the Germans blunder by taking out a ship with so many Americans aboard, and contributing to what eventually became American resolve to enter the war? Or was it the presence of explosives in the hold of a passenger ship that doomed *Lusitania*? Perhaps it was the volatility of the hold that slowed the *Lusitania,* and forced Turner to pursue a straight course rather than an erratic one that might endanger the cargo. One thing is clear: American public opinion quickly consolidated against Germany while forgiving the British its controversial impounding of U.S. merchant vessels. And though America would not enter the war for nearly two more years, it was only a matter of time after the *Lusitania* sank in 315 feet of water off the coast of Ireland before John J. Pershing would be leading the American Expeditionary Force into battle.

British Battle Cruiser
Disaster at Jutland

B Y 1 9 1 6 , T H E F I R S T W O R L D W A R began to look like a war
of attrition. On the Western Front, there was a horrific and
seemingly endless battle for the French city of Verdun, with the
Germans capturing and holding one of the two forts that protected
the city, but unable to rout the French, heroically dug in and resupplied by the famous La Voie de Sacrée, the Sacred Road. Later
in the year, the Battle of the Somme would replace Verdun as the
most enduring symbol of the kind of dug-in, intractable war this
conflict had become. Just as intractable seemed to be the situation
in the city of Hut, where British and Indian forces were trapped
by the Turks in unspeakable squalor, prompting T. E. Lawrence
("Lawrence of Arabia") to offer the Turks a million pounds for the
release of the besieged soldiers. No dice.

The ability to hold out—never mind offensive or defensive
strategies—came to be a major test of a force's effectiveness. Knowing how to deprive armies of ammunition, food, and water became
as important as capturing strategic hill positions or taking a bridge
or owning a riverbank. The Allied naval blockade of Germany,
designed to choke the enemy war effort and also to discomfit
German citizenry and to build anti-war sentiment, was an increasing
annoyance to the Germans. They felt it was an unjustifiable attempt

to starve innocent people, and did not look kindly on anyone who assisted, abetted, or approved of these actions. A popular German cartoon showed President Wilson releasing a dove of peace with one hand while offering a handful of bullets with his other.

Thus, the nefarious German activities in the sea lanes was a serious affair, for Germany and the Allies and their friends. By March 1916, less than a year after the sinking of the *Lusitania*, German submarines had sunk another three dozen unarmed liners, but beyond these stealth operations there had been no significant head-to-head encounters between the British and German fleets. That would change, in a matter of a few hours, in what became known as the Battle of Jutland, in the North Sea. It would be by far the largest naval engagement of the war. And it would be more than simply two navies clashing: two very different philosophies of naval warfare would butt heads as well.

One of the contributing causes of the war of 1914–18 was the Anglo-German race for naval supremacy. Kaiser Wilhelm II envied the British Empire and wanted to rival it in size and influence. To the Kaiser's way of thinking, the British Empire—so far-flung, so powerful, so much a part of the British identity—was made possible because of the might of its Royal Navy. Largest in the world, the Royal Navy had a significant presence in all the word's oceans, and protected British interests from South Africa to the Arctic Circle, from the South Pacific to Hong Kong. So, under the leadership of Admiral Alfred Tirpitz, Germany began to build a navy to rival that of Great Britain.

Tirpitz's British counterpart was Admiral Sir John Fisher, known throughout the Royal Navy as Jacky. Under his direction the British unveiled a new type of warship in 1907. Up to that time battleships had been equipped with a variety of guns. There were large calibers for engaging other battleships and smaller guns for fighting off attacks by torpedo boat destroyers. The number of large guns that could be carried was limited. It was also difficult to identify the shell splashes of the various types of guns.

HMS *Dreadnought* was revolutionary in that her armament consisted of just big guns—ten 12-inchers. This made her the most powerful warship of her day and meant that, overnight, existing battleships were obsolete. Other navies took note, and soon all were building Dreadnoughts, as they were called.

Dreadnoughts became central to the Anglo-German naval race. Jacky Fisher's dictum was: "Build first and build fast, each one better than the last." While this ensured that the Royal Navy outbuilt its German rival, there were penalties to be paid. Because of the haste of construction, new classes of ship were laid down before the faults in the previous class had been corrected.

Speed was the byword in Royal Navy thinking. It permeated everything they did. Ships became ever faster, but it came at a cost—to get speed, weight had to be sacrificed, which meant that the heavy steel-plated armor, which the German ships possessed, would not be something a British ship could count on. This was most apparent in another type of warship introduced by Fisher—the battle cruiser.

The conventional cruiser had two roles in war—scouting for the battle fleet and commerce protection. To this end cruisers were lightly armored, with moderate armament, but were very fast. Fisher believed that speed combined with firepower represented a powerful weapon. If a ship could be developed that had the speed of a cruiser combined with a battleship's armament, it would prove effective against the German Dreadnoughts. Thus the battle cruiser came into being.

The Germans, of course, also built battle cruisers. But because of another fundamental difference in the two navies, the German battle cruisers had the advantage in one very important safety area: numbers of watertight doors.

This is not because of a design flaw in the British battle cruiser, but because of a design necessity. Sailors in the Royal Navy had to be able to live for long periods of time on board, due to the expansiveness of the British Empire. If the sun never set on your empire, your ships of course were going to be called upon to make long voyages. Space for sleeping, eating, relaxing, and storage of provisions for the long hauls affected British warship design, requiring large areas with good access. As a result British warships, with a more open architecture belowdecks, were more vulnerable to sinking—and sinking quickly—without all the watertight doors that distinguished the German ships, which were never envisioned to be too far from port. In fact, there was little or no space on a German battle cruiser for a sailor to sleep. Sleep was done in the barracks on shore.

In the years leading up to 1914, Fisher's love of speed influenced the Royal Navy in another way. Big-ship gunnery concentrated on achieving high rates of fire. But such was the demand to achieve ever more impressive results that safety came to be disregarded.

Gun turrets on large warships had their magazines located deep in the hull. Hoppers took the shell and cordite charge up to the gun-loading cage, from which they were loaded into the breach. To protect against a flash fire, fire doors isolated the main hoist from the turret and magazine. But, to increase the rate of fire, crews removed these, introducing the risk of a fire invading the magazine and exploding the cordite charges.

The Royal Navy's belief in speed above all else would in

time be tested in battle against the numerically inferior German Navy. The British battle cruisers especially would pay dearly for this mistaken philosophy.

When war broke out in August 1914, the Royal Navy's Grand Fleet moved to its wartime station at Scapa Flow in the Orkney Islands north of Scotland. The British hoped that the German High Seas Fleet would sail out and challenge them to battle in the North Sea. The British naval blockade of Germany involved stopping and seizing all merchant vessels bound for German ports. The Royal Navy hoped that this would provoke the German fleet to come out in an effort to break the blockade. In pursuit of this strategy the Grand Fleet spent much of its time on patrol in the North Sea.

The Germans were conscious that the British outnumbered them 22 to 15 in Dreadnoughts and nine to five in battle cruisers. They were therefore not prepared to engage the Grand Fleet in battle until they matched it in strength.

Two years of stealth operations had not weakened the blockade; in fact, it seemed to be beckoning America to enter the war. In January 1916, Admiral Reinhard von Scheer took over command of the German High Seas Fleet. He believed that Germany could win the naval war only by destroying the British Grand Fleet. Von Scheer's more aggressive strategy was to result in the Battle of Jutland.

Von Scheer's plan was to put to sea and lure out the British battle cruisers from their base at Rosyth. Once these had been sunk, he would turn on the remainder of the Grand Fleet, which would inevitably attempt to join up with the battle cruisers. In this way von Scheer hoped to offset the British Grand Fleet's superiority in numbers of ships by engaging it piecemeal.

After a number of failed attempts, von Scheer organized

another coat-trailing operation at the end of May 1916. His battle cruisers would steam off the Norwegian coast. Once the British battle cruisers arrived from Rosyth, they would be destroyed by the German Dreadnoughts following up behind von Scheer's battle cruisers before the main British fleet could arrive from Scapa Flow. The High Seas Fleet would in turn destroy this force.

Admiral Sir John Jellicoe, commanding the British Grand Fleet, sensed from an intercepted radio signal what the Germans had in mind. He decided to preempt them. On May 30, he ordered Admiral Sir David Beatty, commanding the battle cruisers, to set sail from Rosyth and rendezvous with him. The German battle cruisers would thus find the whole of the Grand Fleet ranged against them. This would sure surprise von Scheer.

Despite a screen of U-boats, the Germans did not detect that the whole of the Grand Fleet had put to sea, not just a small contingent. Von Scheer himself sailed in the early hours of May 31, 1916, trailing his lead battle cruisers, under Admiral Franz Hipper, by about 50 miles,

Admiral Beatty and his fleet of battle cruisers arrived at the rendezvous first. Beatty had six battle cruisers, supported by four Dreadnoughts, together with light cruisers and destroyers.

His German opponent, Franz Hipper, with five Dread-noughts accompanied by light cruisers and destroyers, arrived just after 2:00 P.M. Immediately, things started to unravel for the British. Poor signaling procedures allowed the battle cruisers to draw too far ahead of their supporting Dreadnoughts. Both sides opened fire at 3:48 P.M.

The German fire was faster and more accurate, which surprised the British. Beatty's flagship, HMS *Lion*, was hit in one of her turrets, and only the speedy flooding of the magazine below prevented her from exploding. Her consorts were not so lucky.

Indefatigable and *Queen Mary* were hit and blew up within minutes of one another. A third, the *Invincible*, was also sunk.

Beatty remarked to his flag lieutenant: "There seems to be something wrong with our bloody ships today." He was right, but the problem was a fundamental one.

The "big cats," as the British battle cruisers were nick-named, had been found wanting. Their lack of armor could not keep out German shells. Worse, the lack of turret anti-flash protection resulted in magazine explosions. Jacky Fisher's demand for speed above all else had been dramatically shown to be flawed.

The situation was not helped by the superiority of the German shells, which penetrated the British ships' armor before exploding, while the British shells tended to detonate on impact. The Germans were routing Beatty. When Von Scheer and the main body of the German High Seas Fleet arrived, Beatty withdrew northward, knowing that Jellicoe and his 24 Dreadnoughts were steaming their way. Would von Scheer fall for it, even though his entire plan had been to draw the strength of the British Grand Fleet into the fray? Von Scheer did, but once again "there was something wrong with the British ships" that day. The German ships, despite being heavily hit in cases, were difficult to sink. Their heavy armor and numerous watertight compartments enabled them to take punishment and survive.

Even so, von Scheer realized that he was in danger of being cut off from his base. He also appreciated that the British were now taking advantage of superiority in numbers of Dreadnoughts. The Germans therefore withdrew.

To hold the British at bay, von Scheer launched torpedo attacks with his destroyers. While they had no success, their action was enough to make Jellicoe pause for fear of losing any more ships. This gave the Germans the breathing space they needed, and they were able to escape the trap and return to port.

The British Grand Fleet, realizing that the Germans had eluded them, also sailed for home.

In all, the British lost three battle cruisers, three cruisers, and eight destroyers. The Germans lost one old battleship, one battle cruiser, four light cruisers, and five destroyers. Both sides claimed victory at Jutland, but the British were now finally conscious of the weaknesses of their ships, especially insufficient watertight compartments and armored protection, as well as lack of turret safety.

Not until November 1918, at the end of hostilities, did the British Grand Fleet and German High Seas Fleet meet again in the North Sea. It was part of the armistice agreement that the German ships sail out of port and surrender.

While the numerical superiority of the British Navy would ultimately win the day, understanding that the Germans had surpassed them in design was a difficult pill to swallow. It proved to be a costly lesson learned in just a few hours at Jutland. These lessons would be put to good use at another time, in another war.

French Mutiny in the Trenches

N O O N E V I S I T I N G N O R T H E R N F R A N C E today can fail to be struck by the numerous war cemeteries that mark the countryside. Row upon row of crosses and gravestones commemorate the hundreds of thousands of men who fell in the carnage that was the Western Front of 1914–18.

More than 80 years after the end of the conflict, it is difficult to comprehend how the soldiers of both sides stuck it out for so long amid the filth, mud, and slaughter that was the war in the trenches. This was especially so during the prolonged and murderous offensives, which resulted in so much human slaughter.

Yet there was an occasion during the war on the Western Front when the attacking troops did break under the strain and refused to continue their attacks. This was the French assault in the Champagne country in April 1917, known as the Chemin des Dames or Nivelle offensive, after the general who directed it.

Blunders in both the preparation for the attack and in the attack's execution led to unnecessarily high casualties among the attacking French troops. The result was a humiliating mutiny among large parts of the French Army.

When World War I broke out, both sides believed that it would be one of logistics and maneuvering, and that it would not last long. Both were confident of victory by Christmas. But the initial opposing war plans failed to achieve their objectives.

However, a war like this had never been fought before. There were not only new strategies to contend with but new technologies, and one influenced the other. Rapid-fire weapons, like the machine gun and magazine rifle, caused the pendulum to swing tactically in favor of the defensive. A soldier firing his rifle from behind cover was equal to ten men charging at him across open ground. Good positions, well fortified, could be held interminably. Never before had simply digging in proved to be the best offense.

This realization meant that by the late autumn of 1914 the Western Front had become two parallel trench lines stretching from the Swiss border to the North Sea, with everyone in trenches, determined to outlast the enemy across the no-man's-land between them.

During 1915 both the Germans and the French, with their British ally, mounted attacks to break through the increasingly formidable trench systems facing them. All these attacks failed, and the generals on both sides became convinced that the answer lay in artillery. If the opposing trenches were subjected to a heavy enough preliminary bombardment, the defenders would become so numbed that the attack must succeed.

The year 1916 in the West was dominated by two massive offensives. In February the Germans launched an attack against a salient dominated by the historic French fortress of Verdun. They calculated that the French would stop at nothing to prevent Verdun from being overrun and intended to literally destroy the French Army.

They were right. The French poured in reinforcements along the only road leading into the salient. This became known as *La Voie Sacrée*—The Sacred Road. The grim battle for Verdun went on until virtually the end of the year. The total casualties for both sides were one million men, but for no territorial gain.

The Allies had also planned a major offensive for 1916. This was to take place on the chalk lands above the River Somme. But with the pressure so much on the French at Verdun, the offensive became largely a British effort.

A week-long artillery bombardment prefaced the attack. Then, on the morning of July 1, 17 divisions assaulted on a 15-mile front, confident that the guns had destroyed the German defenses. They were sadly mistaken. Much of the barbed wire in front of the German trenches remained uncut, and the Germans had been protected by their deep dugouts. The result was that by the end of the day the British alone had suffered almost 60,000 casualties, of whom over a third were killed.

But the attacks went on. For it was vital to relieve the French of some of the almost unbearable pressure that they were enduring at Verdun. Not until late November was the Somme offensive halted. By that time the French and British casualties had risen to 600,000, and the Germans had much the same.

The winter of 1916–17 was one of the coldest in living memory. While the troops in the front line grappled with this and the normal dangers and discomforts of trench warfare, the high commands of both sides drew up plans for 1917.

Conscious of their huge losses on the Western Front during 1916 and the fact that they were also heavily engaged against the Russians on the Eastern Front, the Germans decided to remain on the defensive. Not only that, but they resolved to shorten their line. They began to construct formidable concrete defenses at the base of the salient bounded by Arras in the north and Soissons in the south. Once this was completed, they would withdraw to it.

In contrast, the Allies were determined to resume the offensive once spring came. The French, who were the senior Allied partner, were conscious that until the Germans were expelled from their territory, the war could not be ended.

But fresh minds were needed to break the deadlock on the western Front. Consequently, the phlegmatic Joseph Joffre, known to his men as Papa and who had commanded the French armies since the outbreak of war, was sacked. The dashing Robert Georges Nivelle, who had been a mere colonel in August 1914, replaced him. Not only was he full of charm and confidence. but he was also fluent in English, which went down well with France's British ally.

Nivelle believed that the main reason for the failure of previous trench offensives was that reserves had not been committed in time to forestall counterattacks. But, like the other generals of his time, Nivelle believed in the power of artillery. For his offensive he intended to deploy a massive amount of artillery to pulverize the German defenses before the attack. This, combined with reserves deployed well forward, would break the German defenses in just one day. Or so Nivelle believed.

Nivelle chose to make his effort between Soissons and Reims, the champagne-producing region of France. The main thrust would be made in the hilly and now heavily fortified Chemin des Dames sector just to the east of Soissons. North of the River Oise, British and French forces would also attack in order to tie down the Germans. This meant attacking the shoulders of the German salient, a salient which they were about to vacate.

Nivelle's boasting about his plan was such that it became common gossip. Security was lax in other ways, and the Germans were able to capture documents about the plan. The massive deployment of French artillery could also not be wholly disguised from the prying eyes of German aircraft and balloon observers.

Consequently, the Germans made their defenses even stronger and brought in no less than sixteen counterattack divisions, which were deployed outside French artillery range.

General Alfred Micheler, commanding the French armies in the region, expressed concern at the growing preparations, but Nivelle brushed these worries aside. Then, in mid-March 1917, the Germans began their withdrawal back to the newly created defenses of the Hindenburg Line. The Allies cautiously followed up. Not only was the German Arras-Soissons salient now no more, but the German withdrawal negated the purpose of the diversionary Allied attacks to the north of the former salient.

However, Nivelle insisted that they go ahead. Consequently, the British attacked at Arras on April 9 and the French at St. Quentin on the fourteenth. Canadian troops succeeded in capturing the dominant Vimy Ridge, but that was the only significant success.

At Chemin des Dames the preparatory bombardment opened on April 7, 1917. Twice it had to be delayed because of difficulties in observation, both in the air and on the ground.

Not until April 11 did the attack itself take place. The French gained some ground, but suffered heavy casualties. They used tanks, but these arrived late, and many were destroyed by artillery fire. Not a single one reached the German front line. Reserves, too, could not be quickly deployed because of the narrowness of the communications trenches.

During the next week the French continued to attack, but made little progress. Casualties grew heavier. Unable to cope, the French medical system broke down, and many died unnecessarily of their wounds. By April 26 it was clear that Nivelle's offensive had failed, but the French attacks continued until the losses became unacceptable. This dawned on the common French soldier more than on Nivelle. Having had enough of what seemed a senseless slaughter, many soldiers refused orders to attack. At the end of the month Nivelle was removed. His successor was Philippe Pétain, who had commanded the French defense of Verdun with such success. He immediately halted the offensive, but this did not lift the spirits of the common French soldier. In fact, dissatisfaction spread like wildfire.

Two Russian brigades fighting with the French had become distracted by news of events back home—Bolshevism has burst into revolution in Russia—and this served to aggravate the situation. Many units refused to return to the front line, setting up camps in the woods. It was not that they had refused to take any further part in the war; they merely wanted an end to the senseless attacks that had killed and maimed so many hundreds of thousands of their comrades. And their complaints echoed a nation that was becoming war weary. The soldiers demanded more leave, better food, and improved care of their families.

By the end of May 1917 half of the French Army was affected by the mutinies. Pétain realized, however, that to put them down by force would totally break the spirit of the army as a whole. He asked the most disgruntled units to send deputations to see him. Pétain listened to their complaints and took action. More regular leave was introduced. Better canteen facilities were set up. Above all, he reformed the French system of defense. This was now to mirror the German model, with depth and the minimum number of men holding the front line.

The French government was determined, however, that the ringleaders be caught and punished. These were selected by the officers and noncommissioned officers alike, with the agreement of the enlisted men. Nearly 3,500 were court-martialed. A number were sentenced to life imprisonment and 554 to death, but only 49 were actually shot.

·   ·   ·

Thus the French Army was nursed back to health. But the mutinies happened only because of Nivelle's blunders. His disregard for security, lack of appreciation of the strength of the German defenses, and his lack of emphasis on logistics, especially medical facilities, had sent tens of thousands of French soldiers to their deaths. But underlying all was that the French Army had suffered too much already and Nivelle's badly managed offensive was the final straw.

Surprisingly, the Germans remained ignorant of the crisis in the French Army. Even so, it was the British who now had to bear the main offensive burden. They, too, would suffer agonies during the late summer and autumn of 1917—in the mud that was the Third Battle of Ypres.

Both British and French managed to stem the five German drives of the spring and summer of 1918, when storm-troop tactics pointed a way of breaking the trench-bound deadlock. Then, with an ever growing American Expeditionary Force, under General Pershing, the Allies took to the offensive.

When the guns were finally stilled in November 1918 all the Allies could hold their heads high—not least the soldiers of France, who had weathered such suffering over nearly four and a half years of brutal and bloody conflict.

The Treaty of Versailles
and the Seeds of World War II

THE GREAT WAR, AS WORLD WAR I was known until a
second world war changed its name, improbably hurried to a
close. Improbably, because who would have guessed that revolutionary movements within two of the combating giants would suddenly change the momentum of the war?

The revolution in Russia officially began in March 1917;
widespread discontent with Tsar Nicholas's running of the war, the
failure to secure any gains, and the extreme cost to the Russian
people in terms of lives and material sacrifice came to a head. While
the Tsar was negotiating secretly with the French in Petrograd—
they both agreed to give each other "complete liberty" in establishing their own borders, the French in the west, the Russians with
their own western frontier—his protecting regiment, 17,000 strong,
was in the streets demonstrating against him. Sailors on the Russian
cruise ship *Aurora* murdered their captain, and took control of the
ship as a Bolshevik vessel. Later that same day, sailors at a naval
base in Kronstadt murdered 40 officers and arrested 100 more.
Police stations in many cities were sacked and burned.

Meanwhile, the Tsar was trapped on a train by revolution-
aries. They would not let him pass or leave. His Commander-in-
Chief, General Alexeyev, asked his high-ranking officers to sign a

telegram to the Tsar urging him, in the interests of restoring the spirit of the Russian troops, to abdicate. Alexeyev argued that only abdication could save the monarchy and allow Russia to continue its war effort. Over three centuries of imperial rule came to an end when Tsar Nicholas—"in the name of the welfare, tranquillity and salvation" of his "warmly beloved Russia," as quoted in Martin Gilbert's *First World War*, stepped down.

Political turmoil ensued. A provisional government, led by Alexander Kerensky, survived only six months. Despite assurance from the Russian Minister of War, General Verkhovski, that the spirits of the Russian Army were nearly restored, by October 1917 it was clear that the opposite was the case. Entire garrisons of troops refused to march; the Bolshevik Military Revolutionary Committee was calling the shots; they occupied public buildings. On November 7, 18,000 Bolsheviks surrounded Kerensky's government ministers as they sat in the Winter Palace. Fifteen thousand sailors soon joined in the throng, and minesweepers and destroyers all came to be anchored in the Neva River near the palace. At ten that night, the *Aurora*, with Bolsheviks aboard and in control, fired a charge at the Winter Palace; soon the palace was overrun. Lenin, who had been in Zurich when the revolution struck, could hardly believe the news: the revolution was complete, and he was elected chairman of the Council of People's Commissars; Trotsky became Commissar of Foreign Affairs. And Russia was now out of the war. A year later, it would be over.

Germany was undergoing some of the same convulsions that shook Russia. The Socialists, aware of what was happening in Russia and anxious to be a part of a worldwide wave of proletarian revolt, were calling for an end to the war and a new government. Hard-liners in Germany also came out of the woodwork, calling for the arrest of those who would dare suggest surrender. Paradoxically, the German war effort was not failing. German soil had not been touched; the German navy was terrorizing the seas and inflicting gigantic losses on Allied shipping; the war in France was going at full tilt, with the outcome by no means clear; and now Russia, the eastern arm of the Allies, was useless.

But America's entry into the war in 1917 was starting to have an effect. Slow to gather and to mobilize, by 1918 General Pershing's American Expeditionary Force was gaining the upper hand. Soon there would be two million American troops engaged. And increasingly, American ships providing safe passage to supply cargoes was improving Allied responsiveness. The Germans were regularly finding themselves outnumbered and more and more isolated as their own allies began to fold. The Bulgarian Army was mutinying, Austria asked for peace talks, and Turkish forces, like the others, were suffering from the effects of the Allied blockade.

But what shook the German prospects the most was a revolution in Germany itself, a revolution that was diplomatic in its way, in October 1918. Kaiser Wilhelm's second cousin, Prince Max of Baden, became Chancellor in the Crown Council chamber in Berlin. But Prince Max insisted on two conditions: the Kaiser must immediately relinquish control of the army and navy, and henceforth only Parliament would have the power to declare war or make peace. General Erich von Ludendorff, head of the German forces in France, had earlier urged the Kaiser to issue a peace offer. Ludendorff was aware that, if not revolution, there was at least revolt, bordering on mutiny, in the German army. "Socialist ideas" and Spartacist ideas (based on the writings of Rosa Luxemburg) were in the boys' heads, he said.

Rather suddenly, it looked like the war could not go on.

Facing the dishonor of having an army refuse to fight and a people refuse to be governed, on October 4, Prince Max telegraphed Washington requesting an armistice. On October 11, German forces began a withdrawal from the Western Front, though it was planning to fight its way back home. It would have to.

The Allies were wary of any armistice that might simply be a pretext for the Germans to bring some order at home and re-group. It seemed that everyone was groping for a framework to bring the war to a halt, but could it possibly be the case?

Back in January 1918, President Woodrow Wilson, in an address to Congress, had laid out what he felt was the "only pos-sible program" for a settlement. It was his famous "Fourteen Points." The points involved removal of trade barriers, armament reductions, adjustment of colonial claims, return of all French ter-ritory to France, restorations of Belgian and Italian borders, evac-uation of the Balkans, and a guarantee of access to the sea for Serbia; a freeing of certain nationalities in the Ottoman Empire, independence for Poland, and a formation of an association of nations to ensure liberty and territorial integrity for all nations. This last would become the League of Nations.

In late October, Wilson, who became the center of nego-tiations for the war's end, received a communiqué saying that the Germans were ready to stop their submarine warfare. He told his British and French colleagues that perhaps they should prepare for an armistice.

The English, French, and American generals convened to discuss what their requests would be. They wanted surrender of all German artillery and railroads, and the surrender of all subma-rines. Meanwhile, sensing that the end was near, the Allies turned up the heat, widening their assaults in Italy and Turkey.

Fighting mixed with negotiating continued on many fronts,

as the Allies moved in, like a boxer cutting the angles on his staggering opponent. And mutinies started to break out on the Central Powers' side like an epidemic: two Austrian divisions refused to fight on the Italian front, German sailors resisted orders from von Scheer to attack the British Fleet, and along the Western Front the German resolve was weakening, as more and more of their troops sought to get home alive.

On the next to last day of October, the Kaiser left Berlin for Spa, a resort town in Belgium. He deferred to the General Council to decide what his fate was. One possibility he offered was that he might abdicate in favor of his son. But no decision was reached.

The American forces pressed their advantage in France. In Germany, revolt was intensifying amidst widespread demand for the end to yet another monarchy. The Kaiser, still in Belgium, responded by saying, "I wouldn't dream of abandoning the throne because of a few hundred Jews and a thousand workers." But his second cousin, Prince Max, had already informed the Allies that the German government was awaiting armistice terms.

By November 9, 1918, the Socialist deputies in the Reichstag were asking for the Kaiser's resignation. When he did not, they called for a general strike in all of Germany. Imperial Germany was about to fall. It was left to diplomats to cipher out the numbers and wording, but the soldiery, at least in Germany, had fairly much laid down its arms.

The next day, November 10, the German government accepted the terms of the armistice. All German soldiers would evacuate the countries of the Western Front and withdraw to the east bank of the Rhine; the German army would turn over guns, artillery, airplanes, railroad cars, engines, trucks, and all military ships at sea. And at eleven the next morning, the eleventh hour of the eleventh day of the eleventh month, all fighting on the Western Front would cease. The war was over.

When American troops marched into Germany the following month, already the German people were deeply resentful of what they considered the harsh terms of the armistice. They felt they hadn't lost a war to an enemy, but lost control of their own revolutionary population, a minority of radicals who had undermined the war effort that would otherwise have been successful. Indeed, after marching through war-torn France and Belgium, with forests charred, villages reduced to rubble, American troops were amazed to see the neat and peaceful German countryside, untouched by battle. Germany did not look like a loser. And increasingly, it didn't want to be treated like one. But worse was yet to come for them. Armistice terms were one thing; the terms of the peace treaty would be another.

In January 1919, the three remaining Allied powers sat down to work out acceptable terms of peace. The Germans were allowed no input. Now it was for Woodrow Wilson, statesman Georges Clemenceau of France, and Britain's Lloyd George to distribute punishment and spoils.

First, the powers split up the colonial holdings of Germany and Turkey. Britain and France, being smaller and less resource-rich than the U.S., benefited nicely. Then came the matter of "reparations of damage." A commission was set up on January 25; every country wanted full repayment for costs and damages to be paid by Germany. Eventually, the agreed-upon price tag came to $56 billion. Then the Allies demanded that Germany admit that the war was caused "by the aggression of Germany." This became known as the "war guilt clause," and is considered the very symbol of German humiliation.

As the daily peace conference talks continued, an anti-German feeling grew more spirited, more intense, as the Allies tended to the burying of their dead. And yet British Prime Minister Lloyd George began to feel that some of the clauses in the peace treaty, in their severity, might be a "a constant source of irritation." But this only led to a spat with Clemenceau, who reminded the Prime Minister that the French people had but an imaginary border with Germany while the British, as "a maritime people who have not known invasion," had the luxury of distance and the English Channel.

On June 22, at the Palace at Versailles, built for King Louis XIV in the 1600s, the German delegates agreed to sign all of the more than 200 articles of peace except for the one on war guilt. And on that day the German navy scuttled the German fleet, in violation of one of the terms of the armistice. Enraged, Lloyd George and his colleagues declared that no alterations were possible and that Germany had but 24 hours to sign all the terms.

Germany signed the Treaty of Versailles on June 28, 1919, with the "Principal Allied and Associated Powers," which represented 27 victorious countries who had been part of the Allied effort. Germany was punished heavily.

The German Army was to be restricted to 100,000 men and was not allowed tanks or guns above 150mm in caliber. The Navy was permitted no new ships larger than cruisers, while an air force was banned. An Allied control commission was to be set up to check that Germany was abiding by these terms. In the event, it was not given the powers to ensure that this was so.

The German Rhineland was demilitarized, which meant that no German forces were allowed to be stationed west of the River Rhine. The French, with much of the northern half of their country devastated by the war, wanted financial reparations. The enormous sums asked for were to ruin the German economy, creating galloping inflation and helping to polarize German politics to the extreme left and right. This would help eventually to bring Hitler to power.

But the peacemakers also realized that nationalism in terms of seeking ethnic self-identity had also been a cause of the war. After all, the spark that triggered World War I had been the assassination of the Archduke Franz Ferdinand by a Serbian separatist in the then little-known town of Sarajevo in the Austro-Hungarian province of Bosnia-Herzegovina in the Balkans. Consequently, the map of Europe was redrawn. In the north, Poland, Estonia, Lithuania, and Latvia were given their independence. The Poles had no seaport. Consequently, they were given part of East Prussia. What became known as the Polish Corridor, giving them access to the port of Danzig, isolated the rump of East Prussia from the remainder of Germany. This, too, was to be a source of major resentment to the Germans and was to be one of the seeds that grew into World War II.

The Austro-Hungarian empire was also broken up. Hungary was split off from Austria proper. The immediate result was an extreme left-wing putsch under Bela Kun, which in turn was supplanted by a right-wing regime under Admiral Miklos Horthy, which would later become a faithful ally of Nazi Germany.

In the troubled Balkans the Allies created a new state, Yugoslavia. This included the former Austro-Hungarian provinces, together with Serbia and Montenegro. The new state would be Serb-dominated. Splits would surface in it during World War II. It would hold together under strong man Tito, but after his death would disintegrate, only to be shakily recomposed under Slobodan Milosovic (where conflict, at the end of our century, threatens world peace once again).

Finally, the peacemakers formed the League of Nations to act as a mediator in future international disputes. But traditional isolationism meant that the USA did not join. The League also had no means of enforcing peace. Consequently, by the 1930s it became increasingly incapable of preventing wars from breaking out.

The Allies celebrated the signing of the Treaty of Versailles with victory parades. Little did they know at the time that they had sown the seeds of not only World War II, but also other conflicts that would trouble Europe into the next millennium. And it should be noted that the United States Senate rejected the treaty, which left Europe on her own to work out its execution. It proved too onerous a task.

Lloyd George had been right: the harsh terms meted out to the Germans in the language of the treaty were such a "constant source of irritation" that eventually a man named Adolf Hitler was able to capitalize on an enraged and humiliated citizenry that felt wronged, and transform such discontent into vicious Nazism. Unable to achieve prosperity, or anything close to it, after the war, Germany readied itself for another.

DAYS OF INFAMY

Part II

The World Goes to War Again—

From the Russian Revolution

to Pearl Harbor

The Germans were unhappy again. Under the leadership of Adolf Hitler, the country attempted to recoup some of the losses of the First World War and to reclaim its place as the dominant European empire. This would involve German forces on two fronts, East and West, which would eventually prove Germany's undoing. With Stalin, in control of the Soviet Union since 1924, having paranoiacally purged his military leadership, Hitler could not resist pressing his forces eastward, hoping to engage and rout a weakened enemy. But with the Russians mustering troops at mind-boggling rates, and fighting heroically in defense of Moscow and Stalingrad, the German effort stalled. On the Western Front, countless mistakes and costly hesitations hampered the effort to parlay the quick vanquishing of France into something larger. And when the Japanese bombed Pearl Harbor, Hitler couldn't resist gambling that if he declared war on the then neutral United States, Japan would help him with his Russian nemesis in the East. All these miscalculations brought the world to the middle of a raging conflict that would only get larger and more deadly.

Stalin's Purges, Hitler's Putsch

THE PEACE ACCORDS, SO PAINSTAKINGLY worked out at Versailles, would not last long, for two major reasons: Germany's deep resentment of the terms, especially the monetary reparations required, and the fact that Russia, a major player on the Allied side for much of the war, because of its revolution in 1917, was not around to benefit from the spoils. As a result, both countries, Germany and Russia, rather quickly began to maneuver and to re-arm. As the historian A.J.P. Taylor pointed out in *Origins of the Second World War*: "The First [World] War explains the second and, in fact, caused it."

The British and French were happy, though. The long, tough Great War had been for them, when all their gains were totaled up, worth the effort. By the time the losers' lands had been redistributed to the victors, Britain and France both were larger and more forceful nations, with expanded holdings. The British picked up the East African colonies of German Tanganyika, giving them a broad sweep of possessions across Central Africa; also, from Turkey Britain secured mandates for Iraq and Palestine. France, in addition to having its German nemesis defanged, picked up Syria and Lebanon, strengthening its presence in the Mediterranean.

Germany, however, in a matter of six months saw its war gains evaporate; not only did it surrender lands it had long held, it ceded territory that it had just conquered. In the summer of 1918, Germany occupied virtually all of western Russia, including the great city of Kiev. With its allies still intact, it controlled the Balkans and Persia. But all that was lost by the time the Treaty of Versailles was signed. And the new socialist government in power in the new Germany, not knowing what to do, began to look for help, in an attempt to restore not only German pride but the German economy. Part and parcel of this was to again expand it borders. So it looked first to military help.

With the country teeming with guns and soldiers, Germany easily mounted an impressive force of volunteers, called the Freikorps. And a veteran of the Great War, Adolf Hitler, found work instructing soldiers of the new army in the importance of obedience to the state. Unfortunately for Germany and the world, the onerous conditions of the Versailles treaty kept the ruling Weimar Republic in such a state of instability that militaristic and increasingly fascistic forces began to foment and threaten the government. Eventually, Hitler would find a prominent pulpit on which to instruct the citizenry about obedience to the state. And he would become very good at it. Several blunders, however, had they not happened, might have averted his rise to power. Turmoil in Russia, always, it seems, Germany's nemesis of first resort, would turn out to impede that new Bolshevik government's ability to fend off the German assault which was still some years away.

Russia was enduring its own civil war, from 1917 to 1922, in the aftermath of the Revolution, which, though surprisingly and so quickly decisive in 1917, still required immense efforts to bring the entire country under its sway. In southern Russia, the Ukraine, from the Black to the Caspian Seas, in Poland, in Finland, in Kiev, Odessa, the Caucasus and in Siberia, the Tsar's White Army and the Red Bolsheviks fought for control of the country. Even the

Allies, basically a small contingent of French, British, and American troops, seized the northern city of Murmansk, with the hopes of abetting a White counterrevolution, but its effort ended in withdrawal. In the end, the deft leadership of Leon Trotsky gave the Bolsheviks the upper hand, and the Russian revolution was more or less complete by 1922.

With the death of Lenin in 1924, however, power passed to a triumvirate—Joseph Stalin, Zinoviev, and Kamenev. They isolated Trotsky, but then Stalin ditched Zinoviev and Kamenev, and allied himself with Bukharin. In 1928 Trotsky, Zinoviev, and Kamenev challenged Stalin's policies. The result was the sending of Trotsky into exile. This gave Stalin almost total power. But it is a power he would come to paranoiacally and ruthlessly abuse. So intent would Stalin become on rooting out any threat to his power that he ordered the arrests of thousands of people on trumped-up charges and had them either executed or sent to labor camps. And he undertook a purging of the armed forces that, in retrospect, proved to be a major tactical blunder, for the lack of military leadership would contribute mightily to Soviet Russia's poor showing in the initial phases of aggressions against Finland in 1939, and against Germany, when it invaded in 1941.

Hitler, however, was not yet in a role of leadership. This was not for want of trying. He would confess later, in 1936, that in the years 1919 to 1923 he "thought of nothing else than a coup d'etat." He tried desperately to spark a revolt, speaking at public meetings about the "criminals of Versailles" and railing about the unfairness of the reparations, the loss of territory, and the national shame. He also mentioned the enemies on German soil—Jews, Marxists, Bolshevists. A fierce currency crisis in Germany had people on edge, and Hitler was determined to make the most of it.

He began to organize a second army within the Weimar

Republic. Hitler became convinced that if he announced a putsch, a German coup, the rest of the army would not oppose him. He was wrong. On November 9, 1923, with sympathizers ready in the War Ministry awaiting his arrival, Hitler's march on the war building was stopped by police. Guns were fired. A man next to Hitler was killed, and Hermann Goering, even back then a Hitler loyalist, took a bullet in the leg. What Hitler liked to think of as his German National Army never got off the ground. At least not then.

Hitler was sentenced to five years in prison. The fact that he was released after only nine months (still long enough for him to dictate *Mein Kampf* to Rudolf Hess) surely was a major blunder for Germany and the world.

Still chafing under the enormous repayment schedules instituted by the Versailles terms, the German economy could improve only slightly in the years after Hitler's failed putsch. When the worldwide depression hit in 1929, Germany was again thrown into chaos and instability. By 1933, with the crisis in Germany deepening, Hitler could call upon his once secret army, which had now reached 400,000 strong, making him a real force in German politics. In that arena, extremist parties of the left and right benefited as social conditions deteriorated, with unemployment and inflation both out of control. The Communist Party and the National Socialist Party vied for the people's consent. By 1932, the Nazis had become the largest party in the Reichstag. The situation became internally violent, with armed Communist loyalists doing battle in the streets with what had become Hitler's private army. The president of Germany, Paul von Hindenburg, hoping to stave off Communist Party control, offered the chancellorship to Hitler. On January 30, 1933, Hitler accepted. Shortly thereafter, von Hindenburg died, and Hitler united the positions of president and chancellor under the title of Führer.

Stalin was equally busy. In 1929, having consolidated his control of the party and, to a much lesser extent, the country, he launched his first Five-Year Plan. While Stalin's main aim was to modernize Soviet industry, he was also determined to make agriculture more efficient. Collectivization had begun under Lenin, but this was now intensified, and it led to enormous suffering among the peasantry, with many being deported to labor camps. In 1932 one of the old guard Bolsheviks, M. N. Ryutin, circulated a pamphlet condemning these extreme measures and calling for Stalin's removal as head of the Communist Party. The following year A. P. Smirnov expressed similar sentiments. In neither case, however, was Stalin able to persuade the Politburo that they should be executed, thus demonstrating that Stalin's power was not as absolute as he wished. He would work on that.

The suffering of the Russian peasantry continued, exacerbated by a severe famine during the winter of 1932–33. Some party leaders now believed that the pressures of the Five-Year Plan should be eased, and they created a liberal faction within the Politburo. The Seventeenth Party Congress, held in early 1934, while extravagant in its praise of Stalin, expressed a majority view that the rate of economic growth projected for the Second Five-Year Plan should be scaled down. This was contrary to what Stalin wanted.

In December 1934, S. M. Kirov, a Politburo member and leader of the Communist Party contingent from Leningrad, was murdered. He was a member of the liberal faction, and a brilliant orator who had become very popular in party circles. No one has been able to prove it, but the suspicion is that Stalin instigated this crime. It sparked a reign of terror.

Under the direction of Stalin ally Genrikh Yagoda, head of NKVD, the secret police, scores of people were arrested, with an emphasis on the old guard Bolsheviks. They were incarcerated in Moscow's Lubyanka prison and coerced or brainwashed into making confessions. A series of show trials followed. The victims were then shot or sentenced to long terms in Siberian labor camps. During 1936–38 alone, 36 percent of the Communist Party's membership was purged, as Stalin's long arm reached out to nearly every walk of Soviet life.

Yagoda himself was arrested in 1937, together with several of his associates in the NKVD. His place was taken by N. I. Ezhov, who pursued the purges even more ruthlessly. Among his early victims was the Red Army's key reformer, Mikhail Tuchachevsky, who had created an impressive modern fighting force. He and his closest associates were shot. Almost all the senior hierarchy and many middle-grade officers in the armed forces were arrested. Reforms were reversed, and mediocre officers received rapid promotion.

Not until the end of 1938 did the pace of arrests slacken. By that time there were some 10 million Russian people in the labor camps, and morale in the party and armed forces was at an all-time low. Nonetheless, Stalin was in an expansive mood, and he and Hitler were headed toward an inevitable conflict.

Hitler, almost tribally wary of the Russians, struck an alliance in 1938 with Mussolini in Italy, who signed the Comintern Pact, uniting Germany and Italy, along with Japan, which had signed a year earlier, against the Soviet Union. This allowed Hitler to act with impunity against Austria and Czechoslovakia. Hitler took control of the Sudetenland, which contained Czechoslovakia's frontier fortifications. This prompted a meeting between Hitler, British Prime Minister Neville Chamberlain, and his French counterpart, Edouard Daladier. Hitler emerged from this "Munich Crisis" with more than he had planned for. It was a monumentally symbolic instance of Allied "appeasement," and it left all parties worried that indeed armed conflict, on a major scale, was in the near future.

Chamberlain, once back in Britain, warned Hitler that further aggression would be risking war. But Hitler was intent on reclaiming the Polish territory that now divided East Prussia from Danzig, a German-speaking but, after Versailles, "free" city.

Hitler moved in nonetheless, threatening the Poles and cleverly engaging the Russians in a deal. A pact was signed between the German and Russian foreign ministers, Ribbentrop and Molotov, in which Russia agreed not to resist a German invasion of Poland in return for a slice of eastern Poland. Poland counted on help from the west, particularly from France in the event of an invasion. But its hopes were in vain. Hitler secretly took common German convicts, dressed them in Polish uniforms, had them surround a German communications outpost in Poland, and then had them shot, the implication being that Poles were attempting to subvert a legitimate German presence on their soil. This staging of a false Polish aggression served as a pretext to move German tanks across the border. The Luftwaffe came after, virtually destroying the Polish air force. Warsaw was encircled and bombed. The Red Army heeded the call to help mop up; in return for their services, Russia demanded the right to base its troops in Lithuania, Latvia, and Estonia, which they annexed to the Soviet Union two years later.

While the Red Army had little trouble advancing into Poland in September 1939, things did not go so well a year later in Finland. Although it had been a Russian territory as recently as 1917, when it won its independence by routing local Bolsheviks, Stalin felt the Finnish border was a little too close to his important Baltic seaports. A long "Winter War" ensued, and the Finns proved tougher than Stalin would admit, but this was perhaps because he could never accept that he had not only decimated his military leadership in his purge, but eroded morale among the troops to a dangerous level. Although the Finns in the end sued for peace and acceded to the Russian demands, the Red Army lost 200,000 men in the fighting, eight times the number of Finn dead.

Even if it could be counted as a victory of sorts for the Soviet Union, the Winter War showed that the Red Army was in trouble. Reforms were initiated, but were slow in coming. The heavy losses further dampened troop morale, and emboldened Hitler to move even faster against Russia when the time came. And the time would come, in June 1941, when the Red Army suffered dreadfully again, only to be saved by the Russian winter and some German miscalculations.

Blunders of Hitler's Luftwaffe

AS ANY WAR PROGRESSES, EVENTS inevitably transpire that signal a mistake, a miscalculation, a moment of hubris, an oversight or outright blunder that could not have been detected beforehand, but which becomes clear in an instant, so clear as to seem obvious from the start. Surely, Stalin's purging of his military leadership came back to haunt him quickly, while the appeasement of Hitler in his aggression against Czechoslovakia in 1938 took longer to dawn on the Allies as a blunder. But when Hitler had unveiled his newly created Luftwaffe in 1935, the world had been impressed, and could not see, and surely Hitler could not, the mistakes made along the way in trying to establish a world-class air force. In fact, the Luftwaffe seemed the equal of the air forces of both Britain and France. And by the outbreak of war in 1939 the Luftwaffe appeared to be more powerful. Its performance during the invasion of Poland that September—a campaign that was over in three weeks—confirmed this impression.

Below the surface, however, the German Air Force was fatally flawed. The Luftwaffe failed to establish the right priorities for new types of aircraft, and increasingly lacked the production resources to produce sufficient quantities of planes. The high command suffered from internal rifts and disorganization. And Hermann Goering, the head of the Luftwaffe, who was enmeshed in a complicated relationship with his Führer, made crucial miscalculations and false assurances. These and other blunders would eventually lead the Luftwaffe, and Germany, to defeat.

The Treaty of Versailles, which ended World War I, severely damaged the war's aggressor—and biggest loser—Germany. It lost 14 percent of its land and 10 percent of its population in a redrawing of borders; along with the land went much of Germany's coal and iron ore deposits, not to mention cattle. Reparations were onerous, too: for terms of up to 10 years Germany was forced to give over much of its industrial production to the Allies. In addition, it was forbidden to have an air force. Nonetheless, Germany secretly put in place the framework for the Luftwaffe, even before Hitler came to power in 1933.

In contrast, by 1935 the air forces of the leading democracies of the world had operated under restricted budgets for many years and had few modern aircraft. The Luftwaffe, starting with a clean slate, was allocated large sums of money, however secretly. Consequently, from the outset its aircraft were modern, making it a formidable force.

The Luftwaffe was given an additional advantage when the Spanish Civil War broke out in July 1936. It was where the Luftwaffe would first cut its teeth. Hitler immediately sent Junker 52 transports to take the troops of leading Spanish insurgent General Francisco Franco from Spanish Morocco across the Mediterranean to Spain. Hitler then formed the Condor Legion, whose fighter and bomber crews, in conjunction with aircraft sent by Italian dictator Benito Mussolini, gained modern combat experience, particularly against the Russians, who supported the leftist Spanish government against Franco. Many German pilots' baptism by fire was against the Russian-made Polikarpov I-16s. By the start of World War II, the Luftwaffe was a tested fighting force. Yet it continued to be dogged by organizational problems.

Air Minister Goering was meddlesome, indolent, and, it was rumored, a drug addict. For a fact, he was regarded as Hitler's leading sycophant, full of extravagant praise for the Führer and averse to delivering bad news. And the loyalty, often blind, between the two men, ran both ways. Goering was reluctant to give the Führer a tactical assessment he did not want to hear, and Hitler proved incapable of ignoring Goering's assurances, no matter how impractical. After all, not only was Goering a war hero from the Great War, but he had taken a bullet alongside Hitler in their failed Beer Hall Putsch of 1923.

Below Goering in the power order came Erhard Milch, the Secretary of State for Air. Although a deft organizational man who earlier had set up Lufthansa, Germany's national airline, he was ambitious, a condition that could prove fatal in the Nazi hierarchy.

Hans Jeschonnek, the Luftwaffe's chief of staff, was next. Possessing a brilliant tactical mind, he unfortunately was a loner, a trait that National Socialism tended to look upon with intense suspicion. Jeschonnek was responsible for operations, intelligence, signals, logistics, training, and organization, but had direct access to Goering only on operational matters. He had no direct control over personnel, which was handled by Goering, who made of deployment and assignment of personnel more a political than a strategic affair.

Aircraft supply and procurement also lay outside Jeschonnek's control, which would hamstring anyone in charge of operations. Matters were not helped by the fact that Milch and Jeschonnek did not get along with one another.

World War I fighter ace Ernst Udet, who had been a film

star in the 1920s, was responsible for aircraft procurement, and answered directly to Milch. Although a glamorous figure, Udet was temperamentally ill-suited for his post. Like so much in the Nazi system of government, "divide and rule" reigned. It was a recipe for disaster.

When Hitler set up the Luftwaffe, he initially saw it as a means of threatening his neighbors and forcing them to bow to his demands. Mass overhead flyovers at the annual Nuremberg Rally ensured that this message got across. In a way, Hitler could be blamed, for once, for thinking too small. As a virtually landlocked country obsessed with expanding its borders east and west, Germany's habitual notion of war was the threatening of neighbors with the intention of gaining some ground for the Fatherland. If it was to be war, Hitler saw it in terms of troops marching somewhere, Poland, Czechoslovakia, France, Norway. The Luftwaffe's primary role would then be to support ground operations. And although to this end the army and the air force spent much time perfecting the techniques of air-ground cooperation—the Blitzkrieg—this policy caused the Luftwaffe to concentrate primarily on dive-bombing at the expense of developing a fleet of heavy, long-distance bombers. It was to prove a grave error when the geography of conflict widened.

For example, German aviation engineers developed the Junkers 87, the dreaded "Stuka," a bomber that proved highly effective during the early Blitzkrieg campaigns. But its slow speed in level flight (especially in coming out of a dive) made it vulnerable to both ground antiaircraft and air pursuit by enemy planes, and it was withdrawn from service in autumn 1943. Goering and his senior Luftwaffe officers demanded that other bombers be given a dive-bombing capability.

Notable among these was the highly promising Junkers 88. But once the necessary strengthening of the wings and fuselage had been carried out, the weight of the aircraft almost doubled, significantly reducing its performance.

None of this mattered very much during the early Blitzkrieg campaigns, in which the Luftwaffe performed impressively in attacking ground targets and destroying hostile aircraft. But when Hitler turned against Britain, attacking over the English Channel, the Luftwaffe's shortcomings became apparent. Not only was dive-bombing unproductive, but the Luftwaffe blundered by grossly underestimating its opponent.

At the end of May 1940, during the German invasion of the West, Goering declared that his air force would destroy the British Expeditionary Force in the Dunkirk pocket. The RAF fighters and the Royal Navy ensured that this did not happen; Goering's efforts fell flat, and nearly 400,000 British and French troops escaped capture and made it by boat across the English Channel. This robbed the Germans of a decisive victory.

When Goering sent the Luftwaffe to pave the way for a German invasion of Britain in the late summer of 1940, he badly miscalculated the RAF's remaining combat power. On August 1 he told his generals, "The Führer has ordered me to crush Britain with my Luftwaffe." This was the infamous Operation Sealion, the German code name for what came to be known as the Battle of Britain. It was not long before Goering and his generals, and their Führer, began to realize that it would take more than the Luftwaffe to bring Britain to its knees, or to the bargaining table.

There were several reasons for the British advantage. With the war in British skies, the Royal Air Force saved much fuel; the

German planes had to fly 50 to 100 miles before engaging the enemy, while British planes could engage as soon as they reached operational height. And the difference between bailing out over friendly soil and choosing the English Channel was not lost on anyone.

But the RAF also had advanced warning and radar systems, much more reliable than what the Germans had, and the full operation of British aviation and munitions meant that they could outproduce the Germans. In the crucial summer of 1940, the Vickers and Hawker factories in Britain were producing 500 planes a month, while the Germans were producing only about 140.

Most fatal to the Luftwaffe effort, however, was a lack of considered strategy. Goering thought brute pummeling would do; he was wrong. In a last-ditch effort, the Germans moved from bombing air fields to bombing the densely populated city of London, but the British would not fold. Unwilling to suffer any more air losses, Hitler called a halt to Operation Sealion. His thoughts turned to Russia.

It was in Russia, however, that the German Air Force's weaknesses, especially its growing inability to meet the demands made on it, really began to be revealed.

The Luftwaffe started the campaign in spectacular enough fashion. On the first morning of battle, June 22, 1940, it destroyed more than 500 Soviet aircraft on the ground and over 200 in the air. By the day's end, 1,200 flying machines, more than 25 percent of the Russian front-line fleet, was destroyed.

But as the German panzers plunged ever deeper into Russia, the Luftwaffe found it increasingly difficult to meet the Army's wide-ranging demands for support. The geography of battle had changed. These calls on the Luftwaffe required more aircraft than it possessed, and production could not meet demand.

The underlying cause of this was Hitler's refusal to put the German economy, especially the munitions industry, on a proper war footing until 1943. The German aircraft industry therefore lacked the resources to produce the ever increasing numbers of aircraft needed by the Luftwaffe.

Goering, however, increasingly blamed Udet, the former film star, for the production shortcomings. Udet became so depressed that he committed suicide in November 1941, although Goering had it officially announced that Udet had been killed testing a new secret weapon.

But it became more and more apparent that one of the Luftwaffe's most serious shortcomings was the lack of long-range heavy bombers. It had nothing with which to strike at the rapidly growing Soviet war industry. This shortfall was the result of blunders by the Luftwaffe high command.

In the mid 1930s development work began on what the Germans called the Uralbomber, a four-engine heavy bomber designed to strike at Russia. However, Erhard Milch ordered all work on the project to cease, ruling that all bombers must be two-engine types because more of that size could be built, improving the production times.

The Heinkel company, however, continued to believe in heavy bombers and developed the He177, with two sets of engines in tandem to circumvent Milch's policy. But there were continual problems with these due to their tendency to overheat. Also, the Luftwaffe's dive-bombing fixation meant that the He177 had to have this capability. Consequently, the He177's entry into service was excessively delayed, and the Germans had nothing with which to strike at the Russian munitions industry until it was too late.

After the surrender at Stalingrad in early 1943, the Germans were steadily driven back, putting the Soviet munitions industry out of range, even to the He177. By the spring of 1943 the tide had clearly turned against the Luftwaffe, especially with British and U.S. heavy bombers increasingly appearing in the skies over the Third Reich. They starkly brought home to the Germans their own lack of a heavy bomber.

Both Goering and Hitler blamed Jeschonnek for the air force's shortcomings, so much so that, like Udet, he eventually committed suicide in November 1943. In two years' time Allied bombers, of the sort the Luftwaffe never managed to develop, punished the Third Reich. There would be more German suicides.

German Hesitation at
Dunkirk and Operation Sealion

IN THE LATE SPRING OF 1940, Hitler had something to prove to the world: that he could march through more than Poland. The previous year, the poorly equipped Polish defenses proved to be no obstacle for a quick, three-week blitzkrieg, a combined air and ground assault by the confident Germans. Now it was time for France.

Hitler felt that he could dispatch the French with nearly as little effort, and that, as a result, the British would come to terms with Germany, and Hitler would then have full use of the great British maritime forces, the perfect complement to the crack German Panzer Divisions and mighty Luftwaffe, which had not yet shown its flaws and was still formidable. Throwing in the Royal Air Force would surely help things along.

The Germans attacked across a wide front, through the Netherlands in the north, through Belgium south of that, through Luxembourg to the extreme south, all forces moving toward northern France. The French armies attempted countermeasures, aided by the Belgian Army. Seeing the vulnerability of France to the steadily advancing Germans, Winston Churchill, only recently having replaced the disgraced Neville Chamberlain as Prime Minister, and amazed that the French had no strategic reserve forces to call upon, agreed on May 16 to send six British squadrons to help shore up the French defenses; already in place was nearly the entire British army, known as the BEF (British Expeditionary Forces). Despite some effective counterattacks, led by a young Charles DeGaulle (against a temporarily rattled Erwin Rommel), the German Panzer Divisions, 1,800 tanks strong, moved through the Ardennes Forest with ease. The Allied plan to break through the German assault and join up with the French forces to the south was obviously in tatters. But against the advice of his on-site commanders, who preached aggression, Hitler, spooked by the counterattack on Rommel and Belgian activity to the north of his Panzer Divisions, issued a "stop order," claiming that his Panzer Divisions needed a rest. What Hitler most wanted to avoid was having his tank corps lured into the wet lowlands near the French coast, which was crisscrossed by dangerous canals. Unbeknownst to Hitler, Churchill had already decided that the fight for France, for now, was lost, and civilian and naval ships began to steam from England through the North Sea to pick up retreating British and French troops.

When the Germans realized what was afoot, Air Minister Goering issued reassurances that proved hollow: he would bomb the coastline and make retreat by sea impossible. In the next week, through June 4, 1940, the Germans did sink a half dozen British and two French destroyers, but more than 337,000 Allied soldiers escaped capture.

It was a timely and brilliant escape. The British could have been pinned and forced to surrender there in Dunkirk had not the Germans hesitated. But getting back across the English Channel was not the end of it for the British; neither was it the end of German blundering.

By June 1940, a virtually defenseless Britain stood awaiting

German invasion. The English Channel had saved them once, but now it seemed no protection at all. Across it, in northern France, most of the British Army's heavy weapons lay abandoned. Despite the success of the escape, the fact remained that 11,000 of its best troops had been killed by the German Army. Another 50,000 soldiers were now prisoners of war. And the RAF had suffered heavy losses during the fighting.

Only the Royal Navy remained strong. However, on its own the Navy was unlikely to be able to prevent an immediate German invasion. Was British surrender, in the event of a German invasion, inevitable? Would the war in Western Europe be lost so quickly?

We will never know, because the invasion did not take place. This was due to a major blunder by Adolf Hitler himself.

Having brought France to its knees, and with much of the Continent now under German control, Hitler was convinced that Britain, now left on her own, would not fight on. Their escape was just pure luck; the British would be sensible, he felt. In any event, Hitler did not want to destroy Britain anyway; he wanted to use her. In this, he terribly underestimated the British resolve to fight.

Hitler was nonetheless poised to drop the hammer. His U-boats were ready to throttle the maritime communications that were Britain's lifeline. The Luftwaffe was ready to bomb towns and cities throughout the British Isles. Surely, Britain would sue for an honorable peace. With France having fallen in only six weeks, Hitler confidently disbanded seventeen infantry divisions and anticipated the end of the fighting in the West, with victory gained at very little cost.

Across the English Channel the mood was very different. Throughout June 1940 Winston Churchill worked tirelessly to rally the British people and organize the defense of the country against German invasion. Contrary to what Hitler believed, peace was not on the British agenda.

Not until July 1, 1940, did Hitler realize he might have to use force to subdue his one remaining active enemy. He ordered preparations for a cross-Channel invasion. But he set no date for it. He stated that it was merely a possible option.

General Franz Halder, Chief of Staff of the German Armed Forces Supreme Headquarters, was responsible for drawing up the plan. Halder began on the mistaken premise that the invasion was little more than a large-scale river crossing. The German Army had proved adept at these during the recent campaign in France. Unaccountably, Halder ignored the fact that the English Channel is one of the most unpredictable stretches of water in the world, as the Allies would learn so well four years later in their own cross-Channel invasion at D-Day.

Halder's plan called for forces from Army Group A to land at Ramsgate and other ports on the Kent coast. Other troops from the same group would land on the Sussex coast and on the Isle of Wight. Divisions from Army Group B would land on the Dorset coast near Lyme Regis. This meant an overall frontage of some 200 miles.

Grand Admiral Erich Raeder, the German naval commander-in-chief, had grave objections to this plan and made them known to Hitler. Raeder was well aware of the trouble the German Navy had during the April 1940 fighting in Norway, when heavy losses were taken. All Raeder had available were two modern battle cruisers, two elderly battleships, four cruisers, and a few destroyers. He did not believe that this was enough to protect an invasion fleet operating on such a wide front. The German Navy also possessed no landing craft or other amphibious shipping capable of landing troops and equipment on hostile beaches. The Royal Navy, on the other hand, still had four battleships, two battle cruisers, two aircraft carriers, and numerous cruisers and destroyers.

Faced with this large British superiority, Raeder could not guarantee the security of the invasion fleet as it crossed the Channel. He told Hitler that the Royal Navy might destroy it before a single German soldier had set foot on English soil. This was not the sort of news Hitler liked.

He overruled Raeder, and on July 16, 1940, he issued a directive for Operation Sealion. All preparations for it had to be completed within a month. It would prove an impossible deadline to meet.

In mid-July 1940, the Luftwaffe had begun to harry British shipping in the Channel and to attack ports in southern Britain. Hitler hoped that these demonstrations by his air force would convince the British that further resistance was useless, making Operation Sealion unnecessary. The British continued to watch and wait. They were unintimidated.

On July 19, three days after he had issued his directive, Hitler made a speech in the Reichstag, accusing Churchill of being the only obstacle to peace. Hitler saw no reason "why this war must go on." His hopes were immediately dashed by the British government's outright rejection of his peace offer. So Sealion proceeded.

The Germans scoured inland waterways in the whole of western Europe looking for flat-bottomed barges that could be readily used for beach landings, assembling them in Dutch, Belgian, and French ports. It didn't occur to the Germans that the barges could not cope with the Channel under their own steam and would have to be towed to their landing points. And there were other makeshift solutions: some barges were hastily fitted with aircraft engines. Many had to be specially adapted to take tanks and other heavy vehicles across the sea.

With all that needed to be done, it became clear that Hitler's deadline could not be met. On the last day of July Hitler held a conference at his Bavarian retreat, the Berghof. Raeder once more advocated a narrower invasion front. In view of the large amount of preparatory work that still needed to be done, he also said that he believed that the invasion should be postponed until May 1941. Hitler, however, ruled that all preparations must now be completed by September 15.

The decision as to whether Sealion should be mounted then or postponed until spring 1941 would depend on Hermann Goering and his Luftwaffe. The planners rightly recognized that an invasion of this scope would succeed only if there was German air supremacy over southern England.

The Luftwaffe was now to mount a concentrated attack to destroy the RAF. Goering called together his air commanders to plan what he called Eagle Day, the massive onslaught that would give the Germans the necessary air supremacy over the invasion area. But poor weather delayed the opening of the attack.

Across the English Channel, every week that the invasion was delayed was a bonus. Defenses along the English south coast grew stronger, and mobile reserves were organized to counterattack the Germans on the beaches. A part-time local defense force, the Home Guard, had been formed at the end of May 1940, and this, too, was rapidly increasing in numbers. And the production of British Spitfire and Hurricane fighters was increasing, too. Indeed, the entire RAF Fighter Command was growing in strength. Even eccentric strategies for defense were being dreamed up; one was to set the sea alight with burning oil to prevent a German landing.

And although the Luftwaffe's operations over the English Channel during July had forced the Royal Navy to withdraw all its warships larger than destroyers to safe anchorage north of Scotland, it would not take long for the Home Fleet to steam south at the first sign of invasion.

A German air offensive against southern England began on August 12, with attacks on fighter airfields and on vital early warning radar stations on the English south coast. Goering, however, made a key error by quickly halting his attacks on the radar stations and concentrating on airfields and aircraft factories. Meanwhile, the debate between the German Navy and Army over the narrow versus wide invasion front continued. Eventually, a compromise was reached. With radar intact, the RAF was able to track the routes of the German planes and anticipate attacks.

The Germans did, in the end, narrow the frontage of attack, although not by as much as the Navy had wanted, with an assault from Cherbourg being canceled. The westernmost landing point was now to be Worthing. This meant that only one army group would carry out the invasion, that commanded by Gerd von Rundstedt, who had little confidence in Sealion.

Recalling that some 150 years earlier Napoleon had wanted to invade Britain but decided it was too difficult, von Rundstedt did not believe that the operation would ever be mounted. When the preparations were reaching a critical stage, he went on leave. His lack of faith and the preparation problems did not bode well. His doubts were reinforced on August 14, when he and a number of other senior officers were present in Berlin to receive their field marshal's batons from Hitler—rewards for the recent campaign in France. Hitler assured the assembled that Sealion would not be mounted if the risks were too great. Invasion was not the only means of defeating Britain, he said.

Hitler had already stated at the Berghof conference at the end of July that Britain's best hope lay in Russia and the United States. If Russia was vanquished, America would soon drop out of the picture, leaving Britain without a future. He therefore intended, come the spring of 1941, to destroy the Soviet Union. Yet Hitler had not abandoned the prospect of invading Britain.

Twelve days after Hitler's speech to his generals, Franz Halder, the author of the original plan, noted in his diary that interest in Sealion had increased, as the forces involved stepped up their training. Meanwhile the RAF and the Luftwaffe were engaged in fierce dog fights in the air. Casualties were high on both sides.

By the end of August, the Germans were convinced that half the British fighter force had been destroyed. Yet RAF Fighter Command was showing no signs of cracking, and its resistance was as fierce as ever. On the ground, efforts were redoubled to ensure that any invasion attempt met with a fierce resistance. RAF bombers also began to strike at the barge concentrations gathering at Channel and North Sea ports.

On September 3, 1940, with no detectable weakening of Britain's air defenses, Field Marshal Keitel, Hitler's chief of staff, issued a directive provisionally postponing Sealion until the twenty-first of the month. Further postponements followed, until on September 14, Hitler put it back until the twenty-seventh, the last date on which winds and tides were likely to be suitable.

Goering had by now turned to bombing Britain by night. But on September 15 he launched one last desperate effort by day to destroy RAF Fighter Command. It was a failure, with the Luftwaffe losing twice as many aircraft as its adversary.

Two days later Hitler postponed Sealion indefinitely and

turned his eye eastward towards the Soviet Union. Contrary to what many observers had believed, Britain had survived and would fight on.

This meant that from June 1941, when his forces invaded the Soviet Union, Hitler was committed to a war on two fronts. His armies would fight an ever more grueling campaign in the East. In the West they had to guard against invasion from Britain, which at some stage surely must come.

This was especially true once America was drawn into the war, something which would not have happened if Britain had gone under in the summer of 1940. Hitler's failure to think ahead and draw up a timely plan that would ensure Britain's early defeat after the fall of France was a grave blunder. When he did finally wake up to the fact, he seriously misjudged the mood of the British people in his belief that the twin threats of the Luftwaffe and U-boats would cow them into submission.

The Pilot Who Bombed London

THERE HAD NEVER BEEN AN air war like that which marked
World War II, and there probably never will be another to
match. The German air assaults in Poland, in France, the Blitz on
Britain, later the Allied bombing of Germany, and the American air
campaign against Japan that spelled the end of the war were unprecedented in the tonnage of bombs dropped. Civilian casualties
were extremely high, centuries-old architecture lost, elaborate human communities erased. It seems ironic in retrospect, painfully
ironic, to realize that when World War II began, bomber crews on
both sides were under strict orders to avoid cities.

And they did so, for the most part, until a single German
crew lost its bearings and dropped bombs on the outskirts of London. Thereafter, the war would see countless merciless bombings
of teeming civilian targets.

When Europe went to war in September 1939, the peoples of both
sides immediately feared the bombing of cities, especially the use
of gas bombs. The Zeppelin and bomber raids of 1914–18 had
triggered widespread predictions that this would happen. And more
recent examples of bombing were cause for concern: the Spanish
Civil War, which began in 1936, witnessed widespread bombing,

particularly the devastation of the Basque town of Guernica by the German Condor Legion on April 26, 1937, forever memorialized in Picasso's great painting.

As war clouds loomed ever larger over Europe, governments took steps to prepare for this aerial onslaught by organizing the building of air raid shelters, the assembling of civil defense groups, and distribution of gas masks. No wonder everyone believed that the war would open with mass bombing. However, the air forces of both sides had a policy in place dictating that they would bomb only military targets.

Early on, the Luftwaffe concentrated on providing support for the German ground forces as they overran Poland, while the British air force contented itself with attacks on German warships and the dropping of propaganda leaflets over Germany. Cities and civilians were left untouched.

The first apparent crack in this policy came in September 1939, when the Poles declared that they would defend their capital, Warsaw, to the last, inviting the Germans to regard the city as a legitimate military target. It was therefore subjected to 10 days' air and artillery bombardment. Warsaw surrendered only after all the public utilities had been destroyed and hundreds killed.

In April 1940, the war began to heat up again, when Hitler invaded Denmark and Norway. A month later, on May 10, came the long-awaited German invasion of France and the Low Countries. It was in Holland that the next crack appeared in the policy of not bombing centers of population.

The German forces invading Holland were keen to overrun the country as quickly as possible so that they could turn south to join in the battle against the French and British. The Dutch strategy was to fall back and defend their principal cities of Amsterdam and Rotterdam. On May 14, after some fighting, the Germans demanded the surrender of Rotterdam, but the Dutch gave no immediate answer. The Luftwaffe was therefore ordered to bomb the port.

While the bombers were in the air, the Dutch surrendered Rotterdam. Radio messages to the aircraft to abort the mission did not get through, and the attack went ahead. The center of Rotterdam was reduced to a sea of flames.

The British thought that the air attack against Rotterdam meant that the Germans had resorted to terror bombing. While the RAF was not prepared to employ the same tactics, the example of Rotterdam did provoke a tentative easing of its bombing restrictions.

German centers of war industry east of the River Rhine were now added to RAF Bomber Command's target list. Inevitably, a few civilians were killed in these raids, but they were not the primary target. Furthermore, the British bombers were too few in number to make much of an impression. But on June 22, 1940, France was forced to surrender. This left Britain on her own.

A triumphal Hitler was convinced that his last remaining enemy must make peace. But across the English Channel, Prime Minister Winston Churchill made it clear that Britain would fight on. Consequently, invasion appeared to be the only option in Hitler's eyes, and preparations for it got underway. The English Channel might seem to the Germans to be just a large river, but before crossing it, they had to gain air supremacy over southern England. Only after destroying the Royal Air Force could the invasion succeed.

From the middle of July 1940 the Luftwaffe tried to do

this by attacking British convoys in the English Channel in the hope that this would draw out the RAF fighters. The RAF, knowing that the main battle was yet to come, refused to be tempted to any significant degree.

On August 1, Hitler issued another directive, which was addressed primarily to Hermann Goering and his Luftwaffe. This was to launch its main offensive against the RAF on August 6, or as soon as possible afterward. Hitler stressed that there was to be no "terror bombing" in Operation Sealion without his authorization. Even so, such a massive air campaign created a real danger of bombing blunders.

Poor weather delayed the main German air offensive against Britain until August 12. The Luftwaffe attacked the RAF fighter airfields and the control rooms that coordinated their operations. It also initially went for the radar stations on the English coasts which provided the crucial early warning needed to intercept the German planes. A major German error during the subsequent battle was not to keep up these attacks until the system was destroyed.

The German bombers had a strong fighter escort built around the now well-proven Messerschmitt Me109. These did have a problem, however. The fuel they carried allowed them only 20 minutes flying over England itself, and this included combat. This meant that the RAF fighters were often able to get in amongst the bombers without interference, and the number shot down began to mount. The Germans, on the other hand, enjoyed strength in numbers, and the air battles were intense.

Another spell of adverse weather forced a lull from August 19 to 24, giving both sides a much needed break. Goering now changed tactics, reducing the number of bombers attacking by day. But he reinforced their fighter escort in an attempt to complete the destruction of the RAF. The remainder of the German bomber force was switched to attacks by night against targets connected with the British war effort so as to stretch the country's air defenses.

The first of these night attacks took place on August 24–25 and was to reveal that the German bomber crews had problems navigating at night. The targets were oil storage tanks in the English Midlands and near Southampton on the south coast. The route would take some bombers close to London.

During the course of this raid a group of twelve Heinkel He111 bombers en route for the Midlands lost their way. Either they miscalculated the wind speed or misidentified landmarks on the ground. Whether they thought they were over the target or they panicked, the crew of at least one of these aircraft dropped or jettisoned their bombs over London, and nine civilians were killed. This was in total contravention of Hitler's orders that cities were not to be attacked without his express permission.

The crews were severely reprimanded for their blunder. Some say that they were immediately transferred to the infantry as punishment. A furious Churchill ordered immediate retaliation with an attack on Berlin the following night. Eighty RAF bombers tried to attack armament factories on the northern outskirts of Berlin. Again, navigation difficulties meant that most bombs fell on farmland to the south. The Luftwaffe kept well away from London during the next few days and nights. But RAF Bomber Command did not observe the same policy toward Berlin. It was now firmly on its list of targets, and planes returned to Berlin on the night of August 28. This time German civilians were killed.

Yet American journalist William L. Shirer, who was in Berlin at the time, thought that Berliners were more concerned that the British bombers were actually penetrating to their city rather than the fatalities that the bombs had caused. This is not surprising, since Goering had earlier boasted in public that no British aircraft would be able to fly over the Third Reich. If they did, he told his audience, "You can call me Maier"—a popular German expression meaning his name would be mud.

Goering's stupid boast helped to fuel anger among the German press, which the next day produced headlines like "Cowardly British Attack," calling the bombers pirates. The Nazi hierarchy feared that this might fuel civil unrest in Berlin. This was especially after a third RAF attack on the night of the September 3–4 caused further death and destruction. The following day Hitler made a speech to the party faithful.

He declared, "When the British air force drops two or three or four thousand kilograms of bombs, then we will in one night drop 150, 250, 300, or 400 thousand kilograms. When they declare that they will increase their attacks on our cities, then we will raze their cities to the ground."

There could now be no turning back. The blunder by a single bomber crew was about to turn the war into a nightmare for hundreds of thousands of civilians. On Saturday, September 7, German bombers attacked the London docks. That night another 247 bombers—three times the number that had been attacking Berlin—raided the British capital again. Two thousand Londoners were killed or injured in these two attacks. In what became known as the Blitz, London was to be bombed every night but one during the next two months. Other British cities as far north as Glasgow in Scotland also suffered.

But none of this could disguise the fact that the Luftwaffe had failed. It had not destroyed the RAF, and hence the invasion Hitler had planned could not take place. As a result, Hitler turned prematurely east to attack Russia and committed his armies to an agonizing and ultimately disastrous four years of gargantuan struggle.

Hitler continued the Blitz until May 1941, but, contrary to his hopes, Britain did not break. Instead, RAF Bomber Command began to steadily pulverize Germany. Later joined by the bombers of the U.S. Eighth Air Force, it became a ruthless offensive that would continue until virtually the end of the war in Europe.

The campaign would cost the lives of hundreds of thousands of German civilians and caused untold destruction. By May 1945 large parts of Germany had become a virtual desert. The horrific destruction caused by aerial bombing in Europe would be repeated against Japan.

Those anonymous and probably bewildered German He111 crews who lost their way over London in August 1940 did, by their blunder of dropping bombs on innocent civilians, set off an irreversible and fatal chain reaction.

Hitler's Declaration
of War on the U.S.

ONE WOULD BE HARD-PRESSED to imagine a more perilous activity than conducting a world war. The scale could not be more vast, and the stakes—the right to govern peoples, the assertion of boundaries, the imposition of social or political ideologies—could not be higher. Conceiving and executing the kinds of strategies necessary to engage the world in such a conflict involves forging alliances with friends, intimidating and deceiving enemies, and the deft placating of the nonaligned. In the late summer of 1941, Adolf Hitler had all of these things under way; and it was his failure to properly read the intentions of friends and enemies alike that proved his personal undoing. It led to the fall of his country, and along the way incurred an almost immeasurable cost to mankind.

Throughout the war Hitler's mistakes were legion, though he had plenty of help. His biggest tactical blunder, without a doubt, was engaging the one enemy he had been determined not to arouse: the United States.

In that summer of 1941, as the Luftwaffe was bombing England, Winston Churchill was pleading with the United States to enter the war. Unmoved, the U.S. held to its policy of neutrality and steered clear of entanglement in what it deemed a foreign conflict. Germany, despite a few strategic mistakes, had been occupying most of France for over a year, including the great city of Paris. Hitler's hope for Great Britain was what he had gained in France: submission. He did not want to destroy the British people any more than he did the French; in fact, he valued British military and industrial might and he wanted it to serve his cause. If Britain would acquiesce, Hitler could put his fuller attentions on his ultimate goal: conquering the Soviet Union. Hitler not only reviled the Marxism-Leninism of the Soviet state; he not only did not trust the giant country to keep its hands off the territories in Eastern Europe; he also wanted to capture the oil-rich lands and vast grain-bearing plains of Russia in order to feed his war machine and his soldiers. The existence of the Molotov-Ribbentrop Pact, signed by the Soviet Union and Germany in August 1939, which pledged mutual non-aggression and also that one would rush to the other's defense if attacked, only made Hitler a little more cautious. He eyed Soviet intentions with great distrust; the Russians moved aggressively toward areas of sensitive German interests, especially in the Baltic. And Hitler ordered plans to be made for an eventual plunge into the Soviet Union.

Meanwhile, the Fascist government of Italy, under Benito Mussolini, was at war with Britain also, and continued to agitate aggressively for leverage in the Mediterranean, and Japan was pushing hard in the South Pacific to secure its access to raw materials. Germany, Italy, and Japan, all bent on pursuing their own advantages, had managed to sign the Tripartite Agreement, in which each determined to leave the other alone but to come to the defense of any of the three that became subject to aggression by another country.

That was the situation on December 7, 1941, with German forces deployed in the West against Britain and in the East against the Red Army, when the Japanese made a surprise attack on the U.S. naval base at Pearl Harbor, destroying much of America's

Pacific fleet. On the following day President Franklin Roosevelt declared war on the Japanese Empire, ominously proposing that December 7 was a date that would "live in infamy," as indeed it would. Luckily for Hitler and Mussolini, or so it would seem, this declaration of war did not extend to Germany or Italy. Britain, which had hoped for some event that would thrust the United States into the war, was to be disappointed. Roosevelt would ask Congress to war only with the country that had attacked, not the allies of that country. Hitler may have sighed with relief. But instead, four days later, on December 11, he declared war on the United States. Another day of infamy. Why?

It was ironic that through his hasty step Hitler succeeded where Britain had so far failed in bringing America into the war. While the U.S. supply of arms to the Soviet Union and Britain and activities by the U.S. Navy in the North Atlantic demonstrated increasing American support for the Allied cause and were a source of irritation to Hitler, American isolationism prevented her from becoming actively involved in the European conflict. A Gallup poll in 1940 showed that 80 percent of Americans were against entering the war. It was Japan that persuaded Hitler to declare war on the United States. He hoped that Japan would then do him a favor in return by moving against the Soviet Union. But he was wrong.

The policy of American isolationism, which goes back to the early nineteenth century, was still going strong. In the mid-1930s, as it grappled with the effects of the Depression, America's determination to stay out of other nations' conflicts was reinforced by three Neutrality Acts passed by Congress, even though this was at a time when European Fascism and Nazism were becoming ever more strident, increasing the likelihood of another European war.

Across the other side of the world, a militaristic Japan was also threatening world peace. In 1937 Japanese forces invaded China and began a war that would last for eight years. Realizing the threat to U.S. Pacific interests, Roosevelt eventually lent Chinese premier Chiang Kai-shek a limited sum of money to buy arms. In fact, it was Roosevelt's keen sense that far-flung conflicts would eventually threaten United States interests that allowed the U.S. to quietly prepare for war.

When war did break out in Europe in September 1939, Hitler was convinced that the U.S. would be a bystander, as it had been in 1914. Even after Hitler had invaded Czechoslovakia, overrun Poland in three weeks, and attacked Denmark and Norway, many Americans hoped that Britain and France would come to terms with Hitler, and that worldwide conflict would be averted.

The blitzkrieg campaign that quickly overran France and the Low Countries in a mere six weeks, routing the Belgians, forcing the British Expeditionary Force to flee across the English Channel, and ending with Germans triumphantly entering Paris, convinced Hitler that Britain could not survive on her own and would quickly surrender. It was a view shared by most Americans.

But British Prime Minister Winston Churchill thought otherwise. Knowing that Britain could not defeat Germany and Italy on her own, he looked to the U.S. as an ally. He began to court Roosevelt, while exhorting his own troops to keep at the ready.

On July 16, Hitler ordered the invasion of Britain, but not before appealing to Britain to end hostilities. Sealion, as we have seen, turned out to be a mistake, or certainly evidence of a German shortcoming. Panzer Divisions on the Continent, working in conjunction with air power, might have proven decisive, but Britain, across the protective waters of the English Channel, would prove able to withstand the mighty, and mightily flawed, Luftwaffe.

Roosevelt was sympathetic to Britain's plight, and knew that the cause of global democracy was at stake. Yet domestically he faced a problem: reelection in November 1940 against a Republican candidate, Wendell Willkie, whose strong isolationism was in step with the overwhelming majority of Americans. Roosevelt proceeded cautiously.

The one active step he did take during that critical summer of 1940 was to trade 50 elderly World War I destroyers for a lease on British naval bases in the Caribbean. Roosevelt also managed to persuade Congress to allow for the calling up of the National Guard for a year's active duty and to introduce a limited form of the draft. And, perhaps most significant, he authorized a massive naval expansion program.

Meanwhile, Hitler, realizing that Britain intended to fight on and not surrender, was forced to make hurried preparations for invasion.

Key to this plan was air supremacy over southern England. However, during the Battle of Britain in the summer of 1940, he failed to achieve this. Or rather, Air Minister and chief of Luftwaffe Hermann Goering failed, by refusing to employ a diversified ground and air strategy in favor of blunt assertion of German air superiority—"by means of hard blows I plan to have this enemy, who has already suffered a crushing moral defeat, down on his knees in the nearest future, so that an occupation of the island by our troops can proceed without risk." But the British, with a higher capacity for producing planes and a keener sensing and tracking system, were able to fight Goering to an aerial stalemate. Eventually, with German fighter and bomber losses mounting, Hitler postponed the air operation. And the heroic efforts of no more than 2,500 British pilots, known as "The Few," saved the country from invasion. And although Britain continued to be bombed as "the Blitz" continued, there was no longer a threat of German occupation, and Hitler turned his attention more fully elsewhere.

He turned east toward Russia, his ultimate enemy. It

would be this radical change in strategy that would eventually lead to Hitler's blunder in declaring war on the United States.

The subjugation of Bolshevik Russia had been a goal of Hitler's since long before he came to power. The Marxist-Leninist philosophy was as dangerous on the streets of Berlin as in the halls of the Kremlin. The notion of the proletariat leading a country was not Hitler's cup of tea; Mussolini, founder of Fascism, which espoused the stern rule of a few, was more to his liking. It was closer to Nazism. Hitler was also sharp to recognize long-standing rivalries. Recalling that Russia and Japan were traditional enemies, stretching back to a war between the two countries at the beginning of the century, Hitler decided to take advantage of this in his relationship with Japan. And he proceeded with canny deliberation.

In 1936 Berlin and Tokyo signed the Anti-Comintern Pact, the object of which was to halt the spread of Marxism-Leninism. In September 1940 relations between Berlin and Tokyo were further cemented. Japan joined Germany and Italy in the Tripartite Pact, which pledged the signatories to come to each other's aid if any one of the three were attacked. Hitler's secret agenda was that Japan would join him when he attacked the Soviet Union.

But while the Japanese maintained friendly relations with Germany, they had a different objective—the creation of an empire in Southeast Asia. In April 1941 they signed a five-year non-aggression pact with Moscow, reducing the high tension on the border between Japanese-held Manchuria and the Soviet Union.

This did not deter Hitler from mounting a massive, four-million-troop invasion of the Soviet Union in June of that year. The effort was called Operation Barbarossa, after the warrior-emperor who, according to medieval legend, lies dormant until Germany is most in need. Hitler still believed that Japan would tie down considerable Russian forces on the Manchurian border.

Meanwhile, as Britain continued to endure the German air attack, American public opinion toward the British cause began to change. London-based U.S. journalists like Edward R. Murrow sent back moving accounts of the steadfastness of the British people under this aerial onslaught. Perhaps then Hitler should have sensed that it might be only a matter of time before the United States became involved. Instead, he proceeded in a fashion that provoked that participation.

Roosevelt won solidly over Willkie in the November 1940 election and was assured of another term in office. He knew very well that sooner or later America would find itself at war, but his fellow countrymen were still very much opposed to it.

In his State of the Union address in January 1941, Roosevelt spoke to the American people of the four essential freedoms at stake in the war—of speech and religion, and from want and fear. In this context America was to establish herself as "the arsenal of the democracies."

Roosevelt followed this up by introducing his Lend-Lease bill in early 1941. The beneficiaries of this would be both Britain and China, who were clamoring for American munitions. Each country lacked the means to make immediate payments, but Lend-Lease meant that they could pay in kind at the end of the war. It was, as Roosevelt explained, like lending a neighbor a garden hose in order to put out a fire. These weapons were to be invaluable to Britain, China, and later the Soviet Union.

Roosevelt also allowed secret military staff talks to be held with the British and Canadians to agree on a common strategy if America entered the war. The crucial decision reached was that, in the event of war with both Japan and Germany, priority would be given to achieving victory in Europe.

Activities were beginning to heat up in the otherwise chilly North Atlantic. U.S. merchant vessels were carrying Lend-Lease materials to Britain, but this laid them open to danger from Hitler's U-boats, then ravaging the sea lanes. In April 1941, Roosevelt set up military bases in Greenland and extended the Pan American Security Zone from longitude 60 degrees west to 28 degrees west. This brought it far north in the Atlantic, close to Iceland, then garrisoned by the British, and effectively involved the U.S. in policing the Atlantic. And that July U.S. Marines began to relieve the British garrison on Iceland. American warships now had justification in escorting vessels this far east.

Hitler was intensely irritated by the American actions in the North Atlantic, but as yet was wary of bringing another player onto the allied team that was against him. With his Panzers driving ever farther east toward Moscow, he did not want to be distracted from the conquest of the Soviet Union. He therefore gave his U-boat crews strict instructions not to attack American ships.

German-U.S. tension rose in September 1941 with the first clash between a U.S. warship, the destroyer *Greer*, and a U-boat. Roosevelt warned the Axis powers that their warships entering the Pan American Security Zone would do so at their own risk. Furthermore, U.S. warships would now escort any vessel carrying Lend-Lease within the security zone. The aircraft and tanks that these ships carried were invaluable in maintaining the British forces in the Middle East and at home. American supplies also took some pressure off Britain's very stretched munitions industry. This fact, and Roosevelt's warning, further increased Hitler's irritation and that of his U-boat crews, who found it difficult in the midst of an action against a convoy to identify U.S. warships. But, desperate to reach Moscow before the onset of the Russian winter, Hitler still refused to allow his U-boats to attack U.S. warships in the North Atlantic.

Even so, as the autumn of 1941 wore on, there were clashes between the two, with American destroyers damaged and even sunk. In China, the Japanese continued to seize and occupy ever more of the country.

The anti-war feeling in America was still strong in spite of the Atlantic clashes and the situation in China. Indeed, Roosevelt was forced to agree to deactivation of the National Guard divisions. But growing American concern that Japanese policies threatened U.S. Pacific interests did enable Roosevelt to get the Neutrality Acts repealed, but only by the narrowest of margins. The American position was that Japanese forces must withdraw from China. To this end a limited embargo on the export of vital raw materials to Japan had been in force since July 1940.

By the autumn of 1941 the Japanese were becoming ever more intransigent in their dealings with America. War between the two countries seemed increasingly likely. Provoked by the U.S. trade embargo, the Japanese had made up their minds that the U.S. Pacific Fleet was the main obstacle to the creation of their empire in Southeast Asia and the Pacific.

Japan's target was the Pacific Fleet's base at Pearl Harbor, Hawaii, but it did not inform Hitler of the plan. The Japanese wanted to remove any danger of their intentions being inadvertently leaked to the Americans. In the end, they took everyone by surprise. The Sunday morning bombing on December 7 caught a sleeping fleet almost entirely at dock; an old target ship, *Utah*, was mistakenly sunk by the Japanese, but so were the *Arizona* and the

Oklahoma; *California* began to sink; and four other battleships were badly hit, all in the first wave of Japanese bombers. A second wave arrived within the hour: the battleship *West Virginia* was destroyed, and the *Maryland*, *Tennessee*, and *Pennsylvania* were badly damaged; another 11 ships were also hit, in addition to nearly 200 aircraft lost, most of them set ablaze on the ground. In the next few days, other islands fell to the Japanese, including Wake and Guam.

Near panic set in on America's West Coast, where a Japanese invasion of San Francisco was feared. In Washington, D.C., on the day after the attack, Roosevelt declared war on Japan. In Berlin, Japanese ambassador Oshima demanded that Hitler declare war on America, citing the terms of their Tripartite agreement. The Führer did relax restrictions placed on U-boats attacking American warships, but hesitated over taking the final step of declaring war. His foreign minister, Joachim von Ribbentrop, reminded him that the terms of the Tripartite Pact bound him to come to Japan's aid only if America had been the aggressor, which clearly it was not.

Meanwhile, Hitler was very conscious of the fact that his armies had become stalled short of Moscow. The coming of winter was partly to blame, though Hitler found someone else to blame. He removed the commander who had floundered in the Russian snow and took over himself. But Hitler's problems were just beginning. Without the expected Japanese agitation from the East, Russian reinforcements were rushing to the aid of Moscow and Stalingrad. And the Japanese ambassador hinted to Hitler that Japan might become involved in the Russian campaign if Hitler would declare war against the United States. That was good enough for Hitler.

Swayed by this, on December 11, 1941, Hitler finally made up his mind. In a speech in the Reichstag, he accused Roosevelt and the American Jewish community of starting World War II and declared war on the United States. It was to be one of Hitler's greatest blunders. Not only did it let Roosevelt off the hook, but the Allies exercised their previous agreement that defeat of Germany and Italy would take priority over that of Japan. American manpower and materiel were to prove one of the decisive factors in the eventual defeat of Nazi Germany.

But Hitler's miscalculation extended still further. His hope that Japan would revoke its non-aggression pact with Moscow came to naught. This meant that the massive Soviet war machine could devote all its energies to the defeat of Germany without having to deploy firepower to its eastern border.

And although it was probably inevitable that the United States would eventually find itself at war with Germany, the fact that America's war effort, almost from the start, could be waged against both Japan and Germany clearly saved time and lives and even more diplomatic wrangling.

Hitler made a series of mistakes along the way, from miscalculating Japan's willingness to declare war on the Soviet Union to allowing Goering to attempt to bomb England to her knees to thinking he could capture Russia in winter. Of course, the biggest blunder is that he made all these mistakes at virtually the same time.

DAYS OF INFAMY

Part III

World War II Gets Ugly—

Disasters at Sea and

Death in Winter

Between declarations of war, where objectives and enemies are officially stated, and the treaties that end these wars, with their hundreds of terms and sharp demarcations of the new order, there is the chaos of war itself, a sometimes shapeless interregnum in which millions of moments qualify as wars unto themselves, with winners and losers. The Second World War ranged far and wide, its theaters of engagement nearly spanning the globe. In far-flung waters and distant cities, men fell for causes they did not understand and for reasons that often amounted to little more than human error. A German battleship scuttles itself for having fallen into a trap, and the commander commits suicide; a famous luxury liner enlisted into the war effort cuts its own escort ship in half, killing 300 men; an overzealous operations commander exposes a convoy in the North Atlantic and pays a dear price. And yet, in the fray of battle, in the aftermath of defeat, who can guess which death or which campaign will be deemed by history as significant? For the German soldiers trapped in Stalingrad, they could surely not have known that their lost cause would be crucial to the reversal of Germany's struggle for domination. Although there are many events that will not even receive the dignity of having mattered much in the end, they are nonetheless as much a part of the picture as anything else, and the very sum of the war to its participants.

The Sinking of the *Graf Spee*

ON MAY 20, 1937, AT Spithead on the English south coast, an official and public naval review was held to celebrate the coronation of King George VI. The might of Britain's Royal Navy, still the largest fleet in the world, was on display. Also in attendance were representative warships from many foreign navies. Among them was a pocket battleship from Germany called *Admiral Graf Spee*.

Who could possibly have known on that day of a peaceful coronation that two and a half years later *Graf Spee* would be scuttled by her crew after an action against three British cruisers? Who could have guessed that a ship's captain would engage hostile warships against orders and then allow himself to be trapped with no means of escape? Certainly, there were people predicting that war was around the corner, but the presence of a German cruiser at a British king's coronation symbolized perhaps the hope that it would not come to pass. Or perhaps the fact that it would. What we know now is that the *Graf Spee* would come to terrorize British shipping and fall to the sea's bottom only because of the most stubborn of blundering decisions by its captain, who sent her there.

Launched in October 1932, before Hitler came to power in Germany, *Graf Spee* and her sister ships *Deutschland* and *Admiral*

Scheer, were called armored ships by the Germans, but were better known as pocket battleships. Their purpose was to ravage maritime trade routes. Their six 11-inch-gun main armament was more powerful than any cruiser. Their high speed enabled them to outrun battleships. And given the otherwise impoverished state of the German navy, these quick and deadly strikers were the stars.

Of course, it was the 1919 Treaty of Versailles that was responsible for the drastic restrictions on the German Navy in both the size of its ships and their number. Thus, when Hitler came to power he had to create a modern navy virtually from scratch. Forced to accept that Germany would be unable to match the Royal Navy in firepower, he set upon developing a small battle fleet with a specific purpose: not to engage other navies, but to sink civilian ships and terrorize maritime traffic.

Hitler recognized that Britain's survival depended on her maritime trade. Throttle this and she could be starved into submission, as had almost happened in the spring of 1917 at the hands of German U-boats. Thus, in August 1939, on the eve of war and with the coronation of King George a distant memory, Hitler gave orders for his navy to prepare for action against British merchant shipping.

The then small force of U-boats was dispatched to waiting positions around the British Isles and in the Atlantic. In addition, *Graf Spee* and *Deutschland* were deployed to holding areas in the North Atlantic. Forty-nine year-old Hans Langsdorff, a naval officer of the old school, commanded *Graf Spee*. She left Wilhelmshaven ten days before the outbreak of war.

Neither *Graf Spee* nor *Deutschland* was immediately committed to action. On September 7, 1939, Langsdorff was ordered to take *Graf Spee* to a waiting area in the South Atlantic. This was off Pernambuco, Brazil. *Deutschland* was simultaneously instructed to cruise off Greenland. *Graf Spee* reached her position on September 12, but received no further orders during the next two weeks. Finally, on September 26, 1939, the order came.

Langsdorff was given permission by German naval headquarters to begin operations against merchant shipping in the South Atlantic and Indian Ocean. Hitler had, however, issued express orders to avoid hostile warships. Langsdorff was warned again three days later not to expose his ship to the risk of a full naval battle.

On September 30, the day after this second warning, *Graf Spee* had her first success. She spotted a merchant vessel—the British steamship *Clement*—off the Brazilian coast. When she tried to make a run for it, Langsdorff sent up his seaplane to stop her.

As *Graf Spee* approached, the *Clement*'s crew abandoned her, but not before transmitting a distress call. Langsdorff then sank the vessel, but radioed Pernambuco to inform the authorities that the crew needed rescuing. This message, like that from *Clement*, was picked up by Allied listening stations. These two signals were the first that the British and French knew of a surface raider at large in the South Atlantic. This was worrying, since the British merchant ships sailing in the area were sailing without any escort. The South Atlantic was one place that it was thought the German menace did not lurk.

Only in the North Atlantic and home waters were merchant vessels organized in escorted convoys. Elsewhere, single vessels would be easy prey for German raiders. Given the news, the French and British naval authorities quickly began to organize task groups to hunt down the *Graf Spee*. These were Force L, built around a carrier and a battle cruiser; Force F, with two cruisers in the Caribbean; Force X with two French cruisers at Dakar; Force H with two cruisers at Simonstown; Force K, with a carrier and battle cruiser sent out from Britain to operate from Freetown; Force Y, with a battleship and cruiser off Brazil; and finally, Force G, made up of four cruisers and based on the Falkland Islands in the South Atlantic. While these forces were being deployed, *Graf Spee* steamed toward the coast of Africa.

On October 5, she intercepted another ship, the SS *Newton Beech*. Further successes followed during the next few days. Langsdorff now rendezvoused with his supply ship, the *Altmark*, transferring prisoners and cargoes and taking on more fuel.

He received information that the British were rerouting ships and decided to move into the Indian Ocean in the hope of more pickings there. Both Langsdorff and German naval headquarters had become aware of the Allied naval forces being deployed to the South Atlantic. He was instructed to leave the Atlantic, in any event, as soon as he felt threatened by their naval buildup. The Germans hoped that a move into the Indian Ocean would also create a useful diversion.

On the same day that Langsdorff received these new orders, he sank another vessel and then steamed south. After meeting the *Altmark* again, *Graf Spee* rounded the Cape of Good Hope well to its south, but a spell of bad weather denied her further success. The seaplane which *Graf Spee* carried to help locate victims now developed a fault. Therefore not until November 14, when he was off the coast of Madagascar, did Langsdorff manage to sink another vessel, *Africa Shell*.

Langsdorff realized that the British were rerouting their ships to avoid *Graf Spee*. He now became impatient with his lack of victims. This ship's engines were also giving him problems. So he decided to return to the South Atlantic. This potentially foolhardy decision was to seal *Graf Spee*'s fate.

Having decided to risk reentering the South Atlantic, Captain Langsdorff was confident that if he did meet Allied warships, the *Graf Spee*'s guns would be more than a match for them. In their pursuit of *Graf Spee* the Allies had sent warships into the Indian Ocean to hunt her down. So when Langsdorff returned to the South Atlantic, the area was temporarily clear. And now with his seaplane once again serviceable, Langsdorff was able to locate and destroy two more merchant vessels.

After taking the second ship's crew on board, but before sinking her, the Germans learned from her papers of an assembly point for merchant ships off the River Plate. Hungry for more victims, *Graf Spee* made for this tempting target. The nearest Allied warships to the Plate were those of Force G, based on the Falkland Islands, off the coast of Argentina.

Commodore Henry Harwood, who was in charge, had two of his four cruisers constantly patrolling off the River Plate and Rio de Janeiro. The other two cruisers refurbished in the Falklands before relieving those on patrol. On December 2, Harwood set sail in HMS *Ajax*. He intended to relieve HMS *Cumberland*, which was off the mouth of the River Plate and badly in need of a refit. As for his other ships, HMS *Exeter* was completing some repairs in the Falklands, and the New Zealand cruiser *Achilles* was off Rio de Janeiro.

Within the next 24 hours Harwood received two signals which confirmed the sinking of *Graf Spee's* latest two victims. He concluded that the German ship had three options—the Falklands, the River Plate, and Rio de Janeiro. The intervals between them were each 1,000 miles. Harwood therefore had only one chance to intercept the raider. He decided to gamble on the River Plate and ordered *Exeter* and *Achilles* to meet him there on December 10.

Meanwhile, Langsdorff received intelligence from Germany

that a small British convoy was scheduled to leave the Uruguayan port of Montevideo. Eager for action, he decided to intercept it, unaware that the Plate was the meeting point for Harwood's cruisers.

Langsdorff's officers were apprehensive about the risk of meeting Allied warships off the Plate, but he overruled them. By December 12, *Graf Spee* was nearby and eagerly awaiting her prey. The British cruisers had now met up and were anxious to see if their gamble would pay off.

Harwood's main problem was that his combined firepower fell well short of *Graf Spee*'s 11-inch guns. *Ajax* and *Achilles* were armed only with 6-inch guns, while *Exeter*'s 8-inch armament was also easily outranged by the German ship. Harwood therefore decided that the only way to fight *Graf Spee* was to split his force in two. *Exeter* would form one division and the two more lightly armed cruisers the other. When day broke on December 13, 1939, the British ships and the *Graf Spee* were once more anxiously watching.

It was *Graf Spee*'s lookouts who made the first sighting. They immediately identified *Exeter*, but thought that her two consorts were merely destroyers—the Montevideo convoy's escort. Langsdorff, ignoring Hitler's order not to engage warships, headed *Graf Spee* toward them and readied for action. The British ships now saw smoke on the horizon, and Harwood sent *Exeter* to investigate.

At 6:16 A.M. Harwood saw *Graf Spee* bear down on *Exeter* and open fire. The British ship soon began to suffer punishment from the German's 11-inch shells, and *Graf Spee* continued to pound. Soon most of *Exeter*'s gun turrets were out of action, and many of her crew had become casualties. Harwood now deployed *Ajax* and *Achilles* to distract *Graf Spee*.

Langsdorff, fearing that they were about to make a torpedo attack, ceased firing at *Exeter* and turned northwest, opening fire on *Ajax* and *Achilles*. *Graf Spee* was then on the move, but continued to fire. Unwisely, *Graf Spee* moved in a zigzag course, which enabled *Ajax* and *Achilles* to close and continue to engage her, scoring some hits with their guns. This did not deter *Graf Spee*'s guns, which struck *Ajax* in return.

To preserve his ships, Harwood was forced to drop back out of range, while *Graf Spee* continued to zigzag.

Langsdorff, who had been slightly wounded, was concerned about the damage that the British cruisers had inflicted and believed his ship was not fit enough to face the long voyage back to Germany. Against his officers' advice, he decided to enter the neutral port of Montevideo and carry out repairs. This second blunder was to trap *Graf Spee* and lead to her doom.

After the Battle of the River Plate, the badly damaged *Exeter* began to limp back to the Falklands, while *Ajax* and *Achilles* followed *Graf Spee* at a respectful distance and then posted themselves at the entrance to the River Plate.

The British Admiralty now ordered Force K, with the battle cruiser *Renown* and carrier *Ark Royal*, which were off West Africa, to make for the Plate. It would take them five days' steaming to get there. Should *Graf Spee* come out before this, she would have little difficulty in dealing with the two cruisers, one of which was seriously damaged.

As it was, her arrival in Montevideo harbor caused an immediate stir. Langsdorff arranged for his prisoners and his battle casualties to be landed. Thirty-seven of his sailors had been killed in the action against the British cruisers. They were given an impressive funeral arranged by the German Embassy. All but Langs-dorff gave the Nazi salute.

Aware that *Ajax* and *Achilles* were too weak on their own to prevent *Graf Spee* from escaping, local British agents set out to trick Langsdorff into remaining at Montevideo. They spread a rumor that the carrier *Ark Royal* and *Renown* were about to arrive. In fact, these two formidable ships were still two days' steaming time from Montevideo.

The German Embassy picked up the rumor and informed Langsdorff. He fell for the British trick and was convinced that he was now trapped. On Sunday, December 17, just four days after the battle, large numbers of the crew began to leave *Graf Spee*. Then, in the presence of a large and excited Uruguayan crowd on the dockside, *Graf Spee* weighed anchor. Many spectators believed that she was going out to do battle.

But while she was still in the estuary of the Plate, smoke began to billow from her. Langsdorff had been ordered to scuttle *Graf Spee* rather than allow the British the pleasure of sinking her in battle. It was an ignoble end for a ship which had up until a few days before had two oceans at her mercy.

Three days later Langsdorff committed suicide in his hotel room. In his farewell letter to the German resident minister to Uruguay, he wrote: "For a Captain with a sense of honor, it goes without saying that his personal fate cannot be separated from that of his ship."

In truth, Langsdorff lost his ship because he had disobeyed the order not to engage enemy warships. He had then compounded his folly by allowing himself to be tricked into being cornered by inferior forces while he still had the chance to escape. It was for these blunders that he voluntarily paid the ultimate penalty.

For the British, the Battle of the River Plate was the one

bright spot in the opening months of the war against Germany. The crews of the three cruisers were given heroes' welcomes when they eventually returned to their home ports. Winston Churchill, then First Lord of the Admiralty, greeted *Ajax* and *Exeter*. So too did King George, who had reviewed the *Graf Spee* during his coronation celebrations just two and a half years before. His Majesty's New Zealand ship *Achilles* and her crew received a similar warm welcome from their admiring countrymen.

Graf Spee had created a threat to the Allied navies that has seldom been surpassed by a single ship in the history of naval warfare. But for Langsdorff's blunders, who can tell what havoc she might have wrought?

The Gray Ghost
of the *Queen Mary*

IN 1967, THE CITY OF Long Beach, California, outbid the great metropolis of New York City by $50,000 for the ownership of a tired but much celebrated luxury liner, the *Queen Mary*. Today, the *Queen Mary* is a hotel, museum, and convention center that is rumored to have ghosts moving about its deep, dark interiors. Indeed, the great ship has had a colorful past, filled with glory and tragedy.

What Long Beach won was a boat that had become a war hero to many, a ship that Churchill said had taken a year off the duration of the Second World War due to its yeoman duty, but which had also cost more than 300 British seamen their lives in a collision that left each captain blaming the other. And it was a ship that, after the war, saw the era of luxury liners fade into the past, made nearly obsolete by the transatlantic airplane.

Built by the shipbuilders John Brown & Co. of Glasgow, the *Queen Mary* was launched in 1936 as the world's second 1,000-foot ship (after the *Normandie*). Accommodating in luxury nearly 2,000 passengers and capable of speeds of up to 32 knots, the ship quickly captured the Blue Riband for the fastest Atlantic crossing, at one point making the eastbound trip three minutes shy of four days. Due to her sleek looks, ten expansive decks, and great speed, she quickly became one of the most popular ships afloat, earning handsome profits for its owners, the now combined Cunard-White Star Line. However, when the *Queen Mary* left Southampton on August 28, 1939, she was packed, ominously, with people trying to flee to America in the face of the threat of war in Europe. As a precaution against being spotted by lurking German U-boats, her portholes were painted over. She remained berthed in New York for six months while it was decided what role she should play. Eventually, after being joined by the *Normandie, Mauretania,* and recently completed *Queen Elizabeth,* it was decided that *Queen Mary* should become a troopship. Her Cunard-White Star Line colors yielded to a coat of battleship gray. For the regal ship, her more memorable, and significant, sailings were all ahead of her. And a blunder was to tarnish her reputation.

With its new coat of paint, the *Queen Mary* sailed for Sydney, Australia, in March 1940, where her luxurious fittings were removed and bunk beds installed. She was given guns for her former sundeck; her engines were retained. She spent the rest of 1940 and 1941 transporting New Zealand troops to the Middle East and Singapore.

When the United States entered the war in December 1941 and the Allies determined that U.S. forces should be built up in Britain, *Queen Mary* sailed to Boston, arriving there in January 1942 for further fitting out. She then returned to Australia, this time with U.S. troops on board. She then did one transatlantic run in May 1942, with U.S. troops, before taking British troops to the Middle East.

She returned to New York in July and then began to regularly ply the North Atlantic route, where she became the preeminent troopship in the war effort. She had two great advantages. One was that she could carry, on average, 15,000 troops at a time. When stretched, with some bunks doing double duty, she was capable of carrying an entire army division, more than 16,000 men in a single voyage, and she still holds the record for the most soldiers and crew ever carried, at 16,683. Her second advantage was that she was very fast, capable of speeds in excess of 30 knots. In fact, she was faster than any U-boat, and thus could travel the treacherous North Atlantic without escort (actually, no escort could keep up with her). With her gray exterior and speedy zigzagging, she became known as the Gray Ghost.

Her elusiveness so infuriated the Germans that Hitler reportedly offered a reward of $250,000 for sinking her. During her war service, the *Queen Mary* would carry more than 1.6 million troops, including more than a third of the 875,000 U.S. troops that sailed for Europe. But it was not all glory for the *Queen Mary*.

On September 27, 1942, she left New York bound for Gourock on Scotland's Firth of Clyde with her normal complement of U.S. troops. Approaching British waters, the *Queen Mary* was provided with an antiaircraft escort. It consisted of the light cruiser *Curacoa* and six destroyers. Laid down in May 1917, *Curacoa* had been present at the surrender of the German High Seas Fleet in November 1918 and had been converted at the beginning of World War II to an antiaircraft cruiser. Her problem was that her top speed was only 26 knots, while Queen Mary always steamed in excess of this.

The escort duly met the liner on October 2, off the coast of Ireland. Both *Queen Mary* and the *Curacoa* were steaming in zigzag pattern to evade U-boats, with the cruiser initially ahead. The liner then overtook its escort. Both captains were convinced that the other must conform to his movements, and the eventual result was that someone zigged when he should have zagged. The huge liner struck the cruiser close to her stern, slicing her in two. With 11,000 troops on board, *Queen Mary* dared not stop to assist in a rescue operation, as it would invite U-boat attack. Consequently, although damaged under the waterline, she steamed on to the Clyde. The *Curacoa* sank quickly, with only 101 of its 430-man crew surviving.

Queen Mary sailed to Boston for repairs and continued to ply the Atlantic for the remainder of the war, but her collision remained a guilty secret until 1945. Then the Admiralty, having exonerated its own ship in an internal inquiry, brought action against Cunard for the loss of the *Curacoa*. The judge eventually found in favor of *Queen Mary*, but the Admiralty appealed. The final upshot was that both ships were found to be at fault, with inadequate communications and ill-prepared evasion strategies being to blame on both sides.

Queen Mary was handed back to her owners in September 1946, and continued to sail the Atlantic until 1967. By then she was losing millions of pounds per year and was thus sold to the town of Long Beach for $3,450,000.

Visitors today to the *Queen Mary*, which is restored to its original colors and is the object of ardent preservationists, can walk within the huge spaces of the once luxurious liner that was once a not so luxurious housing for soldiers going to war. And in its deep bowels, along the long passageway leading to the now forever still propellers, a ghost is said to move. And he is gray.

The Scattering of Convoy PQ17

IN 1941 THE GERMAN NAVY built two battleships so huge
that they were considered "fleets-in-being," meaning that all by
themselves they represented the very essence of a fleet. One of the
ships, *Bismarck*, named for Otto von Bismarck, the nineteenth-
century German statesman who forged the German nation, did not
last long, an omen for German nationhood if there ever was one.

The Royal British Navy was obsessed with tracking *Bismarck* on its very first combat mission. All told, five battleships,
two aircraft carriers, nine cruisers, and eighteen destroyers pursued *Bismarck* around Iceland and back toward Germany. On
May 27, 1941, just five days out of port from the Baltic, *Bismarck*
was sunk, and 2,000 Germans went down with it.

The British Navy switched its obsession to the sister ship
to *Bismarck*, called *Tirpitz* and named for Admiral von Tirpitz, the
architect of the German Navy. The obsession this time was to prove
a disaster for the British Navy, and a serious blow to the attempt
to supply the Russians with war materiel.

The mighty *Tirpitz* spent most of the war lurking in fjords
in northern Norway. From that position she threatened the Allied
convoys carrying vital munitions to northern Soviet ports, munitions that helped to ensure that Russia kept fighting.

It was the Royal Navy's fear that *Tirpitz* would slip out
and attack one of these convoys that led to one of its greatest

blunders of the war. Misinterpretation of intelligence from Norway about *Tirpitz* caused the escort of Convoy PQ17 to be ordered to leave it. The result was that most of the merchant ships in the convoy fell victim to German air and submarine attacks. It was a tragic waste of human life and much needed materiel. PQ17 was the greatest German success of the whole war against an Allied convoy.

In the early weeks of German invasion of the Soviet Union, in June 1941, Russia seemed about to fall. Britain, while welcoming a new ally in the fight against the Axis powers, could offer no direct help. Even so, Britain and the Soviet Union signed a mutual assistance pact in July. Winston Churchill immediately dispatched a convoy carrying fighters and rubber to the northern Soviet ports of Archangel and Murmansk. In addition, the United States declared that the Soviet Union would now be entitled to Lend-Lease, allowing the U.S., still undeclared, to provide military protection for supplies across the North Atlantic.

Three supply routes to Russia were set up. One was by air from Alaska to Siberia. Another was a land route from the Iraqi port of Basra and up through Iran. But the most hazardous of the three and the one that carried the most war materiel was the sea route from Britain up past Iceland and into the Arctic Ocean to Archangel and Murmansk.

The first of the convoys bound for Russia sailed at the end of September 1941. It was designated PQ1 and consisted of 10 merchant vessels which arrived at Archangel without loss. At the same time Averill Harriman from the United States and Lord Beaverbrook flew to Moscow to establish the Soviet priorities for munitions.

Churchill declared to Stalin that he would send a convoy every 10 days, but this proved impossible. The Arctic winter arrived, making conditions ever more grim for those taking part in the Russian convoys. The escorting warships suffered severely from the weather and often needed extensive repairs. The British did not have sufficient numbers of these vessels to provide immediate replacements and hence convoy sailings had to be delayed. Indeed, by the end of 1941 only seven convoys had been sent to Russia, but they all got through without loss.

The Germans, however, had been alerted and began to reinforce Norway. More U-boats and destroyers were deployed. Then, in January 1942, the battleship *Tirpitz* was ordered to Norway. She was followed by the heavy cruisers *von Scheer* and *Prinz Eugen*, although the latter, which had been with the *Bismarck* on her fateful mission, was torpedoed en route.

The British were soon made aware of *Tirpitz*'s presence and realized the implications for the Russian convoys. Churchill declared that she was "the most important naval vessel in the situation today." Efforts to attack from the air failed, however.

In March 1942, *Tirpitz* made her first foray against an Arctic convoy, PQ 12. This had been located by reconnaissance aircraft. The battleship was spotted by a British submarine, but bad weather frustrated her search for the convoy and she returned to port, where she was attacked unsuccessfully by aircraft from the carrier HMS *Victorious*. As a result Hitler ordered more aircraft to be sent to Norway. The odds on the convoys getting through to Russia unscathed were lengthening.

With the coming of spring the Arctic had perpetual daylight, thus robbing the Russian convoys of the cover of darkness. This, and the growing strength of the German forces in Norway, meant that casualties to ships began to rise. Worse, the ice was slow in melting, forcing the convoys to sail close to the Norwegian coast.

But the Soviet Union was once more under increased pressure. The Germans had launched a major offensive in southern Russia designed to overrun the Caucasus and its vital oil fields. Churchill was therefore insistent that the Russian convoys be maintained. Convoy PQ16 sailed on the same night that Churchill made this announcement. It lost six ships before it reached Murmansk.

The next convoy to sail was PQ17. Like the others, its ships gathered at Iceland. In all, it had 35 merchant vessels—22 American, eight British, two Russian, two Panamanian, and one Dutch. They carried a cargo that included nearly 300 aircraft, 600 tanks, and 3,000 trucks and trailers. It was by far the largest of the Russian convoys to date.

PQ17's escort was built around six destroyers and a number of smaller warships. But, aware of the German threat from Norway, the British Admiralty arranged for a covering force to sail ahead of the convoy. This consisted of two British cruisers, *London* and *Norfolk*, and the American cruisers *Tuscaloosa* and *Wichita* and three U.S. destroyers.

Conscious of the threat of the *Tirpitz*, the British Home Fleet was also ordered to sea. The battleships HMS *Duke of York* and USS *Washington*, with the aircraft carrier HMS *Victorious*, two cruisers, and 14 destroyers were to position themselves 200 miles astern of the convoy as distant cover.

On June 27, 1942, Convoy PQ17 set sail from Iceland. Hollywood star Douglas Fairbanks Jr., who was serving on board the cruiser *Wichita*, described the merchantmen "waddling out to sea like so many dirty ducks. . . . Everyone who was watching paid a silent tribute and offered some half-thought prayer." But prayers would not be enough to ensure safe passage for Convoy PQ17.

As the convoy headed north toward the midnight sun of the Arctic, U-boats were patrolling. One of these spotted the merchant ships as soon as they reached open water. Shadowed by the U-boats, the convoy ran into heavy ice, which damaged a number of them. One was forced to return to Iceland. Another had earlier run aground, leaving 33 ships to sail on.

On July 1, a German reconnaissance aircraft spotted the convoy. Those sailing in it now knew that they could expect attacks from the air and by U-boats. There was always, too, the threat of the *Tirpitz*. Fog came to the rescue. Perhaps this would enable the ships to get through safely. It was not to be.

On the following day the fog lifted, and the inevitable reconnaissance plane appeared once more. Early that evening the convoy was attacked by torpedo aircraft. These were driven off by antiaircraft fire, with two shot down.

The next day the convoy avoided attack, but on July 4 the picture began to change. The U-boats moved into the attack and sank two Liberty ships. The escorts managed to ward off the German submarines and convoy PQ17 sailed on.

Back in London, however, the First Sea Lord, Admiral Sir Dudley Pound, had received some disturbing news. Pound was becoming exhausted by the strain of three years of war as head of the Royal Navy and was no longer a fit man. The news he received came from the Government Code and Cipher School at Bletchley Park. They had decrypted a top-secret German naval signal which stated that *Tirpitz* had been located, pulling into a Norwegian port on July 3.

To Pound, this could only mean one thing—*Tirpitz* was preparing to intercept convoy PQ17. In fact, the battleship was merely shifting berths, but the British were not to know this.

Pound realized that he had blundered by placing the distant

covering force, which was powerful enough to take on *Tirpitz*, too far away to prevent the German battleship from attacking both the convoy and the cruisers to its north. He called a hasty meeting of his staff. All but one of them stated that the convoy must stay together. Pound, however, had other ideas. Late that night a series of radio messages were transmitted from the Admiralty:

> MOST IMMEDIATE AND SECRET.
> CRUISER FORCE TO WITHDRAW WESTWARD AT HIGH SPEED
>
> IMMEDIATE. OWING TO THREAT OF SURFACE SHIPS. CONVOY IS TO DISPERSE AND PROCEED TO RUSSIAN PORTS MOST IMMEDIATE. CONVOY IS TO SCATTER.

The convoy commodore and the commander of the close escort were aghast, but there was nothing they could do. The destroyers therefore bid farewell, leaving the ships of PQ17 to face the horrors that lay ahead on their own. The escort commander's last signal to the convoy read:

> SORRY TO LEAVE YOU LIKE THIS. GOOD LUCK. LOOKS LIKE A BLOODY BUSINESS

Douglas Fairbanks Jr., on board *Wichita*, was to say, "It was such a terrible feeling to be running away from the convoy at twice the speed of theirs and to leave them to the mercy of the enemy."

Pound believed that the merchant ships had a better chance of getting through to Russia individually, but he failed to appreciate that the Arctic ice severely limited their scope for maneuver. During the following days the full enormity of his blunder would be brought home to Pound.

On the following day, July 5, both U-boats and the Luftwaffe moved in for the kill. By the end of it, 12 ships had been sent to the bottom. Two more merchant ships perished on the next day, and four more on July 7. During the next few days another four were lost. Eventually, only 11 of the 35 ships that left Iceland made it to Russia, and three of these were sunk on the return voyage.

The reverberations were quickly felt. Churchill condemned the decision to abandon the convoy. American naval commander-in-chief Admiral Ernest J. King was so enraged that he did not want U.S. and British warships to operate together in the North Atlantic. And the Russians were incensed. Stalin accused the Western Allies of lying about the losses suffered by PQ17 and objected strongly when Roosevelt and Churchill delayed the sailing of the next convoy until the autumn. Even though no less than 53 warships were deployed for the protection of PQ18, the Germans still managed to sink 13 of its ships. The Russian convoys were now suspended until the end of the year. Thereafter, with stronger escorts and improved tactics, they continued virtually until war's end.

As for Admiral Pound, the author of the blunders that had destroyed PQ17, a brain tumor forced him to resign in September 1943. He died a month later.

The mighty *Tirpitz*, fear of which had triggered the blunders, never did engage Allied warships in the northern seas, although it continued to lurk. She was subjected to numerous air attacks and was eventually sunk in November 1944 in a raid by Lancaster bombers, with the loss of 1,200 lives.

Death at Stalingrad:
The German Army Gets Trapped

ITLER'S AMBITION TO BLUDGEON THE Soviet Union, to
reform the Russian leadership of its misguided Marxism-
Leninism, to secure for Germany's uses the natural resources of
Soviet territory, became a blind ambition over time. So obsessed
became Hitler that the reversals in battle only strengthened his
resolve all the more. Ultimately, his frenetic campaigns against the
Soviet Union, which saw his armies thrust in four or more major
vectors into vast, unforgiving Russian territory, led to a major turning point in World War II. The Soviet Union gained its first decisive victory, Germany lost its Sixth Army, and Hitler's
commanders began to doubt the word of their Führer.

A visitor today to the city of Volgograd on the banks of
Russia's mighty River Volga will be struck by its massive 200-foot
World War II memorial. This commemorates the dead of Stalingrad, the name by which the city was formerly known. Stalingrad,
then the largest of the many cities named after Joseph Stalin, was
situated in the southern Soviet Union on the west bank of the
Volga, which spills into the Caspian Sea. Nearby, the River Don
sweeps in a big turn, turning from south to west to flow into the
Black Sea. And the city itself, north of the great Russian oil fields,
became a not so natural protection for the Russian war effort. Hitler,

after an obsession with Moscow, then Kiev, then Leningrad, all cities far to the north, determined that he wanted Russian oil. The road would lead into Stalingrad.

Sadly for Hitler, his forces made it into the city but never made it out. German forces first swept into Russia in the summer of 1941. The three-pronged Barbarossa campaign set its sights on Moscow, Kiev, and Leningrad. The German Army, aided by a fierce blitzkrieg from the air and the sweep of Panzers on the ground, made great progress, with hundreds of thousands of stunned Russian soldiers trapped and forced to surrender. But the thrust bogged down just outside of Moscow, as the Russian winter came in December.

Hitler wasn't happy. In the immediate aftermath of the failure to capture Moscow, he sacked a number of his senior army commanders, most notably Field Marshal Walther von Brauchitsch, the German Army's commander-in-chief. Hitler declared that he would personally take over his position and control the Army's operations himself.

Hitler had been meddling in military operations since the beginning of the war. But now he was to exert an increasingly iron grip. It would have ultimately fatal consequences. The German Army spent the winter of 1941–42 on the defensive.

Nonetheless, Hitler was convinced that once the Russian spring came, his armies would again take to the offensive and crush the Soviet Union. But springtime in Russia is as debilitating to ground troops as the Russian winter, as the three-foot snow pack melts and turns the earth into a muddy quagmire. Perhaps for no better reason than an impatience to get moving, Hitler turned his eyes southward to the industry-rich area between the rivers Don and Volga and to the extensive oil fields to the south. Fedor von Bock, who commanded Army Group South, was put in charge of this ambitious operation.

Bock was ordered to subdivide his command into Army Group A under Maxmilien von Weichs and Army Group B under Ferdinand List. While List was to thrust eastward toward Stalingrad to protect Army Group A's open flank, von Weichs would make the advance into the Caucasus, the mountains south of Stalingrad and beyond which were the Russian oil fields. Army Group A launched its attack on June 28, 1942, while List began his offensive 10 days later.

To avoid becoming trapped, the Russians withdrew their forces in the face of the German advance. This frustrated Hitler, who oversaw operations from Radenstein, about 700 miles from Stalingrad. Mistakenly believing that large numbers of Russian troops remained west of the River Don, he halted the advance on Stalingrad and switched most of its armor to Army Group A, hoping to drive south into the Caucasus, closer and closer to the wealth of oil fields. Soon the terrain became desert. The advance was rapid.

The first oil fields, at Maikop, were seized on August 9, but the Russians had destroyed most of the installations. Meanwhile, just five days after he had removed most of its tanks, Hitler ordered the German Sixth Army to resume its advance on Stalingrad. Friedrich Paulus, who commanded this army, had a reputation for obeying orders to the letter. He made no objection, even though his lack of tanks, most of which had been deployed and lost earlier in Barbarossa, meant slow progress. But neither Paulus, nor his men, realized that Hitler was becoming fixated on the city that bore Stalin's name. This was to put them on a road that would end in death and destruction.

Stalingrad was originally known as Tsaritsyn, but changed its name after Stalin assumed power on the death of Lenin in 1924. The justification for the name change was that the new Russian leader had played a major part in the defense of the city during the civil war of 1918–21.

Soon Stalingrad became a flourishing Communist city, acting as a conduit for the produce of the vast collective farms that surrounded it. Stalingrad also became a major industrial center, based on its vast tractor factory, which by August 1942 had switched to the production of T-34 tanks, which would prove to be the best tank in any army during World War II.

Hitler had now switched considerable air support from the Caucasus to support Paulus's advance on the city. This helped the German Sixth Army to approach the outskirts of Stalingrad by August 10, but the Soviet high command became aware of the threat and hurriedly mobilized Stalingrad's citizens to help prepare defenses in front of the city. Among the stout leaders of the Stalingrad Front were Andrei Yeremenko and Nikita Khrushchev.

The first direct German attack on the city came from the air. This was prelude to the ground assault. As attention began to focus on Stalingrad, far to the south, the German offensive in the Caucasus was grinding to a halt. The men of Army Group A had reached the foothills of the Caucasus Mountains. But their supply lines, stretched now beyond 300 miles, were growing more and more vulnerable without sufficient air support. And although on August 23, German mountain troops raised the swastika on the highest peak in the range, Mount Elbrus, Hitler was not pleased. He was looking for more ground advancement, not flag waving on mountain peaks. Thereafter, the advance toward the south gradually petered out.

Meanwhile, Stalin had issued orders that Stalingrad was to be held at all costs. Although strategically, Stalin feared that its capture would isolate southern Russia, he was also fiercely loyal to

the city that bore his name, and in which he had defied Trotksy
in 1928, an event that vaulted his career within the Communist
Party to new heights. Stalin's order was read out to every Soviet
soldier: "Not a step backward." He counted on his best generals,
V. N. Gordov, V. I. Chuikov, and his chief troubleshooter, Georgi
Zhukov, to resist retreat.

Russian reinforcements began to arrive, and the Germans
faced ever stiffer resistance as they approached the suburbs of Stalingrad. Throughout September and October the struggle continued, with mounting casualties on both sides. The combat was
especially fierce in and around the ruins of the tractor factory, parts
of which were occupied by each camp.

Vassili Chuikov and his 62nd Army, who were defending
the city, eventually found themselves clinging to just a narrow strip
of the city on the west bank of the Volga. Chuikov commanded his
men: "Fight as if there is no land across the Volga." All supplies
and reinforcements had to be ferried across the river, which was
under constant German fire.

Winter arrived and heavy German casualties forced the high
command to turn to the armies of Germany's allies. The flanks of
the Sixth Army and Hermann Hoth's Fourth Panzer Army, which
was helping Paulus, were now protected by two Rumanian armies
and a late-coming Italian force.

The Russians took note of this, and Zhukov began planning
a counter-offensive. Though the Russians were often no match in
military strategy for the Germans, Zhukov could see that the strong
German Sixth Army, dug in at Stalingrad, was soon to be protected
by only a fragile shell of a much less imposing military force, Rumanian and Italian.

In the north, Nikolai Vatutin's South-West Front and Konstantin Rokossovsky's Don Front would attack the Rumanian Third

Army, while part of Andrei Yeremenko's Stalingrad Front would assault the Rumanian Fourth Army in the south. On November 19, 1942, the South-West and Don Fronts began their attack. The next day it was the turn of the Stalingrad Front. The offensives sliced through the Rumanians.

On November 23, the two prongs linked up. The German forces at Stalingrad were now cut off from the remainder of Army Group B. The following day Hermann Goering told Hitler not to worry about the Sixth Army being cut off; his Luftwaffe could keep Paulus resupplied by air. Hitler ordered the Sixth Army to stand fast rather than break out. This was to be a fatal blunder.

Goering's boast that air resupply could maintain the German Sixth Army in the Stalingrad pocket was an empty one from the outset. Paulus needed a minimum of 750 tons per day, but the Luftwaffe had a capacity for delivering only a third of this amount. The winter weather meant that this was seldom achieved. Hitler now planned a hasty operation to relieve the Sixth Army.

He placed the man who was generally considered to be Germany's most capable commander, Erich von Manstein, in charge, creating Army Group Don for the purpose. This also took Paulus under its command. But while von Manstein was preparing for the relief operation, the Russians struck again at Army Group B, this time along the River Chir.

They failed to break through, but von Manstein was forced to deploy some of the forces earmarked for the Stalingrad relief operation. This caused the attack to be postponed. At the same time the Russians also attacked the German pocket at Stalingrad, with the aim of splitting it in two. Paulus's men resisted fiercely, and the operation failed.

On December 12, with the Russian offensives halted, von Manstein was finally able to mount Winter Storm, his relief operation. It initially went well, until the Soviet defense solidified. Even so, von Manstein continued to push forward. He proposed that Paulus break out and link up with the relief operation. But the Sixth Army commander, conscious of Hitler's order to stay put, declined.

On December 19, the Russians renewed their attacks on the River Chir, this time concentrating on the Italian Eighth Army. They quickly broke through and captured the main airfield supplying Stalingrad, further eroding Goering's attempt to keep the Germans within Stalingrad supplied. The attack also presented a threat to von Manstein's lines of communications and forced him to halt. Worse, on Christmas Eve the Russians attacked again, this time against the Rumanians in the south. Even Hitler recognized that Army Group Don was in danger of being encircled as well, and on December 28, he sanctioned a withdrawal. This would put the main German forces 135 miles away from Stalingrad. Not only would this make Paulus more isolated than ever within Stalingrad, but the problems of resupplying him by air grew acute.

Now the Russians could concentrate on reducing the Stalingrad pocket. They planned to attack from the west and drive the Germans back into the city itself. But first, on January 8, 1943, they sent emissaries with surrender terms to General Paulus, who rejected them.

Two days later, the final Soviet offensive against the Stalingrad pocket began. By now the Luftwaffe was delivering a mere 40 tons of supplies per day on average, its aircraft taking out wounded on the return journey.

Marauding Soviet fighters shot down ever more German aircraft, aggravating the supply problem. Goering's deputy, Field Marshal Erhard Milch, took charge, but even he could not raise daily deliveries by much. Matters were made worse by the fact that the Russians were now overrunning the airfields within the ever shrinking Stalingrad pocket. Eventually, the Luftwaffe was reduced to the desperate measure of dropping in supplies.

As Paulus's men struggled back into Stalingrad itself, they did so in the knowledge that Hitler had now refused to allow anyone at all to try to break out. The Soviet pressure on the German Sixth Army was remorseless. By the end of January, the German hold on Stalingrad had been reduced to just two small pockets within the city itself. On January 30, the anniversary of Hitler's coming to power, in a spasm of patriotism Goering made a special broadcast in praise of the defenders of Stalingrad, while Paulus declared that he would never surrender. Hitler rewarded him with promotion to field marshal. Knowing that the situation was hopeless, and that no German field marshal had ever surrendered, this was as much as asking for Paulus to commit suicide rather than disobey orders. Hitler was to be disappointed.

On the last day of January, Paulus and the troops in the southern pocket laid down their arms. The strain of fighting a battle that could have only one outcome showed plainly on Paulus's face. The siege had reached an enormous intensity. John Keegan, in *The Second World War*, quotes from the diary of an unnamed officer of the 24th Panzer Division, who wrote:

> There is a ceaseless struggle from noon to night. From storey to storey, faces black with sweat, we bombed each other with grenades in the middle of explosions, clouds of dust and smoke. . . . Ask any soldier what hand-to-hand struggle means in such a fight. . . . Stalingrad is no longer a town. By day it is an enormous cloud of burning, blinding smoke; it is a vast furnace lit by the reflection of flames. And when night arrives, one of those scorching, howling,

bleeding nights, the dogs plunge into the Volga and swim desperately to gain the other bank. The nights of Stalingrad are a terror for them. Animals flee this hell; the hardest storms cannot bear it for long; only men endure.

But they could not endure forever. The surrender of the German Sixth Army at Stalingrad was to be the turning point of the titanic struggle on the Eastern Front. For the first time the Soviets had inflicted a decisive defeat on their adversary.

From then on the Red Army would be continually on the offensive, one which would finally end in the ruins of Berlin in May 1945. Ninety-one thousand German soldiers went into captivity at Stalingrad. They left the corpses of 110,000 in the city. Hitler's fixation with Stalingrad had caused his soldiers to be trapped, and his obstinacy was to be their death sentence. So bitter were Paulus and some of his generals that they became tools of Soviet anti-Nazi propaganda.

Such was the legacy of Hitler's blunder at Stalingrad, a blunder that turned the tide on the Eastern Front.

The Turning of the

Tide in World War II—

From the Battle of Midway

to the North African Desert

With the war raging on three fronts—the Pacific, Western Europe, and Eastern Europe, including the eastern end of the Mediterranean—Allied and Axis powers were stretched to their limits. But in the Pacific, despite some serious early setbacks, the Allied forces began to turn the tide in their favor. The "incredible victory" at Midway and the taking of Guadalcanal were the first signs that the Japanese had more than they could handle in the South Pacific and that the United States had managed a remarkable recovery from the devastation of Pearl Harbor. On the Western Front, Allied strategy began to focus on an amphibious invasion. An early attempt at the French port of Dieppe turned out disastrously, although important lessons were learned and would be put to good use two years later at Normandy. Attempts by Allied forces to attack the "soft underbelly" of the Axis powers, through Italy, came to a standstill when confronted by a German battalion, cleverly dug in at the ruins of a Benedictine monastery. The struggle for Italy was seemingly thankless: it dragged on and on without objectives that were clearly worth winning. What value is taking Rome while Britain is under threat of invasion, France is occupied, and the Japanese are intent on taking island after island in the South Pacific? But the war was wide, the enemy widespread; the journey to victory would consist of small steps, with of course missteps along that way. The sad tale of inexperienced British pilots, lost in the African desert, their bodies not to be found for decades, is eloquent testimony to the lonely sufferings of war, as we shall see.

The Sinking of Force Z

ONE OF THE WORST SETBACKS suffered by the British during World War II was the Japanese conquest of the British colonies of Malaya and Singapore. Among the many disasters of that campaign was the loss of Force Z, consisting of two of the Royal Navy's finest ships—the battleship *Prince of Wales* and battle cruiser *Repulse*. Sent into battle without air cover, they were sunk by Japanese aircraft.

Senior naval commanders blundered by underestimating air power's threat to major warships. The loss of these two ships also confirmed that the aircraft carrier, with its ability to both provide air cover for the fleet and strike hostile fleets at long range, was superseding the battleship as sovereign of the seas.

Malaya is a peninsula extending southward from Thailand into the Indian Ocean; it sits between the two largest islands of the Dutch East Indies, Sumatra to the west, and Borneo to the east.

In 1939 Malaya provided 38 percent of the world's rubber and 58 percent of its tin. Rich in resources, it was a crucial part of the British Empire. Mineral-starved Japan cast its hungry eyes on Malaya and viewed it as critical to its own projected empire, which it was bent on achieving by force of arms. After the end of

World War I the British constructed a naval base on the Malayan
island of Singapore. It became the epicenter for the defense of its
Far East possessions. Large coastal batteries were installed to protect the base from attack from the sea.

During the massive Japanese naval buildup in 1941, the
Dutch and the British both became concerned that their crucial
possessions were in peril. To defend both Malaya and Singapore,
more ships, troops, and aircraft were needed, but with war looming
on the horizon in Europe, the British could spare little. This was
especially true of the Royal Navy, which was loath to reduce its
capital ship strength in home waters and the Mediterranean in view
of the twin threat of the German and Italian navies.

In October 1941, with an increasingly militant Japan making the prospect of war in the Far East more likely, the British
Admiralty finally agreed to reinforce Singapore. The battleship
Prince of Wales was selected, one of the new King George V class
of battleships, built by Cammell Laird & Co. Ltd. in Birkenhead,
England. She was armed with ten 14-inch guns, three rocket pro-
jectors, and room for two aircraft; she carried a crew of over 1,400
men. She was one of the most powerful ships of her day. Commissioned only at the end of March 1941, she had already seen
much service. Less than two months after commissioning, *Prince
of Wales* was part of the squadron force sent to stalk the mighty
German battleship *Bismarck* on her maiden military mission. In an
engagement with *Bismarck* and its escort, *Prinz Eugen*, *Prince of
Wales* took seven hits but managed herself to score three on the
Bismarck.   TIRPITZ!

After retiring (*Bismarck* was soon sunk, sitting in port in
Norway), the *Prince of Wales* brought Churchill to Newfoundland
for an important Atlantic conference with President Roosevelt,
during which time the charter for the United Nations was signed.

By the fall, with the Japanese obviously planning a major thrust in the South Pacific, she and the British cruiser *Repulse* were dispatched to Singapore to help defend the British territories on Malaya.

Repulse was a very fast battle cruiser that had won fame during World War I by routing a German squadron at the Battle of the Falklands. Already moving through the Indian Ocean, and well armed with six 15-inch guns, she rushed to join the *Prince of Wales*, several destroyers, and the aircraft carrier *Indomitable.* These three ships, and their escorting destroyers, would make up Force Z, which appeared powerful enough to match any warships, including battleships, the Japanese deployed against Malaya and Singapore.

Appointed to command Force Z was Admiral Sir Tom Phillips. Known as Tom Thumb because of his small stature, he had not seen combat since 1917, but was highly thought of in the Royal Navy. He had recently been serving at the Admiralty as Vice Chief of the Naval Staff, with specific responsibility for operational matters. But Phillips did have a blind spot. Despite growing evidence to the contrary, he remained convinced that the threat of aircraft to capital warships was minuscule. His conviction that large warships could repel hostile aircraft had little evidence to support it: the Royal Navy itself had had numerous smaller ships sunk by land-based aircraft in both home waters and the Mediterranean. But in Phillips's view these vessels had merely been unlucky or had suffered from poor ship handling.

He believed that the same could not happen to capital ships, which was what the admiralty considered the three ships at the heart of Force Z. Phillips's stubborn refusal to acknowledge the vulnerability of such ships to air attack led directly to his blunders off the coast of Malaya.

• • •

Prince of Wales sailed from Britain, with Phillips on board, on October 25, 1941. Two destroyers would escort her on her voyage east to Singapore. On November 5, however, the Admiralty received news that the carrier *Indomitable* had run aground in the West Indies and was damaged. But no decision was made to halt the *Prince of Wales*. The *Indomitable*, with its fleet of fighters, would have been crucial assets in fending off a Japanese air attack. Without the air cover she could provide, Force Z was critically exposed.

The *Prince of Wales* continued her voyage, calling in at Freetown, Sierra Leone, and later at Capetown, South Africa, for refueling. On November 18, 1941, *Prince of Wales* sailed from Capetown. That same day, the carrier *Hermes* arrived at the port of Simonstown, farther up the South African coast, for a refitting after service in the Indian Ocean. No thought was given to using her to substitute for *Indomitable*.

Prince of Wales sailed on to Colombo, Ceylon, departing there on November 29 and meeting up with the *Repulse* in the Indian Ocean. The two ships now sailed on together, with their attendant destroyers, to Singapore. Lacking its vital aircraft carrier, Force Z was already doomed.

The arrival of Force Z at Singapore on December 2, 1941, was seen as the final element needed to make the island—and Malaya— invincible. Japanese designs on their vital resources could now be thwarted. This was reinforced by the general British view that Japanese naval air power, whether carrier- or land-based, was of a low standard. However, this ignored the fact that the Japanese Navy had more aircraft carriers than any other nation at the time.

Most of these carriers were at sea during that first week of December 1941. They were on their way to strike at the American Pacific Fleet base at Pearl Harbor in a dramatic demonstration of the aircraft carrier's power. The threat to Malaya and Singapore would therefore be from land-based aircraft. Indeed, land-based Japanese naval planes had already deployed to Thailand in preparation for the eventual assault on Malaya. This included 72 Mitsubishi bombers.

On hearing of Force Z's arrival at Singapore, the Japanese deployed more bombers to Thailand to counter this new British threat. As the British had already anticipated, the Japanese plan for invasion involved both a land thrust across the border with Thailand and amphibious landings on Malaya's northeast coast. It was to be mounted simultaneously with the attack on Pearl Harbor and other Pacific targets.

A state of emergency had been declared in Malaya and Singapore on December 1. But the arrival of Force Z the following day served to increase the British complacency that already existed. They merely went through the motions of preparing for war without any real belief that the Japanese were capable of mounting an attack or would do so.

British complacency was demonstrated when *Repulse* left Singapore on December 5 for a goodwill visit to northern Australia to encourage the Australian Navy to join Force Z, even though the previous day the main part of the Japanese amphibious force for the invasion of Malaya had sailed from Hainan, China. Other forces sailed from Indo-China on December 5. At this time Phillips, Force Z's commander, had been in the Philippines, another immediate Japanese objective—discussing how the American and British forces could cooperate in the region.

On December 6, a Malayan-based Hudson maritime patrol aircraft spotted the main Japanese amphibious force steaming west toward Malaya. It was clear that invasion was imminent. Phillips immediately flew back to Singapore, and *Repulse* reversed course.

On the night of December 7, 1941, after the Japanese had scored such a stunning triumph at Pearl Harbor, the complex audacity of their designs on the South Pacific were in full view. Their objectives indeed included Malaya and, as would become clear in the next several weeks, so much more—including Guam, Wake Island, the Philippines. A Japanese task force approached the Malayan coast. Last minute preparations for the landings and the simultaneous attack from Thailand went ahead. The troops approached the beach at Kota Bharu, located mid-peninsula. They stormed ashore during the early hours, quickly penetrating the weak British defenses. Within 24 hours the Japanese had secured an airfield. Japanese aircraft also attacked other airfields in Malaya and bombed Singapore.

Phillips decided Force Z should attack the Japanese shipping at Kota Bharu. But then came news of further landings at Singora, 120 miles north of Kota Bharu, toward the isthmus connecting Thailand and Malaya. These were considered more serious, so Phillips altered his plan and made these his objective.

But because of the Japanese air attacks, which had destroyed a number of aircraft on the ground, the RAF had to evacuate its airfields in northern Malaya, leaving the area without air cover. The only air support it could offer Force Z was one squadron of obsolete Brewster Buffalo fighters based on Singapore, far to the south of the Malaya peninsula.

Phillips was apparently unconcerned that he would have no air cover over northern Malaya. Force Z sailed in the early evening of December 8, aiming to arrive off the landing beaches on the morning of the tenth.

On the afternoon of December 9, a Japanese submarine

spotted Force Z sailing northward and transmitted a sighting report. Japanese floatplanes were launched from cruisers to confirm the position and heading of the British ships. Bombers stationed in Thailand took off to locate and attack the enemy. Phillips's Force Z was spotted. Not only had he lost the element of surprise in his attempt to attack the Japanese transports, he was a sitting duck without adequate air cover.

Sensing his predicament, Phillips decided to abort the operation. At 9:00 P.M. Force Z altered course and began to steam south. Shortly after midnight, however, Phillips received a false report of further landings at Kuantan, well to the south of the original attacks. He altered course to attack the shipping there, but did not tell Singapore, as he was on radio silence. For a time Phillips's whereabouts were unknown to the Japanese.

During the night Force Z sailed on alone. At 3:00 A.M., however, another Japanese submarine sighted it and fired torpedoes, but with no success. Acting on the submarine's information, Japanese air reconnaissance tried again to find Force Z. It failed for the time being, because of Phillips's subsequent change of course toward Kuantan, but the Japanese continued to scour the area.

At 11:00 A.M. a Japanese reconnaissance aircraft spotted Force Z through a gap in the clouds. The Thailand-based naval bombers, numbering 34 land-based bombers and 51 torpedo bombers, zeroed in on the *Prince of Wales* and *Repulse*.

Most of the Japanese aircraft concentrated on *Prince of Wales*, which was steaming astern of *Repulse*. Eventually, they hit her, forcing her to reduce speed. Fifteen minutes later, another wave, this time torpedo bombers, arrived. Again the battleship *Prince of Wales* was hit. Her speed was further reduced, and she began to settle.

Repulse, too, was struck by torpedoes, which jammed her

rudder, forcing her to steam in a circle. The crippled *Prince of Wales* desperately zigzagged in an effort to avoid further damage as the Japanese continued to attack her. With her jammed rudder, *Repulse* was virtually helpless. She suffered further torpedo strikes but miraculously remained afloat, before receiving a fatal hit at 12:35 P.M. She sank.

A final attack was now made by high-level bombers against *Prince of Wales*. There would be no escape. The fundamental flaw in Phillips's thinking had been ruthlessly exposed. A bomb eventually penetrated the ship's deck, causing carnage in the casualty station below. Phillips ordered the crew to abandon ship. Ten minutes later, at 1:20 P.M., the mighty battleship *Prince of Wales* capsized and sank. No less than 840 British sailors from the two ships lost their lives, including Admiral Tom Phillips himself. Two great capital ships sank in less than an hour. The remainder, shocked by the sudden destruction of Force Z, were picked up by the accompanying destroyers.

The effect on British morale in Malaya and Singapore was grievous. The Japanese onrush down through Malaya could not be halted. By the end of January 1942, the British forces had been driven back onto Singapore Island. Two weeks later, on February 15, Britain's once great bastion in the Far East surrendered to General Tomoyuki Yamashita.

The loss of the *Prince of Wales* and *Repulse* was a crushing blow which contributed directly to the final surrender two months later. Phillips's mistaken belief that his ships could operate in a hostile air environment without air cover was exposed as a blunder. The tragedy also confirmed that air power had become decisive in the war at sea. The aircraft carrier, and not the battleship, was now the principal naval surface weapon, as the Japanese themselves would discover at the Battle of Midway.

Japanese Bungling at Midway

IT MUST BE REMEMBERED THAT in World War I the Japanese fought on the side of the Americans and British against the Germans. They campaigned successfully against Germany's Pacific colonies, only to be shut out of any of the spoils at war's end. In fact, they were forced to give back much of the terrain in China that they had won in the Russo-Japanese War of 1904. Adding insult to injury, the Washington Naval Treaty of 1922 enforced a diminished status on the Japanese Navy in the Pacific: they were allowed a navy only three-fifths the size of the U.S. and Britain.

Japan had a history of seeking to resist Westernization, which it saw as a threat to its traditional way of life. Although it relented significantly on the military side and built technologically up-to-date forces, Japan's distrust of the West continued. And, as a small set of islands with a burgeoning population of over 60 million in 1940, it was unable to be self-sufficient in food and resources. Thus the vision of Tojo, the Japanese Premier: to establish Japanese control in its chosen sphere and to defeat any Western nations that would not allow this. And thus Japan's Pacific strategy: to secure access to regions that could feed its people and its industry. America was seen as a threat to these ambitions for several reasons, principal among them the U.S. presence in the Philippines, its close relationship with Chiang Kai-shek, and the likelihood that we would act to protect the interests of other Western countries in the region

On the sleepy Sunday morning of December 7, 1941, nearly 200 torpedo- and dive-bombers, along with an escort of quick Zeros, surprised "Battleship Row" at Pearl Harbor. Two attack sorties inflicted heavy damage on the U.S. Pacific fleet: the *Utah* sunk; the *Arizona* blown up; the *Oklahoma* capsized; *West Virginia* and *California*, too; burning badly were the *Maryland*, the *Tennessee*, the *Pennsylvania*. A dozen smaller ships were hit, nearly 200 aircraft destroyed. On December 8, Roosevelt declared war on Japan.

Flush with success, Admiral Yamamoto, a charismatic, almost legendary naval leader and the architect of the attack, pressed on. The American outposts of Guam and Wake Island fell; the British-held Gilbert Island did as well; then, ignominiously, the Philippines were surrendered and General MacArthur (vowing famously, "I shall return") was removed to safer ground by Roosevelt. By March 1942, the American presence in the Pacific had been reduced to a battered Hawaii and Midway Island, a small supply post in the middle of nowhere.

What would the Japanese do next? Many feared an invasion of Hawaii; others felt San Francisco would be hit. What made the atmosphere all the more tense was the conviction that the Japanese knew they had to move fast, and no one was more sure of this than Yamamoto. Although Japanese propaganda would have it that the American spirit was flagging, that they hadn't the fortitude for war and its sacrifices, Yamamoto understood American production capabilities. He knew that Japan was badly overmatched in the automotive industries, and he had no doubt that the steel production and the assembly lines were now being committed to the war effort. It was only a matter of time. To Premier Konoye he confided in

1941, "If I am told to fight regardless of the consequences, I shall run wild for six months or a year, but I have utterly no confidence for the second and third years of the fighting."

Yamamoto's ambition was simple: draw out what remained of the U.S. force in the Pacific and smash it. Assaulting Midway seemed ideal. It would be a useful resupply spot for the Japanese once they had vanquished the American presence there, and the Americans would fight desperately for it, since it was only 1,100 miles from Hawaii.

It's hard to say when the Japanese made their first mistake, in a series of mistakes that squandered a sure victory and a unique opportunity, but one may as well start with the delays put upon Yamamoto's plan. His eagerness to hit Midway was not shared by many in the high Naval Command. As a result, the operation was continually put off until American Jimmy Doolittle, in April 1942, surprised all of Japan by leading a bombing raid on Tokyo. Fears for the Emperor's life were so intense that the country was ready to respond, and it did so by giving the go-ahead to Yamamoto's Midway plans. As things worked out, one can't help but think Japan would have fared better striking earlier.

Yamamoto assembled nearly the entire Japanese fleet, a huge armada committed to a single operation. Perhaps this was Yamamoto "running wild" while he could. Nine battleships, four carriers, six heavy cruisers, 65 destroyers, nearly 200 ships altogether supported by over 700 planes, with a troop accompaniment of over 100,000 men, including 20 admirals. What they faced was something less than 50 ships, and perhaps no carriers at all. However, the biggest blunder was that the Japanese were a little too persuaded of their own superiority, so they were rather careless in determining the whereabouts of American carrier strength, and they did not consider what would happen to their well-planned surprise if in fact the U.S. knew all about it.

That was a mistake because the Americans, thanks to the advancing field of cryptanalysis and the persistence of one of the analysts, knew what the Japanese were up to. The analyst, Commander Joe Rochefort Jr., working in a underground bunker on Pearl Harbor, was convinced that the flurry of Japanese transmission referring to "AF" were really about Midway. He was convinced the Japanese intended to strike, given the volume and frequency of "AF" references. Admirals Nimitz and Halsey were wary of putting all their eggs in the Midway basket; suppose Rochefort was wrong, and the Japanese were amassing for a strike elsewhere. For the U.S. to be surprised again in the Pacific would be unforgivable. So the admirals pressed Rochefort for proof that the Japanese transmissions were really about Midway.

Rochefort came up with a classic trick: he publicly communicated on open lines that Midway was running out of fresh water. Sure enough, the Japanese picked it up and, in coded transmission, reported that "AF" was running out of fresh water. That was proof enough that something would be happening at Midway, something big, although the Americans didn't quite know what. Then the Japanese made yet another mistake that resulted from their sense of superiority. They felt that, given the numbers, they could afford to risk losses in purely diversionary schemes, with no greater payoff than to keep the Americans guessing. Japanese landings on the far north Aleutians were contested fiercely, and another approach at New Guinea resulted in carriers clashing in the Coral Sea. Two Japanese carriers went down, as did the American *Lexington*. The *Yorktown* was badly damaged—so badly, in fact, that Yamamoto and his admirals thought they had sunk her. They were to learn differently in a very short while.

Some of the subordinate Japanese commanders wanted more time to prepare, especially since the detailed plan was a complicated one. But the high command was impatient for action. Little effort was made to establish the whereabouts of the surviving U.S. carriers. No preliminary air reconnaissance was flown and no submarine screen deployed until the eve of the battle.

On June 3, a Midway-based Catalina airplane spotted the Japanese fleet. That afternoon B-17s were sent to attack it, virtually the entire contingent of Midway bombers, some 25 planes. As they were in the air, the Japanese launched an air attack of their own, bombing Midway mercilessly, and shooting down or forcing into fatal ditches all but two of the American planes. The rout appeared to be on. Admiral Nagumo, who was commander of the four-carrier box contingent, ordered his reserve aircraft to be prepared for a second strike on Midway. The first wave then returned to the carriers to rearm, and it was at this point that U.S. torpedo bombers struck. While almost all were shot down by Zero fighters, they forced the Japanese carriers to take evasive action, which delayed rearming to deal with this new threat.

Meanwhile, two U.S. carriers, the *Hornet* and the *Enterprise*, had moved into the area. Nimitz had positioned them to the northeast of Midway, in hopes of keeping them away from any assault on the island but hoping they could perhaps ambush some unsuspecting Japanese ships. The quickly repaired *Yorktown*, damaged so badly at the Coral Sea, was bringing up the rear. With the Japanese fleet finally spotted, U.S. dive-bombers, which had gone out with the lower-flying torpedo-bombers, couldn't find the carriers. Flying with radio silence and high above the clouds, squadron commanders couldn't follow the evasive action of the carriers. Nearly out of fuel, Lieutenant Commander C. Wade McClusky spotted a Japanese destroyer steaming full speed to the northwest. She must be returning to where the other ships are, he concluded, and followed. And there they were, four carriers in a staggered square, their decks alive with bombs, men, and fuel lines, floating tinderboxes waiting for a match. McClusky and his squadron, as well as a second squadron, hit the carriers with all they had. In six minutes three of the four were in flames and beginning the list that would sink them. The Zeroes, drawn down to low level by the torpedo-bombers, were unable to cope with this new attack. The surviving Japanese carrier then launched an attack on the U.S. carrier *Yorktown* and seriously damaged her (a Japanese submarine sank her three days later). U.S. dive-bombers retaliated by damaging the Japanese carrier. Both sides now withdrew. It was over.

What could have been a key step in Japan's successful attempt to secure its own protected world instead turned the tide in the Pacific. The United States, having defended Midway, would go on to gain back what the Japanese had taken—the Philippines, Guam, Wake Island, and more. The reason the Japanese lost is simply that they saw no reason how they could, which led to the disastrous blunder of overconfidence.

Still, the war for the islands would be a drawn-out affair, and not everything went well for the Allies. The British in particular suffered some stunning defeats, and the Americans, though clearly evolving as the major force in the Pacific, had their share of dark days.

BY 1915, WORLD WAR I was under way, but the United States, following the neutrality politics of President Woodrow Wilson as well as the general will of the people, was not involved. On May 1, the luxury cruise ship *Lusitania*, sailing under the Cunard Line flags, left Pier 54 in New York harbor, outbound for Liverpool. Many wealthy American and British travelers were aboard, intent upon a peaceful voyage, despite warnings from the German Embassy that vessels flying the British flag were fair game to German submarines. On May 7, 1915, off the coast of Ireland, the *Lusitania* was hit by a torpedo from a German U-boat. She sank in 20 minutes, taking nearly 1,200 lives, including 128 Americans. The *Lusitania*'s captain was aware of the danger in the area,

The *Lusitania* seen here coming into the New York Bay. For a time, the British outfitted the cruise ship with guns, but then changed its mind and left her to her commercial routes.

The *Lusitania* went down in 20 minutes off the coast of Ireland, and many of the dead are buried in County Cork.

but did not take the necessary precautions of staying away from Irish headlands, where U-boats lurked; he was also proceeding at only 15–18 knots, while the *Lusitania*, one of the world's fastest ships, was capable of 25 knots. The German U-boat captain believed he was firing at a troop ship; and in fact *Jane's Fighting Ships* had listed the *Lusitania* as a war ship, though the information was outdated. Some of the lives lost on the *Lusitania* found their final resting place on Irish soil, in County Cork. But the most significant legacy of the sinking of the *Lusitania* was that it inflamed American public opinion against Germany, and was a major factor in bringing the United States into the war.

The German Embassy went so far as to take an ad out in New York papers on the eve of the *Lusitania*'s fateful voyage, warning passengers that they traveled at their own risk.

Erhard Milch, Goering's second in command.

UNDER THE TERMS OF THE Treaty of Versailles, which ended World War I, Germany was forbidden to mount an air force. This did not stop Hitler from empowering Air Minister Herman Goering from developing a secret war department, the Luftwaffe. In the early days of World War II, the Luftwaffe proved the class of the air, pummeling Poland and subjecting Britain to interminable and unforgettable bombing raids. But woeful mismanagement in the Luftwaffe ranks of command doomed the Luftwaffe to making numerous blunders—at Dunkirk, at Stalingrad, and in the Battle of Britain—that fatally damaged the German effort at European domination. Erhard Milch, the Secretary of State for Air, was second in command. Although a deft organizational man who earlier had set up Lufthansa, the German commercial air fleet, Milch was too ambitious to be trusted by Goering, and his ideas

Colonel Hans Jeschonnek, Luftwaffe chief of staff, was blamed for the disaster at Stalingrad, when air support could not save the surrounded German army.

were often ignored. Hans Jeschonnek, the Luftwaffe's chief of staff, was next in line. Although a brilliant tactician, he unfortunately was a loner, a trait that National Socialism tended to look upon with intense suspicion. He was blamed for the disaster at Stalingrad and eventually committed suicide. World War I fighter ace Ernst Udet, who had been a film star in the 1920s, was responsible for aircraft procurement, and was directly answerable to Milch. Although a glamorous figure, Udet was temperamentally ill-suited for his post. As the pace of bomber production proved unsatisfactory to the Fuhrer, Udet, who was held responsible, also took his own life, though Goering reported that the movie star was killed heroically, testing a new weapon.

The handsome film star and World War I ace Ernst Udet was in over his head as chief of procurement. His depression over the poor performance of the Luftwaffe led to his suicide.

Darkened by gray paint and chockablock with troops, the
Queen Mary worked as a key transport of U.S. soldiers
across the Atlantic.

WHEN THE *QUEEN MARY* WAS launched in 1936, under the
colors of the combined Cunard-White Star Line, her stacks a
bright orange, her hull black, she was the fastest ship in the world, carrying passengers across the Atlantic in record time and winning the Blue
Riband. But by 1940, the British Admiralty decided that such a fast, big
ship would be better used moving troops. She was outfitted with troop
bunks, guns on the former sun-deck; her tiger colors gave over to a non-
descript gray paint; even the portholes were painted over, giving the
speedy ship, hard to spot in the ocean mist, the nickname "The Gray
Ghost." She could carry 15,000 troops at a time at speeds of up to 30

knots, prompting an enraged Hitler to offer $250,000 to his captains for the sinking of the Gray Ghost. In October 1942, with 11,000 U.S. troops aboard, the *Queen Mary* approached the coast of England, zigging and zagging, along with its escort, the *Curacoa*, in an attempt to evade German U-boats. Due to faulty communication between the cap-

The light cruiser *Curacoa*, which was hit amid-
ships by the *Queen Mary*. Of its crew of 430,
101 perished off the coast of Ireland.

tains of the two ships, the *Queen Mary* cut the *Curacoa* in half. Fearful of
being a sitting duck for preying German subs, the *Queen Mary* did not
stop to assist in the rescue of the British seamen abandoning ship. The
disaster led to an official British inquiry after the war, but no charges
against either captain were filed.

William Hatton, crew chief on the *Lady Be Good*. Unable to find his way back to base, Hatton and his crew bailed out over the African desert. It would be 16 years before their remains would be found and the story of their demise pieced together.

FIRST LIEUTENANT WILLIAM J. HATTON led the crew of an American bomber called *Lady Be Good*, named after the Oscar Hammerstein and Jerome Kern song that won the 1941 Academy Award. Although inexperienced, Hatton and his men, along with two dozen other crews, left North Africa on April 4, 1943. Their mission: bomb the Italian port of Naples in order to damage German resupply efforts in the Italian campaign. Poor communications, night flying and inexperience resulted in the mission being partly aborted, with Hatton and his crew flying blind in an attempt to get back to base. There would be no trace of plane or crew till 1959, when parts of the plane, and later the crew's personal effects, were found in the desert, concluding a long and tragic flight.

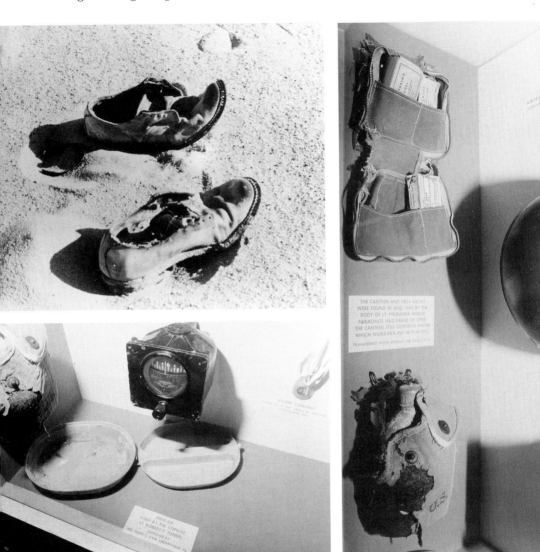

Some of the personal effects found by oil men in the desert, the legacy of a heroic struggle to overcome adversity, inexperience, and poor planning.

THE U.S.S. *INDIANAPOLIS*, A PORTLAND class cruiser, served nobly in World War II, seeing much action in the battle for the Pacific, and even once surviving a dead-on kamikaze hit. But its last trip would be its most memorable, and most ghastly. On July 16, 1945, the *Indianapolis* set sail for the Marianas Islands with a secret in its hold: part of the atom bomb that would be assembled and shortly be dropped on Japan. She delivered her cargo on July 26 and was ordered to make for the Philippines, where she was to prepare for the invasion of

The *Indianapolis*, which played a key role in assembling the atomic bombs which eventually brought Japan to surrender.

Japan, should it be necessary. But she would be sunk by a Japanese submarine, *I-58*. Of its crew of nearly 1200, 350 went down with the ship. For the remainder, an interminable struggle in the sea was made nightmarish by the presence of hungry sharks. When the carnage was over and rescue finally came, there were only 316 left to tell the story. The

Three who survived the attack of a Japanese sub and countless sharks.

Indianapolis's Captain Charles McVay survived, but his torment was just beginning. He was subjected to court-martial proceedings for not taking precautions to evade the Japanese sub. He would commit suicide in 1968, and it would be left to a grade-schooler, who learned of the *Indianapolis* through the film *Jaws*, to start the campaign that would officially clear McVay's name.

The *I-58*, the Japanese mini-sub put six torpedoes into the *Indianapolis*. Its captain would later testify that no amount of diversionary tactics taken by the *Indianapolis* would have saved it from his attack.

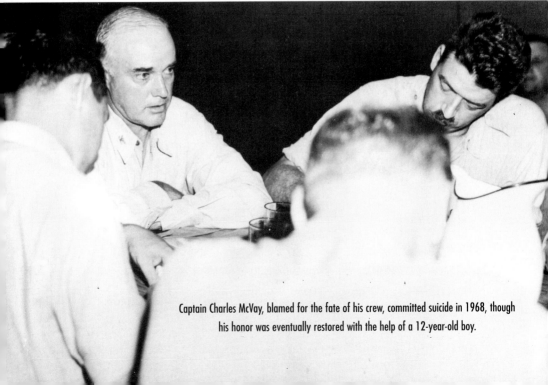

Captain Charles McVay, blamed for the fate of his crew, committed suicide in 1968, though his honor was eventually restored with the help of a 12-year-old boy.

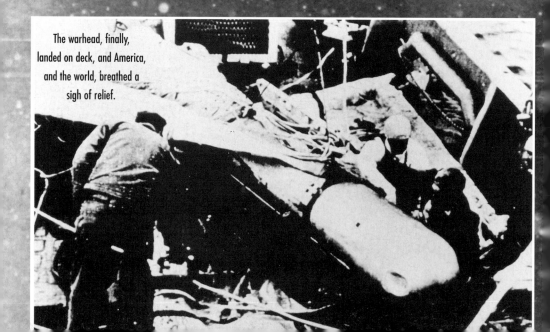

The fourth H-Bomb, under water, being
secured for removal to the surface, in
April 1966.

The warhead, finally,
landed on deck, and America,
and the world, breathed a
sigh of relief.

DURING THE HOTTEST DECADE OF the Cold War, the United States kept nuclear-armed bombers in the air 24 hours a day, which made mid-air refueling necessary. In January 1966 a B-52 collided with a tanker aircraft over eastern Spain during refueling. Both were destroyed, but the B-52 was carrying four nuclear bombs. Three fell on land, and were quickly found. None had detonated; but the search for the missing fourth would take more than three months, and lead to much embarrassment for the United States government, as the possibility that they had blundered into an accidental nuclear explosion, or that the unfound warhead would at any moment detonate or possibly fall into the wrong hands, caused widespread panic. Eventually, the fourth was found, with the help of small underwater search probes, nearly a half mile under water. When the H-bomb was hauled up, undetonated, an American nightmare came to an end, though the accident only served to make Cold War relations more tense.

Arthur Schlessinger and President Kennedy confer in the Oval Office. Schlessinger counseled against an invasion of Cuba. Kennedy persevered, but did so half-heartedly, which led to the fiasco known as the Bay of Pigs.

Early in John F. Kennedy's term as president, he felt compelled to uphold a campaign promise to Cuban exiles that he would aid them in overturning the Castro regime. Presidential aide Arthur Schlessinger advised against an invasion, but Kennedy did not want to be accused by the Cuban exiles of backing out. He was also swayed by CIA declarations that once landings had taken place, the Cuban people would support the invasion and turn against Castro. In April 1961, Cuban exiles landed in the Bay of Pigs, on the northern coast of Cuba. But promised American air support did not materialize, and the small force was overwhelmed by superior numbers of Cuban troops using Russian vehicles and weaponry. The invasion was a failure, and an early blow to the Kennedy presidency. The aggression set the stage for a later showdown, the Cuban Missile Crisis, in October 1962, where Kennedy and Khrushchev squared off in a war of nerves that brought the world as close as it would get to a nuclear holocaust.

Naval Night
Fighting at Guadalcanal

THE BATTLE OF MIDWAY, PERHAPS the most decisive battle in World War II, was still just a battle, not the war itself.
What the Americans achieved was the right to keep claim to a small
atoll with a tiny airstrip. There was still much work to do in order
to turn back the Japanese advance in the South Pacific. Attentions
turned to the Solomon Islands, a string of islands northeast of
Australia.

In August 1942, just two months after the Battle of Midway
concluded, the Americans planned an invasion of Guadalcanal, an
island in the Solomons chain. U.S. intelligence reported that the
Japanese had a small garrison there building an airfield. This was
to be stopped.

The Marine's First Division landed on August 7 easily,
overrunning and scattering the 2,200 Japanese troops there into the
jungle. They also took the three surrounding but smaller islands—
Tulagi, Gavutu, and Tanambogo—which protected Guadalcanal on
three sides. The channel through these three to the Guadalcanal
beaches, narrow and treacherous, especially with enemy battle
cruisers in play, was known as "the Slot."

On this day, however, there were no enemy ships visible.
But when reports of the Allied landing reached Japanese Admiral

Inouye, he rushed a naval task force of seven cruisers and a destroyer into the Slot. What ensued was a series of mistakes by the Americans in command that in all likelihood prolonged the Battle of Guadalcanal from weeks to months. Fortunately for the U.S., the blunders did not turn out as badly as they might have, since the Japanese followed with a tactical blunder of their own, squandering an early advantage.

It's not that the Navy, which was under Vice Admiral Ghormley, did not expect a Japanese naval response to the invasion. They surely did. Ghormley's first in command, and in fact the commander afloat since Ghormley was ashore in New Zealand, was Rear Admiral Fletcher, who had a task force at his disposal that included three carriers—*Saratoga*, *Enterprise*, and *Wasp*. The amphibious force that landed on August 7 consisted of seven cruisers and 19 destroyers, and was commanded by Admiral R. K. Turner.

With the airfield left behind by the Japanese, the Marines took it over and renamed it Henderson Field (after a pilot lost at Midway). But by the next day the Japanese planes came after Fletcher's American carrier force. It was a day of fierce air combat, with both sides giving as good as they got. But Fletcher, fearful of what the loss of American carriers could mean for the attempt to regain the Pacific, not to mention the loss of air cover its planes could provide to the Guadalcanal initiative, decided to withdraw. This was done with the approval of his superior, Vice Admiral Ghormley, but it led Admiral Turner, in command of the cruisers and destroyers operating in the Slot, and the first line of protection for the landed Marines, to withdraw also to open water. Without the carrier support Turner felt he might be a sitting duck.

He was right, but he was wrong to delay. He decided to stay one more night in the area before withdrawing. He planned to move more supplies ashore to the Marines at daybreak, and then head out to open and safer water.

Even though Allies had sighted the Japanese cruisers during the day, Admiral Victor Crutchley did not believe that the Japanese would attack by night. It was thought that the fact that Japanese ships lacked radar and the notion that Japanese sailors had poor night vision would deter such night operations. The Allied ships were therefore not on the alert.

The Japanese Navy was, in fact, highly trained in night fighting, with those sailors with the best vision being selected as ship's lookouts. They had superior shells to the Allies, very effective ship's searchlights, and were well versed in target illumination. Furthermore, all their ships were equipped with the very powerful and highly effective Lance torpedo.

At midnight, a Japanese force of seven cruisers and one destroyer, under Vice Admiral Gunichi Mikawa, slipped past the destroyers patroling the entrance to the Slot and immediately found itself among a part of the Allied cruiser group. His ships launched torpedoes and followed these up with gunfire. Within moments the Australian cruiser *Canberra* was sinking and the USS *Chicago* was badly damaged. Mikawa's force then swung around Savo Island, a bit to the north of Guadalcanal, and fell upon a separate Allied contingent. Within minutes all three U.S. cruisers there were also sinking. The transports were now without protection. But Mikawa feared Admiral Fletcher's carrier force, of whose whereabouts he was unsure. Rather than risk being caught by U.S. carrier aircraft once dawn came, he made good his escape, satisfied that he had given the Allied ships a good thrashing. The Allies had paid dearly for their blunders in underestimating Japanese capabilities and giving so little priority to night-fighting techniques.

In little more than a half hour of battle, during which the Japanese displayed brilliant ship handling and sharpshooting, they sank four cruisers, badly damaged a fifth, and took a destroyer. The Americans were outclassed in the dark. The area of the en-

gagement became known as "Iron-bottom Sound" for all the hulls
that sank there.

Turner managed to escape with what was left of his transport operation, although supplies had been only partly unloaded.
The Marines on the beach, a division of about 16,000 men, were
on their own. No carriers, no transports, no bombardment fleet to
keep the Japanese at bay and help widen the perimeters of their
activity.

A window of opportunity opened for the Japanese with the
American naval task force withdrawn and dispersed. If at that moment they had made an immediate, large-scale reinforcement of
troops on the islands, which could have been done in the absence
of American air defenses, they might have had a good chance to
retake Guadalcanal. Instead, they pursued the task fleet, perhaps a
grander tactical strategy, but in what was becoming an island-by-
island battle for regional supremacy, it was a strategic blunder.

Japanese theater commander Isokoru Yamamoto, architect
of the attack on Pearl Harbor, now pursued a plan to destroy the
U.S. carrier force. The result was the Battle of the Eastern Solomons (August 23–25). The Japanese lost a light carrier and various other ships, but seriously damaged the U.S. carrier
Enterprise, which sent her aircraft to Henderson Field, now operational thanks to the frantic work, under great pressure, of the
Marines. Aircraft from there attacked the reinforcement convoy,
forcing it to withdraw.

Such was the U.S. air dominance around Guadalcanal that
the Japanese decided to continue to take advantage of their naval
superiority at night. They began to run reinforcements down
through the Slot under cover of darkness. The troops were largely
transported in destroyers, and this supply route became known by
the Americans as the Tokyo Express. But their efforts were inter-

mittent and scattershot, not the kind of buildup that could threaten the Marines' hold on the island.

An Allied naval task force was now positioned at the entrance of the Slot to turn back the Tokyo Express. On the night of October 11, it consisted of four cruisers and four destroyers. The Allied tactic was to steam straight ahead and use the destroyers to illuminate for the cruisers' guns. They surprised a Japanese force of three cruisers and two destroyers. Admiral Turner, not quite believing his radar, executed a 180-degree turn before closing in on the Japanese ships. Unfortunately, his destroyers fell out of formation and found themselves between their own cruisers and the Japanese. Even so, one Japanese cruiser and a destroyer were sunk before the Tokyo Express withdrew. But the Americans also lost a destroyer, and one light cruiser was badly damaged. The Battle of Cape Esperance was therefore a draw, but showed that the U.S. Navy still had much to learn. Despite the cruiser losses, the task force was able to land reinforcements on the island.

Yamamoto now deployed his carriers again in an attempt to achieve naval supremacy around Guadalcanal by day. Two of his carriers were badly damaged, but the carrier USS *Hornet* was lost and another carrier, *Enterprise*, was badly damaged.

The Tokyo Express continued its operations by night and had its next clash with the U.S. Navy on the night of November 13. As in the previous engagements Turner had trouble with his radar, and the two forces closed to within 1,000 yards of each other before opening fire. The Japanese had deployed two battleships to bombard Henderson Field, but one of these was sunk, along with two destroyers. But the Americans suffered worse in this point-blank engagement, losing one light cruiser and four destroyers, with two heavy and two light cruisers as well as one destroyer badly damaged.

This meant that the Americans were left with virtually no ships to protect the Slot, and the overall theater commander, Admiral William Halsey, was forced to detach the two fast battleships protecting his carriers. *South Dakota* and *Washington* arrived just in time to face another Tokyo Express foray. This was built around one battleship and two heavy cruisers intent on having another go at Henderson Field. On the night of November 14, the American battleships clashed with this force. *South Dakota* had electrical problems and was literally riddled by Japanese shells, but *Washington* managed to get within 8,500 yards of the Japanese ships and literally blew the battleship *Kirishima* and the heavy cruiser *Ayanami* out of the water. But three U.S. destroyers were lost.

The Americans were feeling better. Perhaps they would not lose control of the seas around Guadalcanal. The fact that they had compromised Japan's efforts to reinforce their jungle-hidden forces on the island would, in the end, persuade the Japanese that the island was lost.

Nevertheless, the seemingly irrepressible Tokyo Express continued to operate, and on November 30 eight Japanese destroyers on a supply run clashed with five U.S. cruisers and four destroyers in the Battle of Tassafaronga. Again, the Japanese came off best, losing just one destroyer to one U.S. cruiser sunk and three badly damaged.

Still, unable to resupply the Japanese forces on Guadalcanal, an evacuation began in January 1943, five months after the Marine invasion. On February 9, U.S. forces finally secured their first stepping stone on the long road toward the Japanese mainland. It had, however, been a costly victory, especially in naval terms. American disregard for training in night fighting had proved a costly blunder, but their protection of their carriers, though prolonging the conflict, had in some measure seduced the Japanese. Rather than taking advantage of the Allied naval absence and staging a counter-invasion of sufficient size, they engaged in a series of sea battles. And though the Japanese sank two precious American carriers, they lost Guadalcanal.

The Disastrous Raid on Dieppe

HITLER WAS WELL AWARE THAT eventually he might have to face an invasion of Europe by Allied forces. And strategically, the Allies knew the same. By gaining some semblance of control over the Japanese in the South Pacific, the Allies could begin to plan just how to approach the European coast. Of course, on June 6, 1944, in the largest amphibious operation of all time, the Allies would assault Hitler's much vaunted Atlantic Wall on France's Normandy coast. It was another major turning point in the war. But the success of D-Day, the fact the Allies got onto the beaches and were able to advance beyond them, was partly due to a disastrous operation that took place some seventy miles farther up the French coast almost two years earlier.

The raid on the French port of Dieppe in August 1942 met with a bloody repulse due to a series of blunders. Delays in mounting the operation led to a loss of surprise. This meant that the German defenses became stronger than expected. There was insufficient fire support, both from the Allied ships off the coast and aircraft above, and the planners failed to appreciate the obstacles confronting the tanks when they got ashore. These blunders would lead to heavy casualties being suffered by the attacking troops, most of whom were Canadian.

. . .

When America entered the war in December 1941, President Roosevelt and British Prime Minister Winston Churchill held three weeks of meetings in Washington, D.C., to formulate an Allied war policy. They agreed that defeat of Germany was the number one priority, while the Japanese menace in the Pacific was to be checked. Defeat of Japan would become the priority only after Germany had been defeated.

With the Pacific Naval Task Force beginning to assert itself against the Japanese, the Allies brought renewed concentration to the war against Germany. Hitler had taken France, and was effectively in control of Western Europe. His campaign on the Eastern Front early in 1942 had not yet run into disaster in Stalingrad, as it eventually would. Churchill and Roosevelt worried that the Russian Army was headed for defeat, and their instinct, following standard military logic, was to do something to divert German attention and resources elsewhere. Since an invasion of Europe had been assumed all along, they thought that perhaps the time had come. The debate, however, was on how to go about it.

The Americans wanted a cross-Channel invasion as soon as possible. The British, who were fighting Axis forces in Libya, wanted priority given to securing North Africa before assaulting Europe. Churchill felt Germany might be most vulnerable through the "soft underbelly" of the Mediterranean basin. Hence, there was an enormous commitment of troops, under General Bernard Montgomery, and materiel, to the war in North Africa.

The Germans had just launched a fresh offensive, pushing southward in Russia toward the oil fields beyond Stalingrad. The Red Army was on the run. Soviet Foreign Minister Vyacheslav Molotov appealed to Churchill and Roosevelt to open a second front in Europe as soon as possible.

At last the British Chiefs of Staff came up with a plan. It would be a 48-hour, cross-Channel operation against the French port of Dieppe. The town had the attractions of being lightly defended and well within range of fighter aircraft based in southern England. On May 13, 1942, the plan was given the go-ahead. It had two critical justifications. First, by presenting the Germans with a threat to their Western Front, it might force them to divert troops from Russia, or at least prevent any more troops or aircraft to be sent to the Eastern Front from France, satisfying Molotov. Second, it would provide the second-front planners with firsthand information on the pros and cons of centering the main invasion of western Europe on a port. Ports were likely to be more heavily defended, but the landing of reinforcements and supplies would be easier than over an open beach.

So critical did this become as a operation in which much could be learned for the future that General Montgomery was removed from North Africa and given responsibility for executing Rutter, as the Dieppe raid was code-named.

Among the troops under Montgomery's command was a large force of Canadians, many of whom had arrived in Britain in late 1939 but who as yet had seen no combat. The Canadians were becoming increasingly impatient to be given a more active role in the war and were fed up with endless training. Montgomery selected General J. H. Roberts's Second Canadian Division, based on England's south coast, for the Dieppe operation.

The plan called for the Canadians to land on the beaches off the port itself, destroy military installations, and then withdraw. Paratroops would then be used to neutralize prominent coastal batteries on the headlands on either side of the port. Dieppe would also be subjected to a preliminary attack by RAF Bomber Command.

A large force of fighters was organized to cover the landings and to tempt the Luftwaffe up into the air so that as many German aircraft as possible could be destroyed. Any amphibious landing in combat relies heavily on the support of naval gunfire, which takes the place of artillery until guns can be landed. The bigger the guns, the more effective the fire.

However, ever since the summer of 1940, after British warships in the English Channel had suffered heavily at the hands of Hitler's Luftwaffe, the Admiralty had enforced a policy that no warship larger than a destroyer was allowed to operate in those narrow waters. Consequently, the Royal Navy was prepared to offer only eight destroyers and a few smaller gunboats to support the Dieppe operation.

An additional aspect of Rutter was the provision for a Canadian battalion equipped with Churchill tanks. The idea was to land the battalion with the first waves of infantry. The tanks were to be equipped with modified exhausts to prevent water from getting into their engines as they waded ashore, but little account was taken of the stony beaches or the sea wall that they would have to climb.

In June 1942, after the necessary landing craft had been assembled, Montgomery held two rehearsals. It was finally agreed that Rutter would be mounted on July 4, 1942. But the first of several fateful delays interfered.

The English Channel was struck by a spell of bad weather that brought high winds and very rough seas. Montgomery was worried that such conditions could put the Dieppe operation at risk. It was decided to postpone the raid for at least a month, until the tides were once more favorable. But Montgomery then thought that the longer the preparation went on, the greater the chance the operation would be compromised, and the element of surprise would be sacrificed.

He was right. German air reconnaissance spotted the

buildup of landing craft in English south coast ports. Hitler personally issued a warning of the likelihood of landings and ordered the defenses on the French Channel coast to be strengthened.

Montgomery was transferred back to North Africa, where he took over command of the British Eighth Army in Egypt. It was Rommel with whom he now would do battle, leaving Dieppe to others. Namely, Rutter was left to the man who had conceived the plan in the first place, Admiral Lord Louis Mountbatten, a cousin of King George VI. Mountbatten now took full responsibility for the raid.

As Commander-in-Chief of Combined Operations, Mountbatten was in charge of the development of amphibious warfare techniques and of raiding operations. He was conscious that there had been no major raids against Hitler's Atlantic Wall for some months. Valuable experience could still be gained from the Dieppe raid for the eventual invasion of Europe. He was keen that Rutter still go ahead, in spite of Montgomery's fears of compromise. It was agreed that it should finally take place in mid-August. There were, however, major changes to the plan, one of which was to prove a serious blunder.

The RAF's heavy bombers would no longer bomb Dieppe before the raid for fear of inflicting casualties on French civilians and perhaps turning the French against the Allies. The opportunity to disrupt the German defenses just before the landings took place was passed up, and the Canadians would have to rely largely on the relatively small guns of the warships.

Continuing uncertainty over the weather led the RAF to cancel the airborne operation against the coastal batteries. Instead, Commandos, an elite raiding force organized by Winston Churchill in June 1940, would be used to subdue the batteries. Among their number were fifty U.S. Rangers, who had been training with the Commandos and would be the first American ground troops to set foot on the soil of German-occupied Europe. The part played by the Commandos and Rangers was to be the one bright spot in an otherwise disastrous day.

In order to maintain its security, the last change to the plan was to give the operation a new code name—Jubilee. But it had already been compromised.

The date of the operation was set for August 19, 1942. Expecting an attack, the Germans continued to strengthen their defenses on the Channel coast. Their intelligence forecast that tide and moon conditions made the landings likely during the period of August 10–19, so the German division responsible for the defense of Dieppe was on a high state of alert. Then, on the night of August 18, minesweepers cleared mines in mid-Channel to ensure that the assaulting ships had a clear passage to Dieppe.

In their wake came the amphibious task force. The Commandos who were to silence the Goebbels Battery to the east of Dieppe ran into a German coastal convoy, with a strong escort. The resultant naval clash caused the landing craft to become scattered, and only 20 Commandos managed to get ashore. Even so, they were able to distract the battery and prevent its firing out to sea.

On the other flank, the operation went according to plan, with the guns of the Hess Battery successfully put out of action.

The preliminary phases of Jubilee had gone well. But as the Canadians prepared to land, the planning blunders were to be brought home with a vengeance.

The main force of Canadians closed on the port of Dieppe. Not able to use heavy bombers, two squadrons of medium bombers had taken off at dawn to attack targets around the port. They were followed by swarms of fighters. As the planners had hoped, the Luftwaffe took the bait. Messerschmitt Me109s and Fockewulf Fw190s took off from airfields all over northern France. Soon fierce air battles were raging over the English Channel, with ships' guns also joining in.

But it soon became clear that the Luftwaffe, operating close to its bases, was faring better than the Allied fighters, which could spend only a limited time over Dieppe before having to return to their airfields to refuel. As the landing craft made their final run in to the shore, the guns of the Allied ships gave covering fire. But, undeterred by this, the more powerful German coastal batteries returned their fire. Soon they were hitting landing craft and even sank a destroyer.

As the surviving landing craft beached, the Canadian infantrymen leapt out. They met heavy fire from the fully alerted Germans and began to suffer casualties immediately.

Worse, the tracks of the Churchill tanks had trouble coping with the deep pile of water-worn pebbles on the beach. This made them easy targets for the German anti-tank guns. Those that made it to the sea wall beyond found it impossible to surmount, and more tanks became casualties. Confusion on the beaches grew, with reinforcements being landed in the wrong place.

General Roberts, who was overseeing from on board one of the destroyers, found it impossible to establish what the true situation was, especially since communications with the shore were poor. With the Canadians taking ever more casualties, Dieppe was rapidly becoming a one-sided battle, even though some troops had managed to advance into the town. Roberts eventually realized that the operation was not going as planned and at 9:00 A.M. ordered a withdrawal.

The confusion caused by the carnage on the beaches and the poor communications hindered the withdrawal. It took over four hours to complete. Of the 5,000 troops put ashore, 3,350 were killed or wounded, 90 percent of them Canadian. Twenty-eight tanks were lost and many landing craft. Hundreds were captured: they now faced the prospect of nearly three years as prisoners of war. If in their anger they sought someone to blame, there was plenty of blame to go around. The failure to win the air battles was bad enough, with the Allies losing over 100 planes, over twice what the Luftwaffe lost. But even worse was the refusal to allow heavy bombers to suppress the coastal defenses around Dieppe prior to the landing. The British Admiralty's refusal to allow ships larger than destroyers to support the raid didn't help matters. And the reliance on the Churchill tanks to advance up the beaches turned into a sorry catastrophe. Every tank was lost.

However, the main blunder was Mountbatten's. The operation should have been canceled in early July. Keeping it on hold for so long had meant that surprise was lost.

One wonders if there could have been a less disastrous way to learn the lessons that were learned at Dieppe. Could there have been a way to pay less of a price to understand how to invade an Atlantic beachhead? When the Allies invaded Normandy two years later, they did things differently. They heavily bombed the German coastal batteries and the road and railway communications leading into Normandy prior to the invasion. A massive naval armada, including battleships, was present to provide fire support. And the Allies avoided landing at a port, thereby saving casualties. Instead, they brought with them their own "floating harbors" to assist in the unloading of tanks and equipment. Finally, the men who stormed ashore on that day were much better trained in landing operations than those who did so at Dieppe.

As for the Canadians, they would soon have their revenge

for the disaster at Dieppe. They took part in the Sicily landings and played a key role in the fighting in Italy. Canadians would also land in Normandy on D-Day, and the First Canadian Army would play a distinguished part in the subsequent campaign in Northwest Europe.

Even so, due to their heavy losses, Dieppe still produces bitter feelings in Canada today—a sad legacy of the blunders made by the British high command.

The Bombing of Monte Cassino

T HE ABBEY OF MONTE CASSINO, built almost 1,500 years
ago, was customarily a place of quiet meditation, where the
members of the resident religious order endeavored to perfect the
quality of their devotions to God. But during the early months of
1944, the abbey, located 75 miles southwest of Rome, was the
scene of some of the toughest fighting of World War II. The abbey's destruction during the battles for Cassino was an Allied blunder that not only wiped out an architectural treasure, but helped
prolong the fighting.

In September 1943, the Allies hit the beaches of southern
Italy. Operation Baytown, on September 3, and a week later, Operation Slapstick, hit at Paranto; Operation Avalanche stormed Sa-
lerno, driving the Germans north into the mountains. If Italy is a
boot, imagine a line across it at about mid-ankle. That is where the
Germans dug in, in a position called the Gustav Line, which extended from the Mediterranean on the west to the Adriatic on the
east. Principal to this line of defense was Monastery Hill in Cassino,
on which was situated the great fortress abbey, where St. Benedict
had established the roots of Christian monasticism in the sixth century. The German defenses featured the crack 15th Panzergrenadier
Division and paratroops that had been dropped in. The area,
mountainous and rocky and now well defended, stood in the way
of General Mark Clark's U.S. Fifth Army, which hoped to advance

through the mountain passes and into the Liri River valley and on into Rome via Highway 6, the main north-south route on the Mediterranean coast.

But Clark ran into problems: mine-strewn battlefields, swollen rivers, and icy mountain peaks stalled the U.S. Fifth. Clark thought he could snake through the valley along the Rapido River's east bank, if only his men could cross. He dispatched the 36th Division, made up of tough Texans, but the warnings of an American engineer proved prophetic, as was dramatically noted in John Keegan's *The Second World War*: "An attack through a muddy valley that was without suitable approach routes and exit roads and that was blocked by organized defenses behind an unfordable river [would] create an impossible situation and result in a great loss of life."

The Texans tried for three days to cross the river, only to lose 1,000 of their 6,000 men. However, Clark's hope for taking Rome zoomed when he learned of the planned invasion at Anzio beach, north of where his Army was bogged down; surely that would divert, if not trap, the Germans on the Gustav Line, opening the door to Rome.

But the amphibious assault on Anzio, called Operation Shingle, proved a failure. Although it took the Germans completely by surprise, General John P. Lucas bungled the operation after the successful landing. Rather than pressing the advantage of surprise and moving the 30 miles into Rome, he contented himself with establishing his troops at a beachhead. Hitler quickly mustered a new division out of men slated for leave and mounted a counter-offensive, called Fischgang. It stymied Lucas's troops, pinning them down on the Mediterranean coast they had taken such risks to land on. Lucas was relieved of his command.

With Anzio failing, Clark more than ever had to find a way to smash through the Gustav Line and on into Rome. Rome was deemed strategically important for a possible assault on France, which had to be launched from northern Italy. Unfortunately, it had now come down to Highway 6 as the only road to Rome; and high above sat the impregnable Abbey of Monte Cassino.

In the next three months, Allied troops stormed Monastery Hill without success. First, U.S. 34th Division struggled to capture features adjacent to Monastery Hill, but learned how tough it is to attack a naturally strong position. The second battle for Cassino took place on February 18, with attacks by the Second New Zealand and Fourth Indian Divisions, commanded by Bernard Freyberg. He mistakenly feared that the Germans might use the abbey as part of their defense and requested that Allied bombers destroy it. Mark Clark, the Army commander, disagreed, but not out of concern for the ancient place of worship: he felt that the monastery in ruins made an even better defensive position. Freyberg insisted on the bombing, however, and Clark was overruled by the Army Group commander, Field Marshal Sir Harold Alexander. Thus, Allied bombers hit the abbey, destroying much of the structure and killing several civilians who had taken refuge in it, thinking surely it was safe. Not a single German soldier was killed or wounded; they had not been using it.

What neither Freyberg nor Clark nor Alexander knew was that the Germans' First Parachute Division, which surrounded the abbey, was commanded by Frido von Senger und Etterlin, who, a lay member of St. Benedict's order, would not allow the paratroops to use the sacred monastery for defense. However, as Clark predicted, the Germans rushed into the ruins of the abbey and the town, allowing the construction of a maze of tunnels and bunkers. And Clark thought the Germans were dug in before!

A month of atrocious weather followed before a third assault was made. Both the Indian and New Zealand divisions failed to extricate the Germans from the rubble of their defense. The Italian campaign was turning into an embarrassment heading for disaster. Eight months (September 1943–April 1944) had passed since the Allied landings in southern Italy, and troops had advanced only 70 miles. Churchill was apoplectic about the lack of progress while Hitler was ecstatic about German resolve. More and more resources were now necessary to bring the Italian venture toward a close. And getting through Monte Cassino was the major priority before anything else. Field Marshal Alexander ordered a halt to the attacks and drew up a new plan, code-named Diadem. Because of the slow pace of the Allied advance, troops had built up to impressive numbers—all the more reason to end the Italian ordeal quickly and reassign the man- and firepower. With the II Polish Corps at full strength, and with the Eighth Army assisted by Indian, South African, and Canadian troops, Alexander called for a concentration of force at Cassino for a breakthrough to the Liri Valley. The Americans would also attack in the west, from their position at the Anzio beachhead. An Allied air offensive would also be launched against German communications. Diadem was launched on May 11. British XIII Corps attacked and finally secured the town of Cassino, but II Polish Corps, tasked with the capture of Monastery Hill, was repulsed. However, to the west the French succeeded in breaking through the seemingly impassable Aurinci mountains and established themselves overlooking the Liri Valley. This unlocked the Gustav Line, and on May 15 the German commander, Albert Kesselring, ordered a withdrawal.

In the end, the protracted battle for Cassino, made even longer by the unwise bombing of a 1,500-year-old monastery, diverted Allied resources and men, and much delayed the inevitable invasion of the south of France, which was not such a loss to Hitler. In fact, it could almost be counted as a strategic victory, because the campaign tied up Allied troops in Italy for close to a year in areas not deemed crucial to the Third Reich.

The Last Flight
of the *Lady Be Good*

I N 1 9 5 9 , A B R I T I S H O I L survey group came upon a crashed World War II bomber in the Libyan desert. Still legible on its sand-blasted fuselage was the aircraft's name—*Lady Be Good*. It was a B-24 Liberator bomber that had disappeared 16 years earlier, leaving no trace.

It took another 18 months to unravel the mystery of what had happened to the plane and to establish the blunders that brought about tragedy for the aircraft's crew, blunders that were symptomatic of a serious flaw in American bombing tactics. The story of the B-24 called *Lady Be Good* begins where it ended . . . in Libya at the beginning of April 1943.

By then, Generals George Patton and Bernard Montgomery had secured most of a string of North African positions; only Tunisia remained partly occupied by Axis forces, the remnants of Mussolini's Italian Army. German Field Marshall Erwin Rommel, the "Desert Fox," had fought and maneuvered cannily, but now, without resupply, was reduced to a small factor.

American, British, and French troops steadily pressed the remaining Germans and Italians into the northeast corner of Tunisia. The fighting, however, was still very fierce. If Tunisia could be secured, the Allies could concentrate on the liberation of West-

ern Europe. To hurry the end, action on the ground was comple-
mented by an air and sea campaign designed to throttle the supply
lines from Italy. The campaign included attacks on transport aircraft
flying across the Mediterranean with reinforcements.

At Solluch, 30 miles south of the port of Benghazi, was
based the 376th Heavy Bombardment Group, known by its members as the Liberandos. This had been operating in the Middle East
with its B-24s since June 1942. It had grown to four squadrons—
512th through 515th.

Newly assigned to the 514th Squadron was a crew led by
pilot First Lieutenant William J. Hatton. They had arrived in theater on March 23 and had yet to fly their first mission. Even so,
the crew had been allocated a Liberator bomber, which they named
Lady Be Good, the title of the Oscar Hammerstein and Jerome Kern
song that had won the 1941 Academy Award.

On the morning of April 4, 1943, the inexperienced Hatton
and his men, together with two dozen other crews, were briefed
for a mission. They were told that they were to take off early that
afternoon to bomb the Italian port of Naples. They were given a
route to follow, which was to take them across the Mediterranean
and the toe of Italy and then along the north coast of Sicily before
turning northeast toward Naples.

Even as the briefing was taking place, the airfield at Solluch
was the scene of frenetic activity as the ground crews prepared the
bombers for combat. Hatton and his crew were naturally keen to
prove themselves, but because it was their first mission, they were
told to follow two other bombers. One after another, the Liberators
took off from Solluch, crossed the Libyan coast, and flew over the
Mediterranean bound for Naples.

During the day a Ghibli—the local name for a sandstorm—
had been blowing. In spite of the ground crews' best efforts, sand

had got into the engines of some of the B-24s. The result was that one after another they were forced to turn back as their engines began to sputter. Nine out of *Lady Be Good*'s group of thirteen aircraft had to abort before they reached the target. They included the two planes which *Lady Be Good* was supposed to follow, leaving her on her own—and on a course to disaster.

Much of what happened to the B-24 *Lady Be Good* after she found herself alone in the skies has been deduced from the information found in her sixteen years later. This included the log kept by the navigator, Lieutenant D. P. Hays.

The few entries in the log, together with the fact that the navigator's instruments were still in their box, indicated that *Lady Be Good*'s crew had been relying entirely on the two aircraft in front to guide them to the target. When these two turned back, the crew did not know precisely where they were. Eventually, they realized that a strong wind had been blowing them eastward and that they were heading north into the Adriatic, too far east of their Italian target. Hatton therefore turned west.

Lady Be Good had by now been airborne for six hours. It was getting dark, and the crew were beginning to feel the cold in spite of their electrically heated flying suits. The wind, too, had swung to the north, and Hatton and his co-pilot, Second Lieutenant Robert F. Toner, were finding it difficult to keep the aircraft on track. They eventually spotted some fires on the ground, which they assumed were the result of the attack on Naples. But, worried about their remaining fuel, they decided not to bomb. Instead, they turned south and headed back across the Mediterranean for home. Radio operator Robert E. LaMotte managed to get a fix from a station on the island of Malta. This gave them a course that would take them to Benghazi.

For the next two and a half hours, *Lady Be Good* flew

onward toward her base. Then Hatton dropped to under 5,000 feet and ordered the crew to look out for the Libyan coast. By now it was midnight. In the darkness the crew did not identify the coast and requested another fix from Benghazi. This was given, and Hays, believing that they still had not reached the coast, calculated the reciprocal bearing and told Hatton to fly along it.

Almost immediately afterward aircraft engines were heard over *Lady be Good*'s home base at Solluch. Flares were fired to attract its attention, but the plane continued to drone on southward and ever deeper into the desert.

What had obviously happened was that by the time Hays calculated the reciprocal bearing, *Lady Be Good* had crossed the coast and was south of Benghazi. The crew were unaware of this and were convinced that they were still over the sea. It was to be their fatal blunder.

Nothing more was heard of *Lady Be Good*, which was the only Liberando aircraft unaccounted for from the Naples mission.

During the next few days the Group sent aircraft to search for the plane, but nothing was found. Hatton and his crew were therefore duly posted as missing, believed killed. *Lady Be Good*'s crew were lost because they relied on other aircraft to show them the way and did not bother to do their own navigation until it was too late. But this was symptomatic of American bombing tactics of the time, and the potential for catastrophic blundering was to be demonstrated more dramatically by another operation in which the Liberandos took part four months after the Naples mission.

This was the attack on the Ploesti oil fields in Rumania, which was mounted by the Ninth Air Force from Libya on August 1, 1943. No less than five B-24 groups were involved.

The Liberandos put up 30 aircraft and were the lead group. To guide them to the target there were a group navigator and his deputy. Unfortunately, while over the Mediterranean the lead navigator's B-24 suddenly plunged into the sea.

His deputy was alongside and, against orders, dived down to see if there were any survivors. Regrettably, laden with bombs, it was unable to regain altitude and fell behind. This blunder meant that the Liberandos had lost their guides. Nevertheless, they pressed on, with the other bombing groups following them. They crossed over the Albanian coast and then Bulgaria.

Reaching the River Danube, they dropped down to a very low level to avoid German radar. Without their expert navigators, however, the Liberandos mistook the initial point, which marked the beginning of the bomb run. Realizing his mistake, their commander broke radio silence, which was again against orders. The Germans were able to figure out then that Ploesti was the target. Fire from the ground became intense, and bomber casualties began to mount.

Then, as the B-24s turned for home, they were jumped on by Messerschmitt Me109s, and many more were shot down or badly damaged. Others crash-landed on their return to base.

As with *Lady Be Good*, overreliance on specialists to guide them to the target had caused the bombers to miss their way and lose the vital element of surprise. But while the Ploesti raid quickly entered the history books, *Lady Be Good* and her crew were remembered only by a few surviving Liberando crews who had been based at Solluch at the time.

In 1959—16 years after her fatal flight in April 1943—the remains of *Lady Be Good* were found in the Libyan desert, some 450 miles south of her base at Solluch. Much of the equipment on board was still in good condition. The British Petroleum oilmen who found her came across not only personal possessions of the crew, but the aircraft's instruments still in working order. There were first-aid packs, even a water bottle, but no trace of the crewmen themselves. Their fate remained a mystery.

The oilmen noted that three of the engines were feathered and concluded that the crew had bailed out when they realized that the fuel tanks were virtually empty. They also identified the names of most of the crew from their duffel bags left on board.

The U.S. Air Force now began to take an interest. A team from the U.S. Army Quartermaster Mortuary System in Germany was sent out to Libya in the hope of finding the bodies of the crew. The team visited the wreck of the *Lady Be Good* and carried out a thorough search of the vicinity and found further artifacts, but nothing else to shed light on what had happened to *Lady Be Good*'s crew. Somewhere out there in the vast and barren expanse of the Libyan desert lay the key to the mystery.

In early February 1960, another oil survey team stumbled across the remains of five of the crew some 80 miles from the crash site. They also discovered a diary kept by co-pilot Robert Toner.

Toner's diary revealed that the crew had indeed bailed out and that one member was missing after they did so. The last entry, dated April 12, 1943, read, "No help yet, very cold nite."

The crew had landed with hardly any food or water, and this, combined with the harsh conditions, proved too much. But the diary also revealed that three crew members had left the others and set off on their own to find help. This triggered another U.S. Army Mortuary Service expedition—Operation Climax—to search for the missing men. This was mounted in the spring of 1960. However, it was two other oilmen who discovered the first of the remains, initially mistaking a skull for an ostrich egg.

The crewman had walked nearly 120 miles on a mere few

cups of water and candy. Five days later the Operation Climax team discovered another collection of bones, but those of the third crewman were never found. Eventually, the remains of the airman who went missing after the crew bailed out were found, in August 1960, by yet another survey team. It was established that his parachute shrouds had been twisted and hence his parachute had not opened properly. He died instantly on hitting the ground. Thus, 17 years after their last flight, the crew of the *Lady Be Good* could finally receive a proper burial. Lost in the desert, they had paid a terrible price for their navigation blunders.

Now at last they could go home, leaving the remains of the *Lady Be Good* to the ravages of the desert that had brought about their agonizing demise.

Part V

Sending Hitler

Home, and Tojo, Too—

Bringing World War II to an End

By 1944, it seemed that the Allies were in control of the war. But what they faced was not enviable: bringing two proud, beaten, and fanatical enemies to heel. Massive bombing of German-occupied France and Germany itself, though doing tremendous damage and killing tens of thousands, could not seem to break the will of the German forces. At last the long-awaited Atlantic invasion took place on D-Day, and though a ringing success, there was still the pursuit of German troops through France and into Germany. Along the way, the resilient Hitler came up with the countermeasure that, against the steepest odds, and with the help of a few Allied blunders, almost worked. It was Hitler's last strategic gasp. He was the target of assassination plots and attempted bombings. He would later take care of the job himself. Germany would surrender in May 1945.

Bringing the Japanese to the negotiating table was even more arduous. Heavy bombing of Japan itself did not work; Japanese soldiers were still fighting fiercely, and kamikaze pilots were still giving their lives in suicidal dives into American ships. Finally, with the atom bomb successfully tested in the summer of 1945, President Truman made the difficult decision to drop nuclear weapons on Hiroshima and Nagasaki. The long war came to an end less than a week later.

Bomber Harris and
the Bombing of Berlin

B ETWEEN THE UNSUCCESSFUL ANGLO-CANADIAN landings at Dieppe and the tide-turning Allied invasion at Normandy two years later, the bulk of the assault on Germany's hold
in the West was by air. Although Stalin still demanded, and still
expected, the Allies to mount the kind of offensive that would engage German troops and not just have them cannily trying to re-
position their key munitions plants and depots and supply lines,
the Allies were not ready to move. Operation Overlord, as D-Day
was to be called, was still in the planning stages.

Perhaps the Allies, specifically the British, should have
known, from their own experience on the business end of such
approaches, how "area bombing"—a euphemism for bombing civilians—can prove costly to the aggressors while serving only to
harden the resolve of the populations being bombed, as happened
during the German blitz over British skies in 1940. Still, with ar-
maments aplenty, a superb air force in the RAF, and the attractions
of engagements that did not involve landing your boys in enemy
territory, the Allies launched an extensive three-year bombing campaign against German-occupied France and Germany itself, extending eventually to Berlin. The extent to which this long expenditure
of weaponry, energy, not to mention higher than acceptable loss of

planes weakened the Allied ability in 1944 to follow up quickly on
its surprise invasion at the Normandy beaches is difficult to declare
with certainty. But what is clear is that the particular strategy of
bombing, pursued under the leadership of Air Marshal Arthur Harris, head of RAF Bomber Command from 1942 to 1945, resulted
in perhaps the one area of most intense Allied shame, or at least
British shame. His blunder, as we shall see, is arguably a tactical
one, eventually damaging, though not fatally, the post-Normandy
advance of Allied forces, but most certainly his actions were considered morally indefensible, as indefensible, in kind if not degree,
as those of Hitler.

The tactical question facing the Allied bombing strategists was this:
should the air assault be directed against German populations concentrated in cities or against specific targets, by the use of so-called
precision bombing? Targeting cities involves less risk to the attackers, in that the areas of attack are wider and, with no specific targets,
success can be measured against a relatively lower standard. Bombing rail depots, ball-bearing factories, and airfields requires reliable
intelligence information and closer-range bombing, preferably in
daylight to aid in accuracy. In addition, sites key to the German
war effort were well fortified with antiaircraft and air support; and
to find and hit such targets usually involved a cordon of fighter
escorts for the bombers. Raiding cities deep within the Fatherland
could be undertaken at night and consequently could be done without escorts. Escorts deep into German territory were problematic
anyway because of the great distance from British airfields, which
small fighters, with lower fuel capacity, were unable to do reliably.

In all fairness to Harris, who became known—and reviled—
as "Bomber" Harris, he was not the sole exponent of area bombing.

Churchill in 1941 was unhappy with the performance of the RAF. The "exchange ratio" from RAF sorties over Germany was unacceptably high—too many planes lost in return for too little damage. The decision was made that there should be, as quoted from *The Second World War*, "an absolutely devastating exterminating attack by very heavy bombers from this country upon the Nazi Homeland." The aim was to kill German civilians, since it had proved difficult to hit the factories they worked in. And when Chief Marshal Sir Charles Portal added the finer point that drubbing the German working class, the "proletariat," would inevitably lead, in paradoxically Marxist fashion, to their breaking with the ruling classes running the German war effort, the plan had a higher rationale. Portal thought that a revolt similar to the Bolshevik uprising that had undone the Russian war effort in World War I would befall the Third Reich. And the Air Staff chose "Bomber" Harris to carry it out.

Harris's efforts were bolstered by the timely arrival of large bombers, called "heavies," to replace the inadequate smaller British bombers in use since the start of the war—Hampdens, Whitleys, and Wellingtons. The new generation of bombers, the Halifax and Lancaster, could carry larger payloads and were considered well enough armored to withstand hits from German fighters.

So Harris took off. He bombed the historic Baltic city of Lübeck and burned it to the ground. He aimed 1,000-bomber raids on Cologne, Essen, and Bremen a month later, in June 1942. For four months he bombed the German industrial heartland of the Ruhr, mounting in excess of 18,000 missions. Then, in July 1943, over four nights his bombers set off a conflagration in the German port city of Hamburg that succeeded beyond his wildest dreams. The combination of hot, dry weather and a strong wind sent up a firestorm in the heart of the city, with oxygen being swirled into the hungry fire at cyclone speed. With water mains broken, the civil defenses on the ground were helpless as the city burned out of control, killing 30,000 of Hamburg's residents and rendering 800,000 homeless. In his diary Goebbels wrote that Hamburg was "a catastrophe the extent of which simply staggers the imagination"—and one might add Goebbels would become something of an expert in the unimaginable. Harris was to achieve the same firestorm effects in subsequent attacks on a half dozen other German cities. This was his kind of tit for tat.

By this time the RAF was not working alone. The U.S. Army's Eighth Air Force, led by Lieutenant General Carl Spaatz, had joined in the attacks, equipped with sharper bomb sights capable of hitting smaller targets and faster and more long-distance fighter escorts, the Mustang, carrying powerful Merlin engines from England.

Emboldened by the carnage he had left behind in broad swaths of charred German cities, Harris turned to a target whose destruction he believed would bring the war to an end. This was the German capital of Berlin.

Toward the end of August 1943, Harris carried out a dress rehearsal. Three attacks were made on the city, but out of nearly 1,650 heavy bombers dispatched, 126 or 7.7 percent were lost. This was unacceptably high, and Harris decided to await the onset of winter, with its longer nights, the introduction of new electronic aids for his bombers, and for the U.S. Eighth Air Force to join in as well. Spaatz's Eighth Air Force was still smarting from its first deep penetration mission into Germany—against ball-bearing plants at Schweinfurt and a fighter factory at Regensburg—and was not yet in a position to begin attacks on the German capital.

Consequently, Harris decided to go it alone and opened his main assault on Berlin on November 18. It was an encouraging start, with only 9 out of 444 bombers failing to return. Seven further attacks were mounted before the end of the year. Poor visibility, unusually heavy cloud cover, combined with ever more effective German night-fighter tactics, saw the British casualty rate rise steadily. In January 1944, in even more adverse weather, Harris launched five more Berlin attacks, with the loss rate rising to 6.1 percent.

The first half of February saw such appalling weather that no attacks on Berlin could be mounted. However, when the British bombers renewed their attack on Berlin on February 15, they lost 42 out of 891 bombers. Harris realized that the German defenses were becoming ever stronger and did not return to Berlin until late in March, when the loss rate reached a staggering 9.1 percent, which was unsustainable. It was his last flourish. The target had proved too big for Bomber Command's capabilities and the defenses too strong.

On the following day General Eisenhower brought the Anglo-U.S. strategic bombing force in Britain under his own control to prepare the way more directly for the Allied landings in Normandy. Even so, Harris carried out one more major attack against a German city on the next-to-last day of March. No less than 106 out of 782 bombers were lost in the mission to Nuremberg. It was RAF Bomber Command's heaviest casualty bill in all of its major raids during World War II.

Harris had overlooked the fact that London suffered very many more German attacks, albeit none as heavy as those against Berlin, during the Blitz of winter 1940–41, but they had not broken the British spirit. There was no reason why Berliners should weaken. The Battle of Berlin was a blunder in its waste of assets, which would have been better concentrated against German communications and oil, and of lives, just as the Battle of Britain had been a blunder for the Luftwaffe.

But more significant perhaps was the soul-searching of the British people that followed. The morality of the area-bombing campaign, with its evocation in the mind of the swirling furnace at Hamburg, in which 20 percent of the dead were children, was deeply questioned up and down the ranks of British citizenry. Lord Salisbury perhaps best summed up the dreadful lesson: "Of course the Germans began [civilian bombing], but we do not take the devil as our example."

Unlike all the other major British commanders of World War II, Arthur Harris was denied a peerage, and his airmen were not presented with a campaign medal of their own. As observed in *The Second World War*, "Strategic bombing, which may not even have been a sound strategy, was certainly not fair play."

Despite bombing in Berlin, public transport and other services were still operating and in place when Allies battled the last of the German Army at the war's end. In Hamburg, the charred and devastated port city, industrial capacity returned nearly to normal within a few months. On the Allied side, 2,400 bombers from the Eighth Air Force were lost, and the RAF losses for the war amounted to over 50,000 men. Surely, without those losses, the force available to Eisenhower a few months later might very well have eased the pressure on the Allied troops landing at the Normandy beaches.

Operation Cobra and
Friendly Fire at Saint-Lô

ALTHOUGH STALIN WAITED A LONG time for the British and Americans to start an offensive on the Western Front, when it came, it was a model of tactical genius, daring, and execution, well worth the wait. On June 6, 1944, Operation Overlord landed, and the noise and fire and fury of the massive amphibious assault reverberates to this day, and will for all of history.

Five beaches covering a 60-mile area on the Normandy coast were landed, code-named Utah, Omaha, Gold, Juno, and Sword. A massive buildup carried out in secrecy then delivered 6,500 naval vessels, including 4,000 landing craft, 7 battleships, 23 cruisers, over 100 destroyers. There were floating concrete docks, large enough to serve as "harbors" for the landing of tanks and other vehicles on the sandy beaches. There was a pipeline (called Pluto) for gas piped under the English Channel to keep the engines running once they hit the beach and beyond. There were 12,000 combined British and U.S. planes in support of the invasion. Glider and parachute battalions were dropped to strategic bridgeheads inland. Beforehand, the Allies had carried out ingenious diversions and deceptions, whereby the Germans, sensing an Atlantic invasion, did not know where it would be. The Allies even managed to mislead the Germans into thinking they had detected plans for in-

vasion farther north, at Pas de Calais. This left the Germans' Atlantic Wall spread perilously thin; and what the D-Day invaders
found were only three German divisions, two of them woefully
inexperienced. Though the morning of June 6 did not go without
some heavy losses for the Allied troops, only one beach, Omaha,
proved extremely brutal on the landing forces; almost everything
else went as planned. Stalin must have been pleased.

Things did not go so swimmingly after that. The Germans
began instant mobilization, with Panzer Divisions moving quickly
to shore up defenses and protect key cities, such as Caen and
Cherbourg. The planned breakout for the Allied troops, up from
the beaches and then on the road to the liberation of Paris, was
code-named Cobra. Instrumental to its success was the heavy
bombing of German fortifications, followed by the entry of British
and American tank battalions. But what its planners were to learn
is that, in the frenetic aftermath of an amphibious invasion, carpet
bombing can prove hazardous to more than just the enemy.

The port city of Cherbourg fell to the Allies nearly as
scheduled. Within three weeks of the landing, the German port
commander, General Karl Wilhelm von Schlieben, asked the Americans to fire artillery at the city's gate so that he could have sufficient
reason (in the eyes of his Führer) to surrender. The Americans
complied. Still, in other areas the lines of German defense began
to stiffen, and the Allied advance off the beaches slowed.

In Brittany, the American ground forces got bogged down
when they ran into an unexpected "natural" obstacle: hedgerows
planted by Celtic farmers two thousand years before as field boundaries. These 10-foot-high hills of entangled roots and dirt, spaced
about 100 yards apart, offered the Germans near-impregnable defenses. The attacking American infantry fell into these deathtraps.
Five thousand American men were lost in what became known as

"the fight in the *bocage*," the French word for the hedgerows, in three days. No amount of bombing could help them.

The first significant use of heavy bombers came into play on July 7, when nearly 450 RAF Lancasters and Halifaxes were used to launch an attack on Caen by Canadian and British troops, who were held up by a series of fortified villages north of the city. But because of fears that these lay too close to the front line, the bombers struck targets on the northern outskirts of Caen. This had little effect on the Germans and merely made life difficult for the attackers as they tried to overcome the resultant rubble.

Eleven days later, on July 18, a much larger force of 930 British heavy bombers and 632 American B-24s was used to open Operation Goodwood, the British armored thrust to the east of Caen. Their targets were the villages that lay in the path of the advance, and no less than 6,800 tons of bombs were dropped. This certainly numbed the German defenders and enabled the attack to get off to a good start. The shock, however, did not last long, and soon the tanks found themselves being engaged by German anti-tank guns on the flanks of the advance. They reached the foot of the Bourgebus Ridge, on which were positioned the German gun lines. Efforts to secure this over the next two days failed, and the situation was not helped by the arrival of rain. This turned the ground, already churned up by the bombs, into a morass that made the moving up of reinforcements almost impossible. Goodwood was therefore halted.

Even so, what this operation had achieved was to draw the German armor to the British sector, giving Bradley's First U.S. Army the opportunity to break through the German defenses in the St.-Lô area to the west. Bradley's plan was for three infantry divisions to carry out the breakout operation on a mere 7,000-yard front. Once they had got through the German defenses, a further three divisions would be passed through them to complete the breakout. Just prior to the attack, fighter-bombers and medium bombers of the Ninth U.S. Air Force and heavy bombers of the Eighth would attack the German forward defenses.

The breakout at St.-Lô was scheduled for July 21, immediately following the conclusion of Goodwood. But such was the reliance that Bradley placed on the heavy bombers that he left it to Eisenhower's air commander, Sir Trafford Leigh-Mallory, to decide when the attack should take place. A spell of bad weather occurred, and the operation was postponed until July 24.

The front line ran along the St.-Lô–Perriers road. Bradley wanted the bombers to hit the German forward defenses immediately to the south of this and for them to approach from the east so that the bomb run was along the line of the road. Keen to take maximum advantage of the immediate effect of the bombing, Bradley was prepared to withdraw his forward troops only some 800 yards for safety's sake. The airmen had their reservations. They preferred to approach from the north so that the target was presented in greater depth. They also wanted the forward troops to withdraw 3,000 yards. A compromise was reached in that the fighter-bombers would have a safety margin of 1,200 yards and the heavies 1,450 yards. Bradley thought that he had gotten his way over the lateral bomb run, but he was mistaken.

Although meteorologists were still doubtful about the weather, the attack was fixed for the morning of July 24. Leigh-Mallory traveled across to France to watch the start of the attack, but, worried about the overcast weather, decided to cancel. It was too late—the bombers had already taken off. Some of the fighter-bombers were contacted in time, but there was no radio link to the heavies. The lead group of heavies, noting the poor visibility, did not bomb, and neither did most of the second. But some 35 aircraft from the second group did drop their bombs, as did the third and final group. But the lead bombardier had trouble with his bomb-release mechanism and dropped his bombs short, and the remaining aircraft followed suit. Since the aircraft were approaching from the north, many of these fell on the U.S. positions and killed 25 and wounded 131 men of the 30th Infantry Division.

The attack had already been postponed, and the bombing meant that surprise had been lost. Bradley, though, was impatient and, encouraged by a more favorable weather forecast, rescheduled the attack for the next day. The airmen stated that they could not recast their plans for a lateral approach in time. To avoid further U.S. casualties, more use of smoke markers and panels to mark the forward positions would be made, and the heavies would bomb visually, which meant doing so from a much lower altitude than they were accustomed.

At 9:38 A.M. on July 25, the first wave of fighter-bombers began their attacks. Then came the B-17s and B-24s. They met heavier flak than expected, which loosened their formations. Smoke from the artillery bombardment obscured their view. Consequently, a significant number bombed north of the road. The result was that 111 U.S. soldiers were killed and 490 wounded. Among the dead was General Lesley McNair, commander of the Army ground forces and the architect of America's wartime army, who had come over to France on a visit.

One of the U.S. attacking infantry battalions was so badly mauled that it had to be replaced. This and the shock inflicted on the attacking troops meant that they were able to advance only a little more than a mile during the opening day. Clearly, carpet bombing had proved a two-edged sword. General Lawton Collins, commanding the breakout, decided to take a gamble and unleash two of his follow-up mobile divisions the following day. Two days of bitter fighting followed before the Germans broke and the break-through took place. On July 30, the town of Avranches was cap-tured, and the way ahead lay open for General George Patton's newly constituted Third Army to exploit.

Nevertheless, a sour state remained after Cobra because of the inaccurate bombing. Eisenhower told Bradley: "I gave them [the bombers] the green light this time. But I promise you it's the last." The blame must be laid at Bradley's door for the blunders of be-lieving that the heavies could bomb more accurately than they did and for failing to confirm the direction of their attack. Never again would they be used so close to friendly forces' forward positions.

Occurring so shortly after the near-perfect invasion, it was a rude awakening for the Allies. There would be other blunders down the road toward Berlin, but not many. What would be clear is that liberating Paris and moving on to victory, and the war's end in Berlin, would take some time.

A Bridge Too Far

THE DUTCH TOWN OF ARNHEM has a special place in the annals of World War II. This legacy is centered on its bridge, which spans the Lower Rhine, and on the British and Polish cemeteries of the surrounding countryside. These cemeteries contain the graves of over 1,400 men who fell in the fighting around Arnhem in September 1944. These men and others who fell to German hands were victims of a series of blunders in the planning of an operation that the Western Allies hoped would bring the war in Europe to an end before the close of 1944.

When the Allies finally broke out of Normandy at the end of July 1944, there followed a heady dash across northern France. It seemed as though the German armies in the West were broken. On August 25, Paris was liberated. The advance continued toward the Belgian border.

Meanwhile, on August 15, 1944, other Allied forces landing in the south of France had begun to advance rapidly northward. A sense of ultimate victory was in the air.

By early September 1944, however, a problem had arisen. Hitler had given orders that the French ports on the English Channel be held to the last. The Allies placed them under siege. But not until September 12 did the first, Le Havre, fall. It would take time to get the docks themselves back into working order.

Hitler's policy concerning the Channel ports meant that the

Allies still had to rely on the port of Cherbourg for delivery of supplies. The result was that the further eastward they advanced, the ever more stretched became their supply lines.

This triggered a bitter debate between the supreme Allied Commander General Dwight Eisenhower and Bernard Montgomery, who was commanding the British and Canadian forces. Eisenhower wanted to advance on a broad front, with Montgomery's 21st Army Group and Omar Bradley's U.S. 12th Army Group pushing eastward side by side toward the German border. Montgomery pointed to the growing logistics crisis and stated that the overstretched supply lines could not support the simultaneous advance of both army groups.

He was right in this. A streamlined supply system had been set up. This was the Red Ball Express—an endless conveyor belt of trucks speeding back and forth along the ever longer routes between Cherbourg and the front. The problem was that the trucks consumed an increasing amount of the fuel that they were carrying. The result was that by the second week in September, both army groups had run out of fuel and their advance had come to a virtual halt. This gave the German armies a vital breathing space in which to recover.

Montgomery came up with a plan which he was certain would unlock the growing stalemate and bring an end to the war. He saw the River Rhine as the main obstacle facing the Allied advance into Germany. If this could be outflanked, the Germans would be left without a natural position on which to base their defense. This could be done if the Allies could get across the Lower Rhine in Holland.

Holland has numerous lateral waterways situated south of the Lower Rhine that the Germans could use to hold up an Allied advance. The crossings over these and Lower Rhine therefore had be seized by coup de main.

The Allies had a force which could do this. This was the First Allied Airborne Army, which was commanded by the American General Lewis Brereton. Three of its divisions—the British Sixth and American 82nd and 101st Airborne—had been used on D-Day.

Since then the Airborne Army had remained unemployed in England, although a number of operations for it had been planned and then canceled. Montgomery now wanted it to play a key part in his plan. Eisenhower agreed and gave his sanction for the operation to be mounted on Sunday, September 17. The detailed plan, however, contained a number of flaws.

Montgomery's plan was code-named Market-Garden. The U.S. 101st Airborne Division was to secure bridges over two canals in the Eindhoven area. The 82nd Airborne Division was to capture the Grave bridge over the Maas and that at Nijmegen over the River Waal. Finally the British First Airborne Division and the Polish Parachute Brigade were to secure the bridge over the Lower Rhine at Arnhem.

General Frederick Browning was in overall command, using as his headquarters the First Airborne Corps, which would also be parachuted in. Known in the British Army as "Boy" Browning, he was married to the famous novelist Daphne du Maurier.

It was vital that ground forces linked up with the paratroops on their objectives as quickly as possible. This task was given to General Brian Horrocks, who was one of Montgomery's principal lieutenants and was commanding the British 30th Corps.

Horrocks had to have good communications with the airborne divisions, but instead of reporting to him directly, they were to report to Browning's headquarters, which would then pass on the information to Horrocks. In truth, Browning's headquarters was superfluous and should never have been deployed. This was the first of a number of planning blunders.

. . .

Crucial to the success of the operation was the capture and holding of the bridge over the Lower Rhine at Arnhem. The Dutch Resistance reported that two crack SS Panzer Divisions—the 9th Hohenstaufen and 10th Frundsberg—were refitting in the area after being severely mauled in Normandy. Allied intelligence largely discounted the threat that they posed to the British and Polish paratroops. While both divisions were still well below strength, they were still powerful and had recently received training in anti-airborne operations. Their presence at Arnhem was to prove crucial to the outcome.

They had to seize the bridge at Arnhem quickly so as to exploit the surprise gained from the airborne drop. But the RAF refused to allow a dropping zone to be selected close to the bridge for fear that the flak guns placed around it would shoot down too many of their aircraft. This was especially important since it was decided that the drop would take place in daylight so as to avoid navigational errors.

Consequently, the drop zone was placed at Wolfhaze, no less than eight miles from the bridge. This open heath land was selected because it could accommodate gliders, in which one of the brigades of First Armored Division would land.

Another problem was that there was insufficient airlift to enable the division, together with the Poles, to be landed at once. First Airborne Division would fly in two waves on day one and a final one on day two. The Poles would not follow until day three. This was a dissipation of force that did nothing to increase the chance of success.

But as the troops taking part in the airborne operation boarded their transport aircraft and gliders on that Sunday morning,

September 17, 1944, they believed that they were about to strike the decisive blow in the war in the West. None had any idea of the likely effect of the blunders in planning.

The landings in the Eindhoven, Nijmegen, and Arnhem areas initially took the Germans by surprise. The 101st Airborne, the Screaming Eagles, quickly captured three out of its four bridges. The 82nd All Americans also enjoyed initial success, but were not able to capture the crucial Nijmegen bridge.

The initial landings outside Arnhem also went well, but when the troops began to advance into Arnhem, they met heavy fire from the Germans, who had reacted very quickly. Even so, one battalion did manage to find its way to the bridge over the Lower Rhine and capture its northern end.

Meanwhile, Horrocks began his advance, aiming to reach Eindhoven by nightfall. Almost immediately his men ran into problems. They found themselves advancing up a single road, with the ground on either side too soft to take armored vehicles. German soldiers armed with Panzerfaust recoilless anti-tank weapons were soon active. This slowed the advance, and in some sections there was a 30-mile backup of vehicles. The difficulties of advancing on this route should have been recognized beforehand. It was another planning blunder.

The consequence was that by nightfall 30th Corps was still six miles short of Eindhoven. Its chances of reaching Arnhem in three days, which was the aim, were receding.

On Monday, September 18, 101st Airborne completed its capture of the bridges in the Eindhoven area, but it was not until that evening that Horrocks' troops linked up with them. The 82nd was still struggling to secure the bridgever the Waal at Nijmegen. Matters were made worse by the fact that a battle group from 10th SS Panzer Division was now holding it.

At Arnhem the final brigade of First Airborne Division landed in the afternoon. The battalion holding the northern end of the bridge hung on in the face of ever fiercer counterattacks. Efforts to reinforce them failed since the other paratroops were becoming bogged down in house-to-house fighting within Arnhem itself.

On Tuesday, September 19, the Polish Parachute Brigade was supposed to reinforce at Arnhem, but fog prevented them from doing so. The British continued to cling onto the northern end of the Arnhem bridge. But most of the drop zones earmarked for supplies were now in German hands. Attempts to get the supplies dropped elsewhere failed because the paratroops discovered that they could not communicate with the aircraft with their ground-air radios—another blunder.

The battle for the Nijmegen bridge continued, but the 30th Corps had by then reforced the American paratroops there. This enabled the bridge to be seized on the evening of the following day. This left the link-up forces just 11 miles from Arnhem, but the British tanks were short of fuel. German attacks on the flanks of the 30th Corps advance created delays in bringing up replenishment, and the advance was temporarily halted.

Not until the twenty-first, day five of Market-Garden, did the fog lift and the Polish Parachute Brigade deploy. They were dropped on the south bank of the Lower Rhine. Although some men managed to get across the river, they were unable to link up with their British comrades.

Within Arnhem itself the situation was becoming ever more desperate. The British hold on the north end of the bridge was finally broken, and the remains of First Airborne Division was driven back to the suburb of Oosterbeck. Thirtieth Corps did manage to reach the south bank of the Lower Rhine, but was unable to get across it.

Finally, on Sunday, September 24, the decision was made to evacuate First Airborne Division and the Poles who had made it across the river. Of the 10,000 men who dropped at Arnhem, only 2,163 escaped. A total of 1,485 were killed, and the remainder taken prisoner.

Arnhem had proved a bridge too far. The blunders in planning, especially in seriously underestimating German capabilities and over-optimism in the time it would take the ground forces to reach Arnhem, meant that Montgomery's gamble had failed. The Allies would be faced with a grim winter campaign. Not until March 1945 would they finally cross the Rhine. Arnhem itself would not be liberated until April, seven months after the battle.

As for the dwindling band of veterans who fought at Arnhem, they remember the battle with pride. They appear to bear no rancor toward those whose planning errors pitchforked them into such a desperate situation.

The Battle of the Bulge

GERMANY WOULD NOT GO EASILY. Despite the dramatic success of the Atlantic landings at Normandy, which so much German effort had been brought to bear to prepare for, and despite a German holding pattern and then gallant retreat hastened by extraordinary levels of Allied bombing, Hitler was not prepared to see his lines moved back beyond the Rhine River. Typically, he looked for the positives. With the Allied advance coming so far through France and Belgium and the Netherlands, his strategizing mind came upon the difficulties the Allies would have in supporting and resupplying in the increasingly extended effort. Although the Allies had taken Antwerp, northern Europe's largest seaport and crucial to the resupply of Allied forces, the port was not operational yet, for the Germans were still dug in on islands in the Schelde River estuary leading into the harbor. In addition, the approaches to the harbor were heavily mined and had not yet been swept. And though Hitler's armies now faced assault from three huge Allied armies—Montgomery in the north, Bradley to the direct west, and Patton to the south—he conceived a counterattack through the heart of it, through the dense forests of the Ardennes, the same forests through which German armies first had made their marches on France in both world wars. Hitler's goal was to break the line of Allied advance, and then swing north and make doubly sure that

Antwerp would not become an operational supply port. In this he hoped to drain the Allied advance of what it needed to continue. This "bulge" he hoped to create was what gave Hitler's last roll of the dice its common name, the Battle of the Bulge. In Nazi circles, however, the thrust was code-named Autumn Mist. Out of the rugged, late-year German weather Hitler hoped a surprise offensive would reverse his failing fortunes. There were blunders on both sides, the first being that Hitler felt he had the wherewithal to pull it off, the second being that the Allies never thought he'd try.

The resupply issue was a key component to strategizing the follow-up to the Normandy invasions. Eisenhower's two most dynamic generals had differing versions of what should happen. Everyone agreed that the heavy inland bombing preceding the advancing Allied forces had as their goal the wiping out of lines of retreat for the Germans. Bridges and roads through France were to be laid waste. That this would hamper the Allied advance was of some concern, but more important, as the Allied march moved into the autumn and then winter months, as it moved toward the Rhine and the north coast, resupplies of oil, gas, food, and men would become essential. Patton's answer to this problem was to drive a narrow yet powerful force right up and into Germany. Montgomery, on the other hand, favored a broader front for strategic purposes, and insisted that the answer to the supply question had to fit that imperative, not the other way around. Although keeping a supply line open to a narrow front was an easier task than accommodating a hundreds-mile-wide front, that did not necessarily settle the issue.

If there was a flaw in the post-Normandy planning, it was allowing this question to take on such significance. The assumption had been that the long lines of resupply, whether for a narrow or broad thrust, would be shortened by the sequential capture of ports along the English Channel coast—Le Havre, Boulogne, Calais, Dunkirk, and Antwerp. This would progressively shorten the distance on land that supplies would have to move. But Hitler made the wise decision to dispatch an entire Army Group to hold those port cities, and they managed indeed to hold Dunkirk till the very end of the war, and to hold key defensive positions in the Schelde estuary leading into the harbor at Antwerp. Not clearing the estuary was an Allied blunder that would add six weeks to the march into Germany. Holding those positions, and thereby keeping Antwerp, whose port facilities, piers, and docks were amazingly intact, from becoming a supply route for the Allies gave Hitler hope. And it was to give the Allies the Battle of the Bulge, for the prospect of regaining Antwerp itself was enough of a prospect to lead Hitler to take his biggest, albeit last, gamble of the war.

Montgomery knew from Allied intelligence as early as September that Hitler intended to "hold out as long as possible astride the approaches to Antwerp," and yet did not reverse himself. Antwerp was behind Montgomery's army. It would not be out of character for Montgomery to want to be the first into Berlin, and Antwerp was indeed in the other direction. Similarly, it was not unlike Patton to want to beat Montgomery there, hence his own answer to the resupply problem. But Montgomery surely blundered by not turning around and assuring that Antwerp, a city held by the British, became a port that could be used for resupply. Instead, Montgomery hatched his Market-Garden plan, involving the successive seizing of bridges into Germany. Although this was essential to getting resupplies along the roadway, there would be little to move over those bridges without Antwerp being opened. The cart before the horse, surely. And with no gas, no horse power at all.

We have seen how Montgomery's plan ran afoul, by going

"a bridge too far." Hitler capitalized and became convinced that his own offensive would save the day. Routing the First Airborne at Arnhem was the first clear-cut German success since the invasion. The Allies were soon to pay for Montgomery's haste to get into Germany. He had left undisturbed the unmechanized elements of the German 15th Army as he passed them in Belgium and northern France. These 65,000 German soldiers would be recouped and moved into the further reinforcement of the harbor defenses at Antwerp.

The Allied drive began to lose steam in the early winter of 1944. Their requirements for provisions was immense. The German forces, meanwhile, were recovering strength, and with the terrain familiar to them, and the weather grim enough to prohibit Allied bombing, they had a growing advantage, at least a needed respite.

Albert Speer's strategy of dispersal of production away from the traditional centers had proven prescient. By September 1944, Germany was producing as much war materiel as they had in any other month of the war. With Panzer divisions being refitted and resupplied, Hitler was optimistic, and that month he issued his orders to begin the offensive. "I have made a momentous decision," he said. "I shall go over to the offensive . . . out of the Ardennes, with the objective Antwerp." If Hitler could retake Antwerp, then just beyond lay his secret V-2 rocket installations, which could begin pounding London.

U.S. intelligence did obtain indications of a German attack. Although all deployments were made by night, the sound of tank engines carries a long way by night. True, a spell of fog prevented air reconnaissance from being fully effective, but Ultra, the British

code-breaking system, was able to glean little because the Germans
had imposed strict radio silence. Even so, they did decrypt one
signal from an air liaison officer attached to Sixth Panzer Army,
which referred to "the coming big operation." It was significant,
not just because the Germans were planning something major, but
also because Allied intelligence had been trying to locate this strong
armored reserve since the autumn.

Yet this signal was ignored. At the higher levels of command there was a belief that the Germans were no longer capable
of a major offensive. Should they mount any form of counterattack,
it would surely be in the Huertgen Forest to the north or against
Patton's Third Army to the south, which was advancing toward
the River Roer.

The Allies were not alone in thinking that Hitler had no
business considering an offensive. Many of his own generals were
unpersuaded that it would work. The plan was to charge through
the forest in the middle of the Allied wall and carry on west and
north to Antwerp, and to hold a German line running from Antwerp south through Brussels to Bastogne. Allied fuel supplies were
to be seized along the way because they were needed; and then the
gap in the Allied line was to be widened, allowing more German
troops back into the territories they had only so recently occupied.
Ultimately, British Second and Canadian First Armies would be cut
off from Bradley and Patton to the south. Hitler planned then to
encircle and destroy Montgomery's forces. The balance in the west
would be equalized, and an offensive on the Eastern Front would
follow, and Germany would be back in business.

Alternatives were proposed to Hitler, but he would have
none of it; his only concession was to delay the opening of the
offensive until December.

The two central commanders of the campaign, which carried the code name Autumn Mist, were General Sepp Dietrich, who would lead two armies into Brussels and then turn north toward Antwerp, and General Hasso von Manteuffel, a bright young tank general, who would proceed a bit to the south of Dietrich in the westward thrust. Manteuffel's first objective was Bastogne. Between them they would have at their disposal eight crack Panzer divisions and two parachute divisions. Their main deficiency was a paucity of fuel.

The offensive began on December 16 after a period of fog and rainy snow. It was slow going for the armored German divisions, but with the weather making aerial detection impossible, they took the Allies by surprise at two points along the Our River near the eastern border of Luxembourg. Tired and recuperating divisions of the Allied forces, part of Bradley's army group, were thrown into a panic. The dropping behind the Allied lines of a paratroops battalion consisting of German soldiers speaking English and wearing American uniforms just added to the chaos. Bradley rushed in reinforcements, Eisenhower roused two reserve Airborne divisions from their recuperation near Reims and brought them into the fray: the 101st, under Brigadier General Anthony McAuliffe, at the French city of Bastogne, and the 82nd under Major General Matthew Ridgway, to bolster the northern flank. To the south, Patton's Third Army, which had been moving eastward toward the Saar River, made a 90-degree turn due north. The Allies lost no time in trying to cut off the bulge before it grew too large.

In the week before Christmas, the Allies seemed to have regrouped. The Germans were denied the town of St. Vith, ably defended by General R. W. Housbrouck, and Bastogne, encircled by Manteuffel's Fifth Panzer Division, somehow held on. Such dog-

ged resistance stole valuable time from the German plan and protected fuel depots, further deepening the problems for
gas-dependent Panzers. By now Patton was charging northward
toward Bastogne. At this crucial moment Hitler made a serious
blunder, one that historians have chalked up to his favoritism toward certain of his field generals. In this case, when a shift in the
weight of the assault to the city of Bastogne might have allowed
Manteuffel to take the city, a key milestone on the road to Antwerp,
Hitler overruled his overall commander, Model, in favor of Dietrich's thrust a bit farther north, which was not faring as well. But
Dietrich, a former SS officer much to Hitler's liking, wanted to
carry the day. Precious help that could have made the difference
for Manteuffel instead went to Dietrich, whose progress was very
slow and who was not in a position, as Manteuffel was, to achieve
a major objective. It proved a decisive mistake, as Patton broke
through Manteuffel and into Bastogne, where a fierce battle raged
till the New Year. Meanwhile, reinforcements for Dietrich found a
Panzer division that had ground to a halt for want of fuel.

The Luftwaffe made a final appearance, sending some 800
planes against airfields in Belgium and France. Though more than
150 Allied planes were destroyed, the Luftwaffe took even heavier
losses, and Allied air power then pounded the Ardennes region all
the way in to Germany.

Montgomery then pressed aggressively from the north, and
Patton chased the remaining Panzer division and ground troops
back toward the Rhine with a vengeance. By January 18, the Bulge
was no more.

The losses for the Germans were astounding: 120,000 casualties, 600 tanks lost, 1,600 planes destroyed, while on the Allied
side casualties were half as high. Hitler had frittered away men and
materiel at a time that he could least afford to. Though Allied

mistakes, mostly of Montgomery's doing, made this terrible affair possible, at a significant loss of Allied lives (mostly American), the war was finally heading to a close. The memory of 86 American prisoners of war being machine-gunned to death on December 17 by the First SS Panzer Division did little to slow the march to Berlin. It would take the peculiar politics of the coming new order to do that.

The Bomb Plot to Kill Hitler

BY MID-JULY 1944 GERMANY WAS in an increasingly desperate situation. On the Eastern Front the Red Army was pressing the German forces back into Poland. In Italy the Allies had
entered Rome and were advancing northward. In France the
German Army was struggling to contain the Anglo-American forces
in Normandy.

Ultimate defeat was staring Germany in the face. In the
eyes of some, only Adolf Hitler stood in the way of bringing the
suffering of his people to an end.

On July 20, a bomb exploded in a conference room at
Hitler's eastern headquarters at Rastenburg in East Prussia. The
target was Hitler himself, but he escaped serious injury. The conspirators, believing that Hitler had been killed, tried to seize the
levers of government in Berlin They were arrested, and many of
them would be subjected to humiliation in a show trial.

The failure of the July 1944 bomb plot was the result of
blunders largely brought about by naiveté on the part of the conspirators. Their vain attempt to eradicate Hitler meant that the war
would drag on until the bitter end.

When Hitler had come to power in January 1933, the general mistaken belief among centrist politicians was that he and his Nazis

could be controlled. But on the night of February 27 there was a fire at the German parliamentary building, the Reichstag. Hitler accused the communists of starting it and used it as an excuse to purge left-wing parties.

In August 1934, Germany's presidential figurehead, the venerable Field Marshal Paul von Hindenburg, died. This was to mark the end of democracy in Germany.

Hitler made himself absolute dictator, and all political opposition was crushed. The Army might have stood in Hitler's way, but its primacy in the defense of the Reich was threatened by Hitler's brown-shirted SA. Ernst Roehm, its leader, was murdered on Hitler's orders. The threat to the Army removed, War Minister Werner von Blomberg was duped by Hitler into ordering all ranks of the armed forces to swear a personal oath of loyalty to him rather than to the German state. This trapped the officer corps.

Hitler began a policy of expansionism. It began in March 1936 with the reoccupation by German troops of the Rhineland, which had been demilitarized under the 1919 Treaty of Versailles. Two years later came union with Austria, which fell under the Nazi sway.

Hitler then turned his eye on Czechoslovakia, demanding that the westernmost province of Sudetenland, which contained a significant ethnic German population, be handed over to Germany. It was now that some senior German officers began to fear that Hitler's expansionism might in the end prove disastrous for Germany.

General Ludwig Beck wrote a memorandum to fellow senior officers expressing his fears, and resigned as Army Chief of Staff. His successor, Franz Halder, agreed with Beck. As war with Czechoslovakia appeared ever more likely, Halder began to plot against Hitler. He drew up a plan with fellow officers Colonel Hans Oster and General Erwin von Witzleben to storm the Chancellery and kill Hitler. But war with the Czechs was averted though the Munich Agreement of September 1938, and Halder canceled his plans.

During the summer of 1939, when war clouds once more loomed over the horizon, a largely civilian and communist-inspired group, called the Red Orchestra by the Gestapo, was formed, but the Russo-German Pact of August threw them into confusion, and they took no action against Hitler.

The swift success of the invasion of Poland and natural German antipathy toward that country also temporarily stilled resistance to Hitler. But when he announced his intention of mounting an early invasion of the West, covert opposition to him resurfaced.

Admiral Wilhelm Canaris, head of Armed Forces Intelligence, conferred with Army Commander-in-Chief Walther von Brauchitsch as to what they should do, but all they could come up with was excuses for delaying the invasion. Some of Canaris's staff then hatched a plot to kill Hitler with a bomb. Other groups also formed among the military, but their existence was unknown to each other.

Then on November 8 came the first real attempt against Hitler's life. The occasion was the anniversary celebrations of Hitler's abortive 1923 putsch in Munich. A lone would-be assassin left a bomb at the Buergerbraukeller beer house, where Hitler was to make a speech. On this occasion the long-winded Hitler made a short speech and left the building before the bomb went off. The result was a tightening of security, and the various resistance groups were forced to lie low.

The invasion of the West eventually went ahead in May 1940, and the dazzling victories of the next two years intimidated the plotters. Not until the debacle of Stalingrad over the winter of

1942–43 did they seriously begin to contemplate the death of Hitler once more.

The main group, known by the Gestapo as the Black Orchestra, consisted of both soldiers and civilians. The figurehead was Ludwig Beck, but it also included Ulrich von Hassell (formerly German ambassador to Rome), Carl Goerdeler (former Mayor of Leipzig), theologian Dietrich Bonhoeffer, General Henning von Tresckow, chief of operations of von Kluge's Army Group Center on the Eastern Front, von Witzleben (now retired), and General Friedrich Olbricht.

Two other groups were loosely associated with them. One of them was led by Helmut von Moltke, great-grandnephew of the victor of the 1870 war against France. Another was built around a circle of young diplomats in the German foreign office.

Apart from the lack of coordination between and within the groups, they suffered other shortcomings. None were used to leading clandestine lives and often committed elementary breaches of security, including keeping diaries and talking openly on the telephone. The Black Orchestra itself was also widely scattered, which did not help internal coordination.

Their efforts to obtain the active support of the senior commanders at the front—men like Field Marshal Gerd von Rundstedt, Commander-in-Chief West, Field Marshal Hans Guenther von Kluge, and Field Marshal Erich von Manstein—also failed. The active field marshals of the old Prussian school considered their oaths of loyalty to be unbreakable. As von Manstein remarked: "Prussian field marshals do not mutiny."

Not even Allen W. Dulles, the head of the OSS office in Switzerland, who had knowledge of the existence of many of the plots, took them seriously. Even so, during 1943 there were a number of bungled attempts on Hitler's life.

Not until the summer of 1944, by which time the Germans were under pressure on every front and eventual defeat was becoming ever more inevitable, did a workable plan for killing Hitler evolve.

The key player was Klaus Schenk von Stauffenberg, a devout Roman Catholic and staff officer who had been badly wounded in Tunisia. He obtained a post in the HQ of the Replacement Army in Berlin, a job which necessitated visits to Hitler's field HQ at Rastenburg, East Prussia—the so-called Wolf's Lair. He would take a bomb concealed in a briefcase to a briefing session for Hitler and leave it under the table.

While most of the senior combat commanders refused to support the plan, the plotters still hoped that one in particular might join them: the great Erwin Rommel, who had for some time been idealized by Nazi propaganda and was as well known to the German people as any other general. But Rommel was in charge of the desperate battle going on in Normandy. Even though he believed that the war in the West was lost, he could not bring himself to join the plot while he was embroiled in trying to hold back the British and Americans. In any event, on July 17, Rommel was severely wounded when his car was strafed by a marauding Allied fighter.

Undeterred, three days later, July 20, 1944, von Stauffenberg succeeded in planting his bomb on his fourth attempt. He left the conference early and flew back to Berlin without checking whether Hitler was dead. The bomb did go off with Hitler in the room. But while it killed and injured some of those present, Hitler though shaken, was not seriously injured. In fact, he was fit enough to meet Mussolini later that day and show him the wreckage of the conference room.

Meanwhile, von Stauffenberg arrived back in Berlin and tried to organize the Replacement Army to take over key points in the city. He also sent messages to all Wehrmacht headquarters, but only in Paris was positive action taken, by the military governor, General Carl Heinrich von Stuelpnagel, a member of the Black Orchestra. He arrested all SS and Gestapo personnel in the French capital.

A key element of the putsch was the crack Gross Deutschland Guard Battalion, commanded by Major Otto-Ernst Remer. This was an Army and not SS unit. One of its tasks was to arrest propaganda minister Josef Goebbels in Berlin. When Remer visited him in his office, Goebbels phoned the Wolf's Lair and established that Hitler was still alive. Remer, being an obedient officer, immediately changed sides and the putsch rapidly unraveled. Von Stauffenberg was arrested by General Friedrich Fromm, commanding the Replacement Army and no longer a supporter of the plot, although he knew about it. Von Stauffenberg was shot that night, along with several others. In Paris, von Stuelpnagel was forced to release all those he had arrested.

The other conspirators were quickly rounded up. The Gestapo was well aware of who most of them were, due to the conspirators' lax security. Those who were serving officers were arraigned before a Court of Honor, presided over, at Hitler's orders, by von Rundstedt, the figurehead of the old Prussian military ethos. This was because traditionally no officer could be tried by a civilian court. Those who were suspected of complicity were expelled from the armed forces.

Those who were aware of the conspiracy but had not taken part were also drawn into the net. Rommel, still recovering from his wounds, was eventually forced to commit suicide to save his family. It was officially announced that he had died of his wounds, and he was given a state funeral. Field Marshall Guenther Von

Kluge was summoned back to Germany. Although he had only known of the conspiracy and not participated, he also committed suicide en route.

As for the remainder, they were victims of a show trial presided over by the notorious Nazi Judge Roland Friesler. These trials ended only when the court building was bombed in February 1945, killing Friesler himself.

Most of those found guilty were hanged from meat hooks in Berlin's Plottensee prison, the executions being filmed for Hitler's pleasure. Others were sent to concentration camps.

The conspirators represented some of the finest men in Germany. But because they were idealistic by nature, they lacked the necessary ruthlessness to ensure that their aim of ridding Germany of Hitler was achieved. Their blunders were essentially those of amateurism, and it was this that spelled failure.

As brave as they were, the conspirators' failure merely meant that the Nazi regime exerted an even tighter hold over the country, leaving no chance of another attempt on Hitler's life being made. Only when the Russian guns were pounding at the center of Berlin did Hitler finally take his own life. By that time Germany was almost a wasteland.

USS *Indianapolis*
in a Sea of Sharks

WAR, OF COURSE, IS ALWAYS hell, but observers know well that there are occasions when the violence and suffering seem to reach levels that transcend all the rest: Fredericksburg during the Civil War; the Battle of the Marne in World War I; the ravages on the Eastern Front in 1942; the genocide in the concentration camps; the fierce hand-to-hand combat on Okinawa in 1944. But one occasion near the very end of the Second World War, though not involving anywhere near the numbers of deaths as those incidents mentioned above, seems to share in their transcendence, as a spate of violence of another order, something that has an element of the unreal that makes you think of Hollywood and the overheated imaginations of desperate screenwriters. Such is the case with the USS *Indianapolis*.

Indeed, it was Hollywood, or should we say it was Steven Spielberg, who brought the *Indianapolis* back into the public mind when his film *Jaws* appeared in the seventies, scaring summer swimmers out of the water. In that film, based on Peter Benchley's best-selling book, Captain Quint, played by the actor Robert Shaw, reveals over cups of rum to his shipmates just why he has an obsession with capturing killer sharks. In a monologue spiced with deft storytelling, crude expressions, and horrid details, Captain Quint relates the tale of the *Indianapolis*, on which he says he served during World War II. Those who are hearing the story for the first time might be forgiven for not believing it. But it was and is terribly true.

Commissioned in November 1932, the Portland-class cruiser *Indianapolis*, built by the New York Shipbuilding Corp. in Camden, New Jersey, had a highly distinguished peacetime career, serving as the ship of state for President Roosevelt's tour of South America in 1936. The outbreak of World War II found her in the Pacific. She was assigned to Task Force II and took part in operations around New Guinea, then up in the Aleutians through the spring of 1943, when she became Admiral Raymond Spruance's flagship. Under Spruance the *Indianapolis* participated in the Battle of the Philippine Sea, and was also active around the Gilbert Islands, the Marianas, the Marshalls, and the Carolines, gaining 10 Battle Stars in all. In March 1944 she was detailed to Vice Admiral Marc Mitscher's fast-carrier attack force in operations against the Japanese home islands.

By this time the United States was starting to gain the upper hand in the Pacific corridor, retaking the Philippines as MacArthur indeed made his return. As the Japanese navy began to get stretched to the limit in terms of supplies and firepower, the U.S. pressed its advantage, invading an archipelago of strategic islands to the north, with the view of getting closer and closer to Japan and eventually launching an invasion of Japan itself. Iwo Jima was taken, gruesomely, with huge casualties on both sides; and then on to Okinawa, an 80-mile-long island only two hours' flight from Japan.

So desperate were the Japanese at this point that, with fuel in short supply, they decided to fly attack planes one way, not wasting the fuel for a return. Thus, the pilots were told to seek out the enemy and crash into them. This was *kamikaze*, which meant divine wind. A kamikaze plane was to hit the *Indianapolis* just before the Okinawa landings in March 1945.

The kamikaze plane hit at the bottom of the hull and exploded; still, the *Indianapolis* could stay afloat, and headed for San Francisco under her own power for repairs. When repairs were complete, she set off back into the Pacific under Captain Charles B. McVay III with a very secret cargo.

In the meantime, U.S. troops had secured Okinawa and, under the strategic planning of General Curtis LeMay, was setting fire to Japan with thousands of incendiary bombs dropped from B-29s, flying low under cover of night. Tokyo, Yokohama, and five other industrial cities were bombed relentlessly, exacting over a quarter of a million casualties and more than two million buildings destroyed. President Harry Truman waited for the Japanese to surrender, but they fought on. Something drastic had to be done. Something atomic.

The effort of more than 120,000 people working stateside on the Manhattan Project, which had as its goal the development of a massive nuclear weapon, had paid off. Truman knew in June 1945 that he had the firepower to deliver a devastating blow to Japan. And the *Indianapolis* was to be part of it.

Crew members did not know what was in the 15-foot-long wooden crate, and the heavy bucket that accompanied it they thought might contain gold for the purposes of buying Japan out of the war (it was a plutonium suspension). On July 16, 1945, the *Indianapolis* left Mare Island Naval Shipyard, California, and in 73 hours she arrived in Tinian in the Marianas Islands, carrying parts of the atom bombs that were being prepared for use against Japan. She delivered her cargo on July 26 and was ordered to make for

Leyte in the Philippines, where she was to prepare for the invasion of Japan, should it be necessary. The authorities were aware, however, that a Japanese submarine was in the area and that it had sunk the destroyer *Underhill* on July 24.

Indianapolis's Captain McVay was highly experienced and had already won the Silver and Bronze Stars. He was warned that a Japanese sub was in the area, but not told of the loss of *Underhill*. He knew that his ship lacked submarine detection devices and requested an escort. This was not forthcoming, since the authorities feared that this would demonstrate to the Japanese the U.S. ability to crack their secret naval codes.

Indianapolis therefore set sail on her own, and McVay's only defense against submarines was to steer a zigzag course, which he had been ordered to do at his discretion. On the evening of July 29, McVay ordered the zigzagging to cease after dark and only to resume it should the moon appear; he felt that the zigzagging was dangerously slowing his progress through dangerous waters. The ship was located by Japanese submarine I-58, which was carrying *Kaiten* Kamikaze minisubs. Sometime shortly after midnight it fired six torpedoes, two of which struck the cruiser on her starboard side—one under No. 1 turret and the other under the wardroom. They immediately destroyed her radio communications. This meant that the *Indianapolis* was unable to put out a distress call. Although *Indianapolis* only had a three-degree list it quickly became clear that she was going down by the head, and McVay was forced to order abandon ship.

Of the 1,196 crew members, 350 went down with the ship. And there is some sense in which they can be counted among the lucky. The 850 who survived the torpedo strike found themselves in the kinds of waters that fired Captain Quint's imagination: they were shark-infested. The survivors were forced to endure five days in the water, and although they spotted a number of planes, they were unable to attract their attention. These included a USAAF C-54 transport, which saw what he thought as tracer and starshells in the early hours of July 31. He assumed that it was a naval engagement, but the Army authorities on Guam, where it flew from Manila, dismissed the report on the grounds that it was U.S. Navy business. Furthermore, U.S. intelligence intercepted I-58's radio message reporting the sinking, but dismissed it as a false claim. Eventually, on August 2, the pilot of a USN Lockheed Ventura aircraft on routine patrol from Peleliu spotted them and radioed his base. Two Catalinas then arrived and rescued nearly 60 men. Finally, destroyers appeared on the scene. They recovered the remainder of the 316 *Indianapolis* men who were still alive and took them to Guam. More than 500 men had died, many of them eaten by sharks.

Admiral Nimitz ordered a board of inquiry, which convened on Guam on August 13 (by now Hiroshima and Nagasaki had been hit by atomic bombs), but not until two days later, August 15, the day of the Japanese surrender, was the ship's loss publicly announced. After the USS *Arizona*, the Indianapolis represented the second-greatest loss of life from a single ship.

Unprecedented in U.S. naval history, Charles B. McVay, who survived the ordeal, was tried in a Navy court-martial on December 3. He was charged with inefficiency during the abandonment of his ship and for hazarding it by failing to zigzag. Among the prosecution witnesses summoned was Commander Mochsitura Hasimoto, skipper of I-58. He stated that he would have sunk the cruiser even if she had been zigzagging. This was supported by U.S. submarine skipper Captain Glynn Donaho, who stated that zigzagging was of "no value to surface ships." Even so, the court found McVay guilty of the second charge, and he was sentenced to loss of seniority, although it recommended clemency, in view of McVay's previous distinguished record. On the recommendation of Admirals King and Nimitz, Secretary of the Navy Forestall remitted the sentence.

McVay served until 1949, retiring as a rear admiral, but was never given another seagoing command. In 1968 he committed suicide. As for the man who sank his ship, Hashimoto later retired within a Shinto shrine.

The survivors of the *Indianapolis* continued to fight for justice for their captain, and on August 2, 1995, a memorial to the ship was unveiled in Indianapolis. It took a 12-year-old boy, Hunter Scott from Pensacola, Florida, to unearth the true story. Inspired by Captain Quint's gruesome monologue in *Jaws*, he researched the story for a school history project. He found that McVay had been made a scapegoat for blunders by others—especially the failure to provide the cruiser with an escort and of not mounting a search once she was overdue at Leyte.

It is sad that Captain McVay did not live to see his exoneration; it is the kind of dramatic irony, though, that gives the story of the *Indianapolis* a distinctive Hollywood feel.

Part VI

Of Cold Wars and Holy Wars—

Superpower Standoffs

and Desert Storms

As at the end of the First World War, the Second World War's closing called for a re-alignment. In the very last stages, when the eventual outcome was clear, there were three summit meetings of the victorious powers, at Tehran, at Yalta, and later at Pots-dam. In these sessions, particularly the last two, spoils were distributed, alliances reaf-firmed, and each party—the Americans, British, and Russians—watched each other warily. And just as the Treaty of Versailles ending World War I sowed the seeds of what become the Second World War, Yalta and Potsdam put in motion what would become the next war, a very cold one. Though the Cold War moved the world as close to annihilation as (one hopes) it will ever get, its peculiar tensions kept certain kinds of aggression in check. The threat of nuclear war had a way of forcing diplomatic solutions onto situa-tions that during the era of conventional warfare might have simply erupted into an invasion of tanks or aerial bombing. When the Cold War ended, religious and ethnic tensions in the Middle East, which had been kept in check by being subsumed into the larger East-West detente, came out into the open, and flamed. One would hope that as historians pick through the remains of the Cold War, they don't one day find the seeds of World War III.

Yalta and the Seeds
of the Cold War

BEFORE GERMANY SURRENDERED IN MAY 1945, before the surrender of Japan in September of that year, before the end of World War II altogether, another war had unofficially begun. It was a different kind of war, just as the Great War was different from those that preceded it, and as World War II was different from its predecessor; it was a war that would last for more than four decades, one that proved to be changing in shape, and which perhaps continues to this day. History now knows it as the Cold War.

The statesman and Roosevelt intimate, Bernard Baruch, in a speech before the Senate in 1946, first coined the term: "We are in the midst of a cold war which is getting warmer," he said, referring to the cooling embers of the war just ended, and knowing that they could be fanned into flame.

The term commonly refers to the post–World War II rivalry between the United Sates and the Soviet Union, but in reality that rivalry would play itself out in countless skirmishes between countries big and small, from the superpowers to the Angolas, Vietnams, and Nicaraguas of the Third World; between political parties in Europe, the Middle East, and South America; it would play itself out in televised hearings in Washington, D.C., in which Senator Joseph McCarthy would challenge the loyalties of hundreds of

Americans; it would lead to violent unrest in French and German universities; it would lead to armored invasions, subversions of governments, purges, pogroms, exile, political prisoners, space programs, and, most significant, an atomic arms race. "Cold" hardly does justice to the heat and fire that the Cold War inspired. Still, it is a term that aptly describes the unprecedented nature of the way ideological and territorial disagreements were conducted in the presence of atomic force.

But in 1945, with the die cast in Germany as Russian troops made their deliberate way toward Berlin, pausing to allow the German army to brutally gut Poland, the heads of the Grand Alliance—Winston Churchill, Joseph Stalin, and an ailing Franklin Roosevelt—met at Yalta, the ancient Black Sea resort once favored by the tsars of Russia. Each delegation took over a separate palace. Their mission was to construct a post-war future. And that they did, as the look of the future came to them quickly. In the next four years, by 1949, the ideological and strategic differences that emerged at Yalta, and which were ineffectively resolved there, would result in Soviet invasions, the unveiling of the Marshall Plan, the Truman Doctrine, the founding of the CIA, the formation of NATO, and the division of Europe into East and West, of which Berlin would become the greatest and most enduring symbol, for which Churchill would provide the chilling term: Iron Curtain.

What happened? How could a conference seem to fail so miserably when all parties could look to another conference, which produced the Treaty of Versailles, and see how it contained within it the seeds of a second great war?

Each of the three members of the Grand Alliance (which was to be so short-lived) had different objectives at Yalta. Roosevelt was primarily interested in seeking Stalin's agreement to declare war on Japan and hopefully hasten the end of that conflict. Stalin wanted the honor due his country for the disproportionate effort it had made in defeating Germany, and in addition, he wanted the security of his western borders guaranteed. Churchill wanted to be assured that Germany could not rise again to march all over Europe, and sought enlistment of the vanquished France in that effort. Each player had different suspicions: Churchill and Roosevelt were wary of unbridled and immediate Soviet expansion into the Balkans and Iranian oil fields; Stalin feared that the Anglo-American interests would seduce European economies in places where communist party loyalists were positioned to make legitimate gains, such as France, Italy, Czechoslovakia. Churchill feared that Roosevelt would not commit American might to the long-term preservation of democracy in Europe.

It hardly seemed to be a meeting of allies, and quickly devolved into what it was: a talk among the new combatants of a new order.

General Douglas MacArthur was desperately counting on the Soviet Army to suppress the mainland Japanese forces prior to an Allied invasion that was meant to bring the Pacific war to a close. At this point the Manhattan project leaders could not assure the delivery of the atomic bomb that would eventually settle matters. In order to get a commitment from Stalin, the Soviets were granted at Yalta shipping rights (including warships) into the Mediterranean, through the Dardanelles; Stalin also won the promise of Sakhalin and the Kurile Islands in the Sea of Japan. In addition, the issue of reparations of the Soviet Union from Germany was tabled, since Churchill felt strongly that the burden of repayment on Germany after World War I had led to the discontent and humiliation that brought the madman Hitler to power. Instead, Germany was split into four zones of influence, among the three of the Grand Alliance and including France, much to Stalin's disgust, who felt the French had folded on the Western Front and deserved nothing. But Churchill, not persuaded that a long-term American military presence in Europe could be guaranteed, insisted on the French hand. In return, Churchill and Roosevelt were to get Stalin's signature to the Declaration on the Liberated Europe. The key paragraph, which pleased Roosevelt but gave Churchill some trepidation, read as follows:

> The right of all peoples to choose the form of government under which they will live, the restoration of sovereign rights and self-government to those peoples who have been forcibly deprived of them by the aggressor nations. To foster the conditions in which the liberated peoples may exercise these rights, the three governments will jointly assist the people in any European liberated state or former Axis satellite in Europe where in their judgment conditions require: (a) to establish conditions of internal peace; (b) to carry out emergency measures for the relief of distressed peoples; (c) to form interim governmental authorities broadly representative of all democratic elements in the population and pledged to the earliest possible establishment through free elections of governments responsive to the will of the people; and (d) to facilitate where necessary the holding of such elections.

Martin Walker, in *The Cold War*, goes on to add, "This is the text upon which all future accusations of Soviet betrayal and bad faith were made." And yet it is likely that what Roosevelt particularly had in mind in pressing for these conditions is Poland.

The Polish question loomed large for Roosevelt, not least for the reason that there were seven million Polish-American voters back home. And more so because Stalin knew very well that it was through Poland that his country had been attacked time and again, by Germany twice and even by Anglo-American forces in 1940. Stalin wanted Poland as a further buttress to his western border. And yet Stalin's acquiescing to these terms were deemed to be Yalta's triumph.

The optimism about Yalta died with Franklin Roosevelt on April 12. Harry Truman became president and quickly was persuaded by Secretary of State Stimson and Averill Harriman, the American Ambassador in Moscow, and the policy analyst George Kennan, that the Russians were already in flagrant noncompliance with the terms of Yalta. But until the war with Japan was brought to an end, anti-Soviet sentiments, at least publicly, must be carefully controlled.

Meanwhile, the noose was tightening around Germany. With Patton and Montgomery marching through northern Germany, Berlin was about to be entered. For some reason, however, the Anglo-American forces stayed their hand and let the Russians take Berlin. World War II in the west ended at midnight, May 8, 1945.

At the same time, Russia was pushing for a pro-Soviet government in the wasted Poland, and in Rumania and Bulgaria as well. A second summit among the three powers was held outside of Berlin, at Potsdam, an old Hohenzollern palace. Stalin, Churchill, and the bulldog Truman convened in an atmosphere of acute distrust. Before the conference was over, Churchill would be voted out of his prime ministership, to be replaced at the table by the new British prime minister, Clement Atlee.

Truman had already begun to upset Stalin and Churchill. He canceled the Lend-Lease program abruptly, reversing all the aid going to Europe and to Russia. Although aid still flowed to Britain, it was now in the form of a loan, at an interest rate the British felt was unjust. Reason for Truman to be even less accommodating, to the Russians at least, was provided him on July 16, the eve of the Potsdam summit, when he was told that the first atom-bomb test, at Alamogordo, New Mexico, was a rousing success. Truman now had the key to ending the war in Japan, and very little reason to capitulate to Russian aggression. It was a new ball game.

The United States dropped the atomic bombs on Hiroshima (August 6) and on Nagasaki (August 9). The Soviet Union, rather transparently, declared war on Japan on August 9, and awaited its chance to bargain for some of the spoils of the Pacific war. On August 15, a cease-fire was declared, and Japanese forces laid down their arms. On September 2, on the battleship *Missouri*, the Japanese government officially surrendered to General Douglas MacArthur. The war that had accounted for at least 15 million military dead, and over 30 million civilian dead, was now over.

America almost immediately began sending its war forces home, at the rate of 100,000 troops a week. But in Washington and in diplomatic circles, the awareness of another war was the main topic. While some, including Truman and Secretary of State Stimson and new Under-Secretary of State Dean Acheson, advocated perhaps showing some trust in the Soviets, going as far as to establish the Atomic Energy Commission, which would share certain information about the atomic bomb, there were plans being drawn up to bomb 20 Soviet cities should the need arise. Clearly, the post-war era dawned on a world not at all at peace.

After six years of world war, where were we? The fascism of Germany, of Italy, of Spain, of the countries they had managed to bring under their influence, whether under duress or willingly, had been defeated. The imperialist and expansionist Japan, intent on securing for itself the means to provide its small island complex with the kinds of natural resources and territorial protection it deemed necessary for its survival, had also been put down. But by what? What forces of ideology, of government, had won the day? Therein lay part of the problem of navigating the years that followed. For the forces that triumphed, no matter how expertly allied in their war effort, no matter the depth and breadth of their sacrifice and heroism and expenditure of bodies and monies and materiel during the war, were of many different colors. The United States was a huge but young country, committed to electoral democracy, well endowed with natural resources and (thus far) steady government. Britain was a small country with a parliamentary democracy and an ancient royal family, and a vast but increasingly precarious empire, a country dependent on that empire for the resources and markets and goods it could provide. France was riddled literally by war's impact, and riven by the divided loyalties and accusations of betrayal and collaboration that can befall a country quickly overrun in war and subjected to cruel occupation. Russia, a country with a style of government less than 30 years old that itself was formed in the crucible of a world war, that proceeded along lines in direct opposition to those of its allies, a form of government that though mobilized to defeat fascism, was in itself adamantly non-democratic, and philosophically committed to a world in which its communist philosophy of proletarian revolt was against the economic gospel of its fellow vanquishers: capitalism. These differences were the oppositions that made the Cold War run.

In the early years after the war, in fact, despite what the American and British leaderships felt about Soviet aggression on a variety of fronts, there was a strong popular view that the Russians were equal heroes in the war just ended. The Red Army (renamed the Soviet Army in 1944) had indeed fought with heroism and an

almost unimaginable degree of sacrifice. *Life* magazine pronounced
the Russians as "one hell of a people," and Joseph Stalin was almost
made cuddly, as "Uncle Joe" to our more familiar Uncle Sam, or,
as *Look* magazine put it in a cover story in 1944, "A guy named
Joe," as if he were a silent, everyday neighbor we had come to
understand and admire. In addition, Uncle Joe's chosen political
philosophy, that of Marxism-Leninism, had hordes of adherents all
over the globe. One must remember that capitalism and imperialism
had strong detractors, understandably so, given the many depres-
sions and crises that the free market had foisted upon the world,
and the feudal societies that the various tsars and Ottomans and
Hapsburgs had found necessary for the maintenance of their ways
of life.

Indeed, in the late 1940s there were already strong communist parties in France and Czechoslovakia and other European
countries; the Labour Party in England embraced elements of
socialism, if not communism, in its call for nationalization of key
industries. Anti-imperialism was part and parcel of the move toward
anti-colonialism in areas like Egypt and India, where self-
determination, as articulated in the Yalta agreement, became political rally cries for escape from the British Empire.

So when Russia, in the immediate post-war months, followed up its virtual annexing of eastern Poland with the setting up
of pro-Soviet governments in Bulgaria and Romania, it was not
something that the democratic world could count on to receive
universal condemnation. That's not to say that Harry Truman was
happy. In January 1946, Truman read aloud to his Secretary of
State a letter he had drafted, laying out his grievances about Stalin's
activities:

> At Potsdam we were faced with an accomplished fact and
> were by circumstances almost forced to agree to Russian

occupation of eastern Poland, and that part of Germany east of the Oder river by Poland. It was a high-handed outrage. There isn't a doubt in my mind that Russia intends an invasion of Turkey and the seizure of the Black Sea Straits to the Mediterranean. Unless Russia is faced with an iron fist and strong language, another war is in the making. Only one language do they understand— "How many divisions have you?" I do not think we should play compromise any longer. We should refuse to recognize Rumania and Bulgaria until they comply with our requirements; we should let our position on Iran be known in no uncertain terms . . . and we should maintain complete control of Japan and the Pacific. We should rehabilitate China and create a strong central government there. We should do the same for Korea . . . I'm tired of babying the Soviets.

Walker, in *The Cold War*, goes on to observe about Truman's language: "[T]his was the vocabulary of a permanent American overseas commitment and an unending military expenditure which would prove difficult to sell to a U.S. Congress and a fast-demobilizing American public still thrilling to the novelty of peace."

Lines began to harden on both sides. Stalin started to publicly describe World War II as "the inevitable result of the development of world economic and political forces on the basis of modern monopoly capitalism."

Despite living in a world where the Soviet message was not necessarily evil to all ears, the American diplomatic community began to gird itself for a long test of will. It was at this time, early in 1946, that George F. Kennan, now in charge of the American Embassy in Moscow, issued his famous 5,500-word "Long Telegram," issued in telegraph-speak, with its economical syntax, but leaving nothing out when it came to limning the evil intentions of the Russians:

> At the bottom of Kremlin's neurotic view of world affairs is traditional and instinctive Russian sense of insecurity. . . .
>
> Marxist dogma, rendered even more truculent and intolerable by Lenin's interpretation, became a perfect vehicle for sense of insecurity which Bolsheviks, even more than previous Russian rulers, were afflicted . . .
>
> Everything will be done to set major Western powers against each other. Anti-British talk will be plugged among Americans, anti-American talk among British. Continentals, including Germans, will be taught to abhor Anglo-Saxon powers.
>
> In general, all Soviet efforts on unofficial international plane will be negative and destructive in character, designed to tear down sources of strength beyond reach of Soviet control.

Kennan's telegram created a firestorm in diplomatic circles. Churchill rushed to meet with Truman and to lend his support to Kennan's view of the Soviet threat. In a speech in Truman's home state of Missouri, Churchill coined the term that would come to represent the West's notion of Russia's insecurity: the Iron Curtain.

> From Stettin in the Baltic to Trieste in the Adriatic, an iron curtain has descended across the continent . . . Far from the Russian frontiers and throughout the world, Communist fifth columns are established and work in complete unity and absolute obedience to the directions they receive from the Communists' center. Except in the British Common-

wealth and the United States, where Communism is in its infancy, the Communist parties or fifth columns constitute a growing challenge and peril to Christian civilization.

Nowhere in this rhetoric, either from Truman or Churchill, can be found saber rattling. In it is testament perhaps to the wisdom that comes from just having waged a war that incurred almost unimaginable hardship and tragedy, that the policy which emerged from all of this was not akin to a military response to the Soviet aggression, but an economic one. It has come to be called the policy of containment, and it was carried out under many guises, but the two earliest and most prominent were known as the Truman Doctrine and, shortly thereafter, the Marshall Plan.

Containment, a policy for which George Kennan is credited, called not for military challenges to the Soviet encroachments, but rather relief to those strategic areas where the Soviet message might meet with welcoming ears. The Truman Doctrine therefore called for $400 million in aid for Greece and Turkey, accompanied by the right to send U.S. troops to administer reconstruction. The Marshall Plan called for nothing less than the recovery of Europe, a plan that was unveiled in a speech by General Marshall delivered at Harvard University in 1947.

As Martin Walker has observed, this was the West's seizing of the "moral high ground" in the Cold War debate. But the Soviet foreign minister, Molotov, saw the recovery plan for Europe as a pretext of Anglo-American dominance on the continent, and an attempt to delegitimize the communist parties in various European countries. There was to be a wider conference in Paris about the reconstruction of Europe, but Moscow forbade its puppets from attending. The eagerness of Czechoslovakia to get some real assistance in recovering from the war was to be its undoing. There would be a communist-led takeover, which included the death of the foreign minister, Jan Masaryk. Whether he committed suicide by jumping to his courtyard or was pushed is irrelevant; he was certainly "putsched."

Stalin responded to this Western attempt at unity by calling the first meeting of the Cominform, the Communist Information Bureau. He convened a meeting of the Communist party leaders of Poland, Czechoslovakia, Hungary, France, Italy, and Bulgaria. It was filled with Communist perspectives on the crisis in the colonial system that was threatening the Western capitalism economies and on the Truman Doctrine itself, which was deemed as a manner to deliver monies to "reactionary regimes."

The Cominform managed to mobilize a response to the West's efforts. Labor strikes were called in France and Italy, and the Communist party workers there responded.

Viewing this attempt at destabilizing the fragile democracies of Europe, the United States, still with no taste for saber rattling, still committed in spirit to the idea of letting the Soviets have their way if only it was contained, embarked upon a path that came to define, for many, the Cold War: clandestine intelligence gathering by the newly founded agency, the CIA. The Cold War went underground, a secret war.

More solidarities developed: the North Atlantic Treaty Organization, NATO, was formed after the Russians firmly took control of Czechoslovakia in 1948. The four-part zoning of Germany ended, the French, American, and British sections uniting in division against the Russian sector. An airlift of supplies was begun, lasting 11 months, bringing necessary relief to the Western sectors of Berlin. In June 1948, the state of West Germany, anti-Soviet, pro-West, was formed. For all intents and purposes, Europe was now divided. Russia had East Berlin as part of East Germany, all of Poland, Czechoslovakia, Hungary, Romania, and Bulgaria, all behind the "iron curtain."

In the following year the Soviets would conduct their own first nuclear bomb test. The Cold War entrenchment had set in like a permafrost. It would take 40 years to thaw.

In all of this, and given the retrospect we are now afforded, can one assign a blunder? Knowing what we know now, and some of which we will lay out in subsequent pages, was there another way? It is hard to say. But since the Marxist-Leninist experiment in communist government more or less came to a close in 1989, after 72 years of striving, one has to mark that as a failure. In those first crucial years after so gallantly aiding in the defeat of fascism, did the Russians sow the seeds of their own demise? One can look at the immediate Western response to the Soviets' need to expand, as they did aggressively even before the war was over and pursued even more so in the decades thereafter, and look to what they may have gambled away: the opposition's policy of containment, in which it seemed the Western powers, though revolted by Soviet conduct, were willing to grudgingly accept co-existence as a political reality. Perhaps it was the Soviets' refusal to similarly accept co-existence and instead push the age-old tenet that communism required world domination to survive that was a major mistake. The West was prepared to give the Soviets room, but only so much room. It was not enough for Stalin, not enough for Khrushchev, and by 1952 the policy of containment was something with which the American public was no longer happy. Truman did not run for a third term, and a hero of the Second World War, Dwight Eisenhower, swept to the presidency, bent on repulsing Soviet expansion wherever necessary. The Cold War was indeed, as Baruch had said, getting warmer.

From Korea to
Dien Bien Phu to the Tet Offensive

TWO SUPERPOWERS, BOTH IN POSSESSION of atom
bombs and each in possession of opposing social and political
ideologies, stare at each other. But this is the Cold War, where
there is little enthusiasm for nuclear destruction, invasions, bombing
raids, or military challenges at sea. What there is, however, is a
boundless appetite for diplomatic maneuvering, propaganda, spy-
ing, subversion, and, most important, war by proxy. But during the
standoffs, if one side miscalculates another's reaction, events can
quickly escalate into war. Just this very thing happened in Korea,
when an overconfident General MacArthur felt Mao Tse-Tung was
bluffing when he claimed he would attack if the U.N. forces crossed
a certain line. MacArthur's misreading led not only to a long military engagement involving the U.S. and China, but brought Russia
into an alliance with China against its former ally in World War II.
MacArthur, a great hero of the Second World War, would be removed from his post by his president.

Although the Cold War started in Europe with the partitioning of
Germany, it quickly went global. The United States, the protector
of the still recovering Allied countries, found itself "unhappily but

increasingly supporting and then supplanting its European allies' colonial pretensions," as Martin Walker eloquently put it in *The Cold War*. Moscow, on the other hand, could not afford to abandon any nascent Communist-inspired and anti-capitalist political movements.

The first stage on which the war by proxy would perform was in Korea. The Korean War would last for the better part of four years; actual Russian and American troops would eventually become involved, tossing proxy to the winds. The war would be followed, within the decade, by a blundering French initiative in Vietnam that would spell the end of the French colonial presence in Indochina. Unfortunately for America, the U.S. was now expected to step in wherever Communism threatened to make headroads. It would be 15 years before America would be able to wriggle out.

In the aftermath of Japan's surrender, there was the problem of determining the fates of not only Japan itself but of the regions the country had once occupied. As Japanese troops laid down their arms along the vast Asian littoral, from Manchuria and Korea in the north, through Hong Kong, Burma, Indochina, Indonesia, all the way to the Philippines, the question of reoccupation and by whom had to be faced. Many of these areas had indeed experienced the "colonial pretensions" of American allies: the Dutch in Indonesia, the French in Indochina, the British in Hong Kong and Malaya. The British had already seen the light of the new world and given India its independence only two years after the war ended. But not everyone was happy to see lands and peoples set free. America feared in particular political vacuums among Asian countries into which Communist China might surge like dam water. There was an ideological struggle going on for the soul of China, making the entire region unstable. And as we know, instability often leads to aggression.

In October 1949, Mao Tse-Tung, after routing Chiang Kai-shek's army, proclaimed the People's Republic of China and then signed a treaty with Stalin, the Sino-Soviet Treaty of Friendship and Alliance and Mutual Help. Although the U.S. Navy's Seventh Fleet was sent to protect Chiang's forces on the island of Formosa (Taiwan), the American response was restrained in the absence of any actual Soviet involvement. Still, the loss of China was a terrible blow to American hopes for stability in the region. With Mao and Stalin now allies, something had to be done to gain a foothold for democracy. Rather quickly this would lead to an impressive resurrection of the Japanese economy and its rearmament. In addition, America was now on alert for other Communist aggression in the region.

Korea extends like a shrimp into the Sea of Japan. It is attached to mainland China. Japan annexed the area from Russian control in the Russo-Japanese War in 1905, and freedom for Korea was guaranteed at the Potsdam conference. But a tug-of-war about whom the occupying and defeated Japanese troops would surrender to led, unwisely, to the division of the country into North and South. In a hastily drawn plan, the 38th parallel was determined to be the line north of which soldiers would surrender to the Soviets and south of which they would surrender to the Americans. Afterward, the Soviets declared the 38th parallel to be a political boundary.

Free elections were held in Korea, but Stalin would not allow the elections to be carried out in the North. The Republic of South Korea was therefore proclaimed, with Seoul as its capital, but the Soviets did not recognize the government. Instead, it set up a puppet government in the North, and set upon a scheme of harassing the South with sabotage and terrorism.

In June 1950, the harassment took the form of an invasion. Communist North Korea had a well-equipped and well-trained army, thanks to the help of the Soviets and to Soviet hardware, including a brigade of Russian T-34 tanks and 180 Russian Yak planes. Among its 130,000 troops was a hard core of nearly 25,000 very experienced Chinese Communist soldiers. They quickly moved into South Korea and captured the city of Seoul. The invasion of South Korea was complete.

The Americans were completely surprised. Only four days earlier, the State Department's Dean Rusk had told the Senate that there was "no evidence of war brewing." But the U.S. response was quick. Truman ordered air strikes, without even bothering to consult with his allies. The United Nations voted to support a military action of defense of South Korea. Conveniently, the Russians were not present to cast their veto: they were boycotting the Security Council until Mao got a seat on the council, too, instead of Chiang Kai-shek. So the U.S. managed to mount their intervention under the flag of the U.N.

General MacArthur, commander of U.S. forces in the Far East, was put in charge of mounting an air and sea force assault in support of the South Koreans. Some tentative first steps and early setbacks, which even included the capture of U.S. Major General William Dean, were overcome by a brilliant amphibious assault at Inchon, near the 38th parallel itself, in September. MacArthur, who had been named Commander-in-Chief United Nations Command by this time, drove the North Koreans all the way back through North Korea itself to the Chinese border, even though Mao had threatened Chinese retaliation if the U.N. troops passed the 38th parallel. MacArthur's tactics were considered brilliant, but he miscalculated when it came to the Chinese intentions. He thought surely they were bluffing and told Truman so. The Inchon invasion was to be the last hurrah in a glorious military career. In the coming months, the U.N. forces would endure humiliating reversals and defeats, and the Chinese Army would move in huge numbers. Truman would relieve MacArthur of his command by April of the following year.

Mao did indeed take offense at MacArthur's deep drive to the Chinese border, and mounted an invasion plan, but not before making it clear, over and over to Stalin, that he expected Russian help. As the promised Soviet weaponry failed to materialize, Mao was forced to delay the invasion. When the help did come, and the invasion commenced, it became a confrontation between Americans and Russians who just five years earlier had together victoriously marched into Berlin. That's not to say it was easy to see that it was Russian vs. American, because the 150 Russian MiGs that Mao had been waiting for were painted with Chinese colors and were manned by Russians in Chinese uniforms with Chinese papers.

Over the next three years, Seoul would change hands three times. A Chinese offensive would force wholesale evacuations of U.S. troops by air, trapped without support. Negotiations would begin as early as 1951 in Panmunjon, located in the no-man's-land between North and South, searching for a resolution to the conflict. In the end, the 38th parallel would remain the line of demarcation between North and South Korea. Although the Communist forces would suffer 1.6 million casualties compared to the half million on the U.N. side, it was a costly setback for world peace. The superpowers had been engaged, and Russia had a fierce and huge ally in the Chinese. The United States had spilled blood on Asian soil; there would be more to come.

One of the first acts of Mao's government after signing the Sino-Soviet treaty with Stalin was to recognize Ho Chi Minh's Vietminh as the legitimate government of Vietnam, which in 1949 was still largely under French control. Although the United States had at first little reason to support an outpost of the French colonial empire, the new Soviet-Chinese alliance made it so, if the French could not hold, there would be strategic reasons for moving in.

In 1953, the French seized upon a strategy to subdue the indigenous communist Vietminh in French Indochina. The surrender of the French garrison on May 7, 1954, marked final defeat for the French. At the international Geneva Conference that followed, the formation of communist North Vietnam and Western-backed South Vietnam would be officially recognized. That the French managed to allow themselves to be trapped at Dien Bien Phu was the result of a serious operational blunder by the French commander-in-chief in Indochina, General Henri Navarre. It stemmed from his misappreciation of the military strength and ability of the Vietminh, led by a brilliant North Vietnamese logistician. And the fact the French victory _loss_ at Dien Bien Phu occurred, disastrously, on the eve of Geneva proved that the North Vietnamese general wasn't a bad politician either.

Throughout the conflict the French had been frustrated in their efforts to bring the Vietminh to general battle. In the summer Navarre mounted a massive countrywide offensive to break the back of the Vietminh, but failed to do so. He therefore tried a different tactic. This was to occupy a locality that the Vietminh would be forced to attack, and then destroy them when they did so. He selected the village of Dien Bien Phu, 220 miles west of Hanoi and close to the border with Laos. It lay astride one of the Vietminh major resupply routes. But the remoteness of Dien Bien Phu, lying as it does in the T'ai Mountains, meant that airborne troops would have to be used to seize it and that resupply would have to be entirely by air. This was a serious planning blunder.

The first wave of paratroops were dropped on November 23, 1953, and they quickly secured the village and surrounding area. Further waves were dropped during the next two days. Two airstrips were quickly prepared and reinforcements were air-landed. Among the reinforcements were a number of guns and ten U.S.-built Chaffee tanks. The garrison commander, General Christian de la Croix de Castries, was confident that these would provide him with superior firepower. He then set about constructing a number of fortified redoubts. Some of these, especially Gabrielle in the extreme north and Isabelle in the extreme south, were dangerously isolated.

General Vo Nguyen Giap, the Vietminh commander, who years later would be lauded as a brilliant military strategist, noted what was happening and began to concentrate his forces. Soon they outnumbered the 15,000 French by over three to one. More significant, his men, contrary to French belief, managed to manhandle no less than 200 guns, together with numerous mortars, into position surrounding Dien Bien Phu. These began to bombard the French positions on New Year's Eve and continued to do so for the next 10 weeks. Vietminh antiaircraft guns also shot down and damaged an increasing number of French aircraft.

On the night of March 12, the northeastern redoubt, Beatrice, fell to the Vietminh. Two days later, Isabelle had to be evacuated, which meant the loss of the southern airstrip. The other airstrip was now under constant artillery fire, and the last French transport took off from it on March 27, leaving Dien Bien Phu totally isolated. In desperation, the French parachuted in more reinforcements during early April, but by now there could be no doubt as to the end result. De Castries was forced to surrender on May 7, with 11,000 survivors, many of them wounded. It was the end of France's Far East empire.

The United States had already pumped over $1 billion in

military aid to the French. According the French foreign minister, Georges Bidault, John Foster Dulles even offered nuclear strikes on the Vietminh, but Eisenhower overruled the notion. "You must be crazy. We can't use those awful things against Asians for the second time in less than 10 years. My God."

What the French and Americans settled for in Vietnam was what was settled for in Korea: a partition, north and south, a second iron curtain falling in Asia. In the coming years, of course, this agreement would prove unsuitable to the Chinese Communists, and the United States would find itself embroiled in a civil war in Southeast Asia which managed to cause a near–civil war back home, with camps of strident partisans aligning on opposite sides of the Vietnam issue.

The French had blundered by inviting an engagement with the enemy that they could not defeat. For General Giap and his Vietminh troops, it was a last-ditch effort to get the French out; their desperation, and cunning, led to their triumph. Thirteen years later, an American general, General William Westmoreland, would similarly misread the same General Giap, at Khesanh, and set the stage for the campaign that had everything to do with the eventual American withdrawal: the Tet Offensive.

In the fall of 1967, Westmoreland, commander of the U.S. forces in Vietnam, saw a development that he welcomed—a planned buildup of North Vietnamese forces that indicated an attack at some key American outposts in the countryside. This was the kind of engagement Westmoreland wanted and knew he could win with the American superiority in firepower. What he didn't want was to be caught fighting in the cities, and neither did his men. American B-52s pounded the hills and jungles, raining tons of bombs and na-

palm and leaflets into the inferno. By November 1967, Westmoreland, on a trip to Washington, declared that "the enemy's hopes
are bankrupt." Soon enough, Westmoreland's confidence would
rise even more, as the North Vietnamese made a move into the
rolling hills around Khesanh, which Stanley Karnow in *Vietnam: A
History*, describes as "a region as lovely as the hills of Tuscany."

U.S. intelligence reported that four North Vietnamese infantry divisions along with two artillery and armored units were
heading for Khesanh. Since peace talks were about to commence
in Paris, and it was General Giap the Americans were dealing with,
comparisons to Dien Bien Phu began to fly. Was this a timely
massive assault meant to embarrass the Americans and perhaps
wring concessions out of them at the peace talks? After all, Giap
had seemed to sense the weakness of the French commitment to
French Indochina in 1954; with American will, at least at home,
wavering, perhaps he perceived that the time was right for a crippling blow to an American fortification.

American officers began reading up on the events at Dien
Bien Phu. American newspaper and broadcast journalists began to
make Khesanh–Dien Bien Phu comparisons. Westmoreland himself
listened to a lecture on the French experience. But he was convinced that American power would overcome the North Vietnamese
effort, whenever and however it arrived. And President Lyndon
Johnson, whose own will was shortly to be broken, would confess
to General Earle Wheeler, "I don't want any damn Dinbinphoo."

Khesahn would be no "Dinbinphoo," as it turned out. The
American position was too strong, unlike the poor location that
doomed the French. And though it is still under debate, it seems
unlikely that General Giap intended it be such—he was planning a
diversion rather than a last-ditch effort to cripple American morale.
In fact, Giap had another more involved plan of attack in the works
that would accomplish his goal: make America sick of the war.

· · ·

Tet is the lunar New Year. In 1968, the North Vietnamese themselves had called for a truce to be observed during Tet. Instead, on January 31, they broke their own truce and attacked over 100 cities up and down the length of South Vietnam; they attacked the American embassy in Saigon; they took radio towers. They murdered and pillaged and executed. They assassinated American officers, German doctors, French nuns.

While the American military leadership was feeling chipper about having repulsed Giap at Khesanh, which they did, the wide-scale results of the Tet Offensive, broadcast back into American homes in gruesome detail, began to stir public opinion and public distrust of the American generals, particularly of Westmoreland. For if the enemy presence was as low in numbers as Westmoreland insisted, how could an assault of this breadth and effectiveness be carried out?

A CIA analyst, Sam Adams, would later charge Westmoreland with deliberately skewing the numbers in order to justify the increasing American involvement in Vietnam. Adams specifically referred to the doctoring of numbers prior to the Tet Offensive. The controversy eventually led to Westmoreland suing CBS and Adams for defaming him in a television documentary, but the charges were dismissed. For whatever reasons, it is clear that the Tet Offensive caught the Americans flat-footed. The ensuing chaos in the streets of not only Saigon but dozens upon dozens of South Vietnamese cities—bodies burning, public executions, ripped American flags—had its effect back in American towns and cities, and in American hearts. In March, Lyndon Johnson would announce that he would not seek reelection. In April, Martin Luther King Jr. would be killed. In June, Robert F. Kennedy, whose conviction that the U.S. should withdraw was inspired by the images of Tet, would fall to an assassin's bullets in a hotel kitchen in Los Angeles.

With Vietnam, it is hard to talk of blunders. Is it a war that should have happened at all? If not, the blunder was involvement in the first place, followed by blunders of escalation; but then, when these are followed by blunders, like the Tet Offensive, that somehow lead to an end of the conflict, is that truly a blunder or some kind of blessing? As with many things, it depends on which side you are on. But surely, history will not forget Westmoreland's misrepresentation of the balance of forces in Vietnam, and he will be held responsible to some significant extent for prolonging a war that could not be won.

The Bay of Pigs

WHEN JOHN F. KENNEDY WAS elected president in 1960, the Soviet Union perhaps was at the top of its game, if world opinion mattered. And the reputation of the United States, embarrassed by the U-2 incident, in which a U.S. spy plane had been shot down over Soviet territory, and suffering a slight vacuum in leadership due to Eisenhower's failing health, was in something of an eclipse. Shortly after Kennedy took office, despite his campaign promises of strong-arm tactics against the Soviets, things would get even worse. The young president's first test spiraled into disaster on the Cuban beaches at the Bay of Pigs as a plan initiated under Eisenhower but implemented by Kennedy went awry. The short-term result was that it made American policy look hypocritical at best, bungling and inept and dangerous at worst. Less than two years later, with the incident having cemented the bond between Cuba and the USSR, Khrushchev would be emboldened to base missile sites on Cuban soil and threaten the U.S., only 150 miles away, with nuclear strike capability.

Cold War strategies evolved rapidly during its 40-year duration; and by the early 1960s, the prevailing wisdom had moved from containment to standing for ground (as in Korea) to clandestine activities to the acknowledgment that the Cold War was an economic war as much as anything else.

When Kennedy first came to office, he was advised as much in a letter from British Prime Minister Harold Macmillan. If capitalism were to fail to show steady economic growth, then "Communism will triumph, not by war, or even subversion, but by seeming to be a better way of bringing people material comforts."

The letter went on to discuss a "new form of capitalism," which seemed to profess the importance of mixed economies with heavy government spending. The Kennedy circle could smell the Keynsianism in Macmillan's note, and sent for their favorite economist, John Kenneth Galbraith, to assist in the analysis. It's difficult to say if the new White House crew took Macmillan's message seriously; Galbraith was kept waiting for some time after his arrival as the presidential staff turned the White House upside-down: Macmillan's letter had been lost. Finally, it turned up in three-year-old Caroline Kennedy's nursery. But one thing is for sure: the U.S. strategy toward Cuba couldn't have been further from what Macmillan recommended, and he surely was not surprised at the outcome.

In fact, it is fair to say that Kennedy pursued the opposite tack. Costly expenditures for defense were increased; half of the vast Polaris, Minuteman, and B-47 bomber forces were to be on 15-minute alert at all times. The building of private bomb shelters was encouraged, and the building of public ones was subsidized. This hardly seemed a means of making the American way of life seem triumphant. Rather than exporting the wherewithal to help tottering societies, the U.S. was looking for ways to forcibly remove leaders such as Patrice Lumumba in the newly independent Congo, and doing so clumsily, handing the Soviet Union public relations field days. The U.S. in 1961 seemed about ready to misstep elsewhere—in Angola, Laos, and Cuba. It would do so in Cuba.

Cuba had attained independence from Spain as a result of

the Spanish-American War of 1898. Until the end of the 1950s
most Americans regarded Cuba merely as a holiday paradise. The
poverty of many of its people went unnoticed. Yankee dollars were
the backbone of the Cuban economy and underwrote the dictator-
ship of General Batista. Some Cubans resented the American dominance of the island, and during the mid-1950s a guerrilla
movement developed in Cuba's hinterland. Fidel Castro, a young
lawyer, was its leader.

Castro resented Batista's seizure of power in 1952 and led
an abortive uprising against him. After imprisonment and exile he
returned to Cuba in 1956 to set up his revolutionary movement.
Playing on the unpopularity of the Batista government and adopting
guerrilla tactics against the army, Castro's movement gained increasing popular support. Eventually it controlled most of Cuba. Batista
was forced to flee on New Year's Day 1959. A week later Castro
and his guerrillas entered the capital, Havana, in triumph.

Castro declared that he would honor all existing agree-
ments. These included the U.S. leasing of the Guantanamo military
base, which it had garrisoned since 1903. As a result, America
moved quickly to recognize the new regime. Castro, however, still
had to do battle with pro-Batista guerrillas.

Castro increasingly suspected that guerrillas were being
supported by the United States. Washington, on the other hand,
feared that, in spite of Castro's denials, the regime had a Communist agenda. With the Cold War gaining momentum, a pro–
Eastern Bloc government in America's backyard was unacceptable.

American fears that the Castro regime was extremely left-
wing seemed confirmed when Castro embarked on a wholesale program of nationalization. This included the seizing of one billion
dollars worth of U.S. assets on the island. In retaliation, Washington refused to grant Cuba economic aid. Castro immediately turned

to Moscow and through Soviet Foreign Minister Anasta Mikoyan secured a $100 million dollar loan.

Castro used some of this Soviet money to buy weapons directly from the Soviet Union and from other Eastern Bloc states. But his increasing nationalization plans drove thousands of Cubans into exile in America, where they soon gained the support of a sympathetic U.S. government.

In March 1960, a recommendation by CIA chief Alan Dulles to arm and train Cuban exiles was accepted by President Eisenhower. The CIA set up secret training camps for Cuban exiles in Guatemala and Panama as a first step toward the liberation of Cuba. In Guatemala, Cuban exile Brigade 2506, over 1,400 men, got CIA help in preparing for an invasion of Cuba. As Castro suspected, the CIA was also giving clandestine support to the guerrillas within Cuba itself.

With the Cold War growing in intensity, Kennedy accused the Eisenhower administration of complacency and demanded a more aggressive stance against Moscow. He singled out Cuba and made the restoration of democracy to the island a primary issue.

In the meantime the CIA was developing its plan for Cuba. Cuban-manned U.S. aircraft were to land exiles on the island. They would destroy Castro's air force and set up an alternative government. Active U.S. intervention would consolidate the new regime.

On January 22, 1961, almost as soon as he was installed in office, John F. Kennedy was visited in the White House by General Lyman Lemnitzer, Chairman of the Joint Chiefs of Staff, and CIA chief Alan Dulles. They briefed him on the CIA's Cuba plan.

Presidential aide Arthur Schlesinger advised against invasion, especially since he believed that it would be difficult to cover up American involvement. Kennedy, however, was conscious of his election demand for aggressive action against increasing Communist influence in the world. He did not want to be accused by the Cuban exiles of backing out. He was also swayed by CIA declarations that once the landings had taken place, the Cuban people would support the invasion and turn against Castro. Apart from Schlesinger, no one else at the meeting raised a dissenting voice. Kennedy made no decision, except to tell the CIA to continue planning. He appointed his brother Robert to oversee this.

The CIA then warned Kennedy that Castro was about to receive Soviet combat aircraft. It was after this, on April 4, 1961, that he decided that the invasion should go ahead. The CIA also reiterated their confidence in the Cuban people supporting an invasion. Unfortunately, they had tailored their intelligence to justify their strategy.

The final plan called for CIA B-26s, crewed by exiles, to bomb Cuban airfields and destroy Castro's air force. A 1,500-man invasion force would set sail from the Nicaraguan port of Puerto Cabezas. It would land in the Bay of Pigs in the Giron area. Further B-26 attacks would support the invaders.

To distract Castro's forces, the CIA put out rumors that the main attack would be in the Oriente province, at the east end of the island, and a diversionary landing was to be made there. There would also be a parachute drop at Giron. A U.S. Navy task force built around the carrier *Essex* would be offshore, and the exiles were led to believe that this would support them.

On April 14, the invasion fleet of six transports set sail from Puerto Cabezas. The following day eight B-26s attacked airfields in Cuba. They destroyed three aircraft, inflicted 51 casualties, and damaged buildings. The strike alerted Castro to the imminence of invasion. He ordered a mobilization of the country and immediately rounded up a large number of suspects, including most of the CIA agents in Cuba. Cuba also raised the matter at the United Nations.

The Cuban ambassador directly accused the United States of being behind the air attack. United States Ambassador to the U.N. Adlai Stevenson rejected this, stating that defecting Cuban pilots were responsible.

In truth, Stevenson had been kept in the dark that this defection had been staged by the CIA, who put Cuban markings on their own planes. The planes themselves, contrary to what Stevenson had stated, had taken off from Florida. Those who flew them were Cuban exiles employed by the CIA.

In spite of the Cuban protest, on the afternoon of April 16, 1961, President Kennedy gave the final go-ahead for the invasion. But he canceled the diversionary Oriente landing and the two air strikes scheduled for the day of the invasion. The die was now cast.

In the early hours of April 17, the landings began. The Cuban exiles were convinced that once they got ashore they would take part in a march of triumph to Havana. CIA frogmen were the first to land, swimming in to mark the beaches. But they became involved in a fire fight with local Cuban militiamen. Castro was quickly told of the attack. He ordered forces to be deployed to the Bay of Pigs. Meanwhile, the exiles seized the townships of Playo Largo and Giron and began preparing the airstrip at the latter so that aircraft could land.

Just after dawn, however, some of Castro's aircraft appeared over the beachhead. They attacked the anchored transports and hit two of them. The remainder withdrew, promising to return at nightfall. They never did so. This air strike was at the same time as the parachute drop on Giron. It was thrown into confusion.

Castro had taken personal charge of operations to repel the

invaders. Cuban troops, some in newly acquired Soviet armored vehicles, were soon racing toward the Bay of Pigs. By nightfall they had surrounded the beachhead and were exchanging fire with the exiles.

There were casualties on both sides, but as more Cuban troops arrived, it became clear to the exiles that things were not going according to plan. The Bay of Pigs was about to turn into a fiasco.

On the day after the invasion the exiles found themselves increasingly pinned down as Castro's forces surrounding the beachhead grew to 20,000 men—almost twenty times the strength of the exiles. Bitterly disappointed by the failure of their ships to return to the Bay of Pigs, the exiles now looked to the U.S. task force for support. That afternoon their hopes were raised when U.S. Air Force F-100 Super Sabres overflew the beachhead, but these took no offensive action.

That evening, as Castro's forces began to attack into the beachhead, the CIA pleaded with Kennedy to allow *Essex*'s aircraft to carry out attacks. The President would sanction only another B-26 strike next morning, with an escort from the carrier. Six unmarked jets from *Essex* overflew the beaches at dawn on April 19, but the exiles' B-26s had arrived too early. Most were shot down. No more air support would be forthcoming.

As the day wore on, it became clear to the exiles that Castro's forces were too strong and that they were trapped. They began to surrender. In all, 1,189 Cuban exiles were captured. A further 114 had been killed. Castro was quick to take advantage of the dismal failure of the Bay of Pigs invasion. Now he could, with justification, portray the United States as the enemy, and the vast majority of Cubans accepted this. Indeed, the whole sorry saga merely served to dramatically strengthen his regime.

As for Kennedy, after a few days of indecision, he was

forced to admit U.S. involvement in the operation. He accepted that blunders had been made, but said that the American role had been restrained. He ended with a warning to Cuba about any excessive Soviet influence.

Castro was certainly not going to let the matter rest. In April 1962, the captured exiles were all sentenced to thirty years' imprisonment. Castro then went further. On May 1—one of the most important days in the Communist calendar—he publicly announced that Cuba was now firmly in the Soviet camp. What the Bay of Pigs had aimed to prevent had now come to pass.

Soviet Premier Nikita Khrushchev was quick to take advantage of this. He had two motives. One, to protect the Communist government in Cuba, which had been achieved without the help of the Soviet Army, particularly endearing the Fidelistas to the old-line Bolsheviks. And two, to achieve some nuclear balance. Khrushchev was aware that Soviet missile strength was not at parity with the Americans', and that his own borders were surrounded by nuclear warheads aimed at Soviet cities. Khrushchev had nothing nearly so close. Missiles in Cuba would change that.

In September 1962, the Soviet cargo ship *Omsk* arrived in Havana. Under cover of night, its cargo of medium-range missiles was unloaded. A second shipment arrived a week later, with longer-range missiles in the hold. Nine launch sites were under construction on the island; when completed and armed, the Soviets' missiles would have a range of over 2,000 miles, which would bring them within reach of all Strategic Air Command bases and most major American cities, including Washington, D.C.

By October 14, U-2 spy planes verified beyond a doubt the existence of the bases. For the next two weeks nuclear war was imminent. Kennedy met nearly around the clock with his closest advisers to devise possible responses. The options were four: pre-emptive bombing of the missile bases, appeal to the United Nations to intervene, full-scale invasion of Cuba, and a naval blockade.

Kennedy decided on the fourth option, the blockade, which for diplomatic reasons he chose to call a "quarantine." The crisis reached a head on October 27, when Soviet ships paused as they approached the 500-mile quarantine line. Five days before, on national television, President Kennedy had announced the quarantine, stating emphatically that the armed forces were prepared for "any eventualities." He promised "a full retaliatory response upon the Soviet Union" if the missiles were not removed. Just before the Soviet ships neared the quarantine, Kennedy, through secret diplomatic channels, received the first of two message from the Kremlin. It was conciliatory in tone, and asked for public assurances by the United States that it would not invade Cuba or assist in any such invasion. In return for this, the missiles would be removed. But the next day, on the twenty-seventh, Moscow radio broadcast the same terms, with an added condition: the U.S. must remove its "analogous weapons" from Turkey, which threatened Kiev, Minsk, and Moscow from across the Black Sea.

These messages gave Kennedy some room to maneuver, and his response, suggested by his brother Bobby, gave Khrushchev room as well. The United States responded publicly to the first message, declaring no intention to harm Cuba and, through diplomatic channels, agreed to dismantle 15 rather obsolescent Jupiter missiles in Turkey. Kennedy appeared to have stood his ground, and Khrushchev appeared to have gained two key concessions. A nuclear holocaust was averted by the intuitionist and courageous strategizing of these two world leaders, neither of whom would be on the world stage for much longer.

The Cuban missile crisis was at an end, although it did nothing to improve U.S.-Cuban relations. They were to remain bitter for years. Even after the end of the Cold War mutual suspicion remained, and the relationship between the two countries has only recently shown signs of a thaw.

As for the Bay of Pigs prisoners, in December 1962 the Kennedy administration managed to secure their release, but only after supplying Castro with 53 million dollars worth of food and medicine.

The Bay of Pigs operation stands out as one of America's major foreign policy blunders of the Cold War era. The CIA made the fundamental error of shaping its intelligence to justify its strategy toward Cuba. This clouded its thinking, especially in its belief that a small force of exiles could overthrow the Castro regime without active American help. The Kennedy administration failed to control the CIA, and he was naive in believing that it could distance itself from the Bay of Pigs. The penalty for these blunders was paid by the Cuban exiles themselves. But it was the courage, canniness, and vision of both Kennedy and Khrushchev in the following year, during the very hottest moment of the Cold War, that averted the blunder to surpass all blunders: nuclear war.

The Spanish H-Bomb Crash:
Collision in the Air

THE ENTIRE 45-YEAR PERIOD of the Cold War between the Western democracies and the Communist Eastern bloc was dominated above all else by the nuclear arsenals built up by both sides. Although wise diplomacy and test ban treaties and disarmament programs would ultimately diminish the threat of a superpower nuclear confrontation, there was still the possibility of an accident unleashing terrible destruction, something that nearly happened in the air over Spain in 1966.

Nuclear weapons came in the form of missiles that could be launched from land, air, or from under the water. The forces responsible for these weapons on both sides were maintained at a high state of alert so as to be ready for a surprise nuclear attack.

One element of the U.S. nuclear triad was the mighty Boeing B-52 bombers of Strategic Air Command—SAC. In 1961 Operation Chrome Dome was initiated. B-52s armed with nuclear bombs were airborne every minute of the day or night, ready to attack Soviet targets on a given order.

There was always a risk that one of these aircraft might crash with nuclear weapons on board. This risk was heightened by the fact that, to keep the B-52s airborne for the required length of time, they had to be refueled in the air.

In January 1966 a B-52 collided with a KC-135 tanker aircraft over eastern Spain during refueling. Both aircraft were destroyed, but the B-52 was carrying four nuclear bombs. Three fell on land and one in the sea. The refueling blunder and a poorly conducted search operation not only cost the United States millions of dollars in ridding the area of radioactive contamination and locating the bomb in the sea, but caused it much political embarrassment.

SAC's Chrome Dome missions operated in two areas. One was centered on the Arctic, with the B-52s flying north via Alaska, Canada, and Greenland. The other took the bombers across the Atlantic, over Spain and the Mediterranean to Turkey's borders with the Soviet Union.

A B-52 with radio call sign Tea One Six took off on a Chrome Dome mission from Seymour Johnson Air Force Base, North Carolina, on January 16, 1966. It was armed with four 2,250-pound B28 thermonuclear bombs. Tea One Four was to fly the southern route to Turkey. After six hours' flying they approached the Spanish coast and were refueled by a KC-135 Stratotanker based at an air base at Torrejon, Spain.

Thereafter it flew on to Turkey and patrolled close to the Soviet border until relieved by other B-52s at dawn on January 17. Tea One Six was scheduled for a second air-to-air refueling over Spain on its flight home. This was to be carried out by a Stratotanker with call sign Troubadour One Four, which was on temporary duty from the U.S., over Palomares on the Almeria coast in southeast Spain.

Tea One Six and Troubadour One Four made a successful rendezvous. Troubadour One Four recommended a higher than normal speed during the refueling, which the B-52 captain did not object to, even though his autopilot was giving him slight problems. As it closed with the tanker, Tea One Six's speed increased. The tanker crew warned that it was about to overshoot, but it was too late.

There was a collision. The B-52 started to break up. The tanker flew on a little way and then exploded. None of the four-man crew survived. Five of the seven men on board the B-52 did manage to eject, four of them surviving.

Another air refueling of a B-52 was taking place in the same area at the time, and the crews were the first to alert the authorities to the disaster. The news passed rapidly up the chain of command and reached the White House just 90 minutes after the collision. President Lyndon Johnson immediately ordered everything possible to be done to find the four thermonuclear bombs.

The Spanish authorities were informed, and a U.S. Air Force disaster-control team immediately left the United States for Palomares.

Press agencies were already reporting the collision but, to the relief of the American authorities, made no mention of the bombs. A joint Department of Defense and State Department communiqué was then issued. This admitted that there had been a collision between a B-52 and a KC-135, but gave few other details.

A B-52 BOMBER FROM THE 68TH BOMB WING AT SEYMOUR JOHNSON AFB, NORTH CAROLINA, AND A KC-135 TANKER FROM 910TH AERIAL REFUELING SQUADRON AT BERGSTRON AFB, TEXAS, CRASHED TODAY SOUTHWEST OF CARTAGENA, SPAIN DURING SCHEDULED AIR OPERATIONS. THERE ARE REPORTS OF SOME SURVIVORS FROM THE CREWS OF THE AIRCRAFT. AN AF ACCIDENT INVESTIGATION TEAM HAS

BEEN DISPATCHED TO THE SCENE. ADDITIONAL DETAILS
WILL BE AVAILABLE AS THE INVESTIGATION PROGRESSES.

The damage-control team arrived at the sleepy village of
Palomares and began their search. Their arrival was to disrupt the
lives of the inhabitants more than they could have possibly imag-
ined. They immediately began to search for the bombs, but did not
explain to the villagers why some team members were wearing protective clothing and operating Geiger counters. Matters were not
helped by the fact that few of the team spoke Spanish and none of
the villagers had any English.

The first bomb was found very quickly. Its parachutes,
which were used to drop it, had opened, enabling a soft landing.
It was virtually undamaged and was emitting no radiation. The
following day, January 18, two more bombs were found. The high-
explosive detonators on both had exploded, but there had been no
nuclear detonation. Nevertheless, there was evidence of plutonium
contamination.

At the time, the U.S. Air Force had a policy in force that
prohibited it from providing comprehensive radiation-detection
equipment in the event of an incident involving plutonium weapons
in a remote area of a foreign country. Security was the reason
behind this, but it was now to prove a shortsighted policy.

The search teams at Palomares were equipped with unre-
liable detectors and too few of them. This made the task of establishing the extent of the contamination harder than it might have
been. Nevertheless, five possible contaminated sites were established. Sites 1, 2, and 3 were where the three bombs had landed.
Site 5 (there was no Site 4), connected Sites 2 and 3, and was the
village of Palomares itself. Site 6 was located where the B-52's tail
section had come down. All but Site 1 were found to contain radiation.

Concurrent with the radiation survey was an operation to recover the wreckage of the two aircraft, which was scattered over a wide area, and to establish the cause of the midair collision.

Of greatest concern, however, was the whereabouts of the fourth bomb. No trace of it could be found in the immediate area. Back in the United States, complicated mathematical calculations were made, using the likely trajectory of the bomb to work out where it might have fallen. This established that it could have landed in the sea. A U.S. Navy task force was therefore hurriedly organized to search the waters off Palomares.

By the end of January 1966 there were nearly 700 American personnel based at Camp Wilson, the tented base that had been set up near Palomares to deal with the incident. Some were involved with the contamination problem. Having eventually established the area of dangerous contamination, an operation was put into effect to remove the soil from the most affected area, which was five and a half acres in area. The soil put into sealed barrels and shipped back to the United States. No less than 285 acres of land was plowed up and the vegetation either stored in special pits or burned.

This could not be hidden from the prying eyes of the media, and U.S. authorities were forced by degrees to admit that the B-52 had been carrying nuclear weapons, but stressed that they had not been armed. Nevertheless, the Soviets were quick to make propaganda out of the incident, and even many European newspapers carried reports that did not show the United States in a favorable light. The situation was not helped by the fact Camp Wilson and Palomares were declared off limits to the press, which then had to rely on official communiqués.

By early February 1966, two operations were in progress to find the missing bomb—one on land and one at sea. Both were hindered by out-of-date maps and charts. There were, however,

Spanish witnesses to the midair collision who claimed to have seen a canister attached to parachutes come down in the sea. The most important of these witnesses was a local fisherman who had been fishing in the local waters at the time. He was able to pinpoint the spot with confidence and had tried, without success, to recover the object himself. Yet the Navy gave this firm lead insufficient priority and continued to search over a wide area of sea. The operation on land also continued.

Admiral William Guest, in charge of the naval operation, eventually did realize that random searching was unproductive, and on February 17, designated search areas came into force, with the area in which the Spanish fisherman claimed that the bomb had come down being given top priority. To assist the search, the task force employed a variety of methods, including sonar systems and underwater television cameras. These were employed both from an underwater platform and from a Cable Controlled Underwater Recovery Vehicle, Curv II. Divers were also used, although they were limited to shallower waters.

Most interesting was a series of submersibles. These were under development for the U.S. Navy for deep-sea recovery operations. *Deep Jeep* was on station only for eight days before one of her electric propulsion motors failed, and she had to be shipped back to the States. The *Cubmarine* was a two-man vessel that performed very well, although she was of limited endurance and could not operate in depths over 600 feet. The largest was the *Aluminaut*, which could carry a crew of six and could dive to 15,000 feet. However, she needed extensive routine maintenance and could operate only on a smooth seabed. Finally, there was the *Alvin*, which could take up to three people and dive to 6,000 feet. She was also able to operate effectively in the canyon-like seabed of the primary search area. It is therefore not surprising that it was *Alvin* that first located the missing bomb, on March 1, 42 days after the original incident. The bomb had slid down into an underwater canyon and had come to rest at a depth of 2,550 feet. Not for another two weeks, however, was *Alvin* able to confirm that this was indeed the bomb.

Only now was the search on land finally called off, but retrieving the bomb from such a depth was to prove a challenge in itself. *Alvin* and *Aluminaut* carried out the preparatory work, which was to guide grappling hooks into the parachute canopy. The bomb would then be towed to clearer waters before being lifted to the surface. The first attempt, on March 24, failed, which did not help the United States' already tarnished international image. Not until April 7, this time using Curv II, was the missing Bomb No. 4 finally swung on board USS *Petrel*, 80 days after it had plunged into the sea.

Besides the loss of a B-52 and a KC-135, the Palomares incident had cost the United States government some 80 million dollars. It also suffered a great deal of political embarrassment, which was not helped by its "neither confirm nor deny" policy toward the media.

Chrome Dome flights were immediately scaled down and were forbidden by the Madrid government from overflying Spain. Indeed, as Secretary of Defense McNamara pointed out, they had become unnecessary at the time of the Palomares incident. America had a fully comprehensive ballistic missile early warning system in operation. This meant that on-alert bombers could be launched from the ground rather than having to be airborne. Furthermore, the manned bomber was now only a small part of the U.S. nuclear armory, which was overwhelmingly made up of missiles. Thus Chrome Dome was superfluous and, given the risks of accident involved, should have been halted before the incident took place. That it had not been was the underlying blunder of Palomares.

The Failed Gorbachev Coup

THE LAST FEW MONTHS OF 1989 were one of the most remarkable periods in the history of the twentieth century. They
marked the collapse of Communism in Eastern Europe and were
symbolized by the breaking down of the Berlin Wall, which had
physically separated the Communist east from the democratic western part of the former German capital.

These dramatic events also eventually resulted in the crumbling of the once mighty Soviet empire. The decisive blow took
place, however, twenty months later. Although this effectively
brought an end to the Cold War, it was not decisive in and of
itself. The two, and then three (with China) giants of East and
West, had engaged in a long policy war of attrition and accommodation which miraculously let Communism fail on its own merits
and not by a radioactive conflagration.

The late sixties, of course, were marked by extraordinary
tensions. The United States continued to build up its forces in
Vietnam, with diminishing returns. The domestic scene in America
looked as violent as could be seen on television from Southeast
Asia: cities burning, flags burning, riot police bludgeoning citizens,
young, white, affluent college students taking over university ad-
ministrations; love-ins, be-ins, rock 'n' roll, LSD, violent assassi-
nations of leaders who carried messages of peace.

The Cold War players again changed: Nixon in America, Leonid Brezhnev in the Soviet Union, with Mao still reigning in China, but sporting a distinctively cooler tone to the Russians, which Nixon would cleverly exploit by playing his famous "China card." The Vietnam War, which featured the North Vietnamese Army aided by Vietcong rebels in the South, with massive Russian weaponry and Chinese troops, faced the Americans, who were unable to persuade their NATO allies that this was a war worth fighting. The U.S. commitment grew deeper as first Johnson, then Nixon, who replaced him in 1968, acted on assessments of the progress of the war that were half fantasy and half untruths. The enormous financial burdens of the war became a distinct political problem, forcing Nixon in 1971 to put a freeze on domestic wages, oil and gas prices, and a tax on all imports. The formation of OPEC sent oil prices soaring and engendered panic among American allies. The Yom Kippur War broke out in 1973, and the U.S. was forced to come to Israel's aid with no help from its allies, who were loath to antagonize the oil-producing countries.

As America's ability to enlist its friends in what it deemed key strategic conflicts began to dwindle, the balance of power seemed to be shifting to the Soviet Union. By 1980, the Soviet Union had industrial might. Having fortuitously discovered massive amounts of natural gas in Siberia, it only benefited from the rise in petroleum prices. It was outproducing the U.S. in steel production, oil, iron ore. It was flush with enough money to buy foodstuffs from imports to keep its populace happy.

As a result, there was a gradual change in the governments of both the U.S. and Britain. Conservative and more hawkish leaders came to power and dominated the decade of the eighties: Margaret Thatcher in England, Ronald Reagan in the U.S.

As Harold Macmillan had told John Kennedy as long ago

as 1961, the Cold War would become an economic competition, and the more or less social-democratic policies of Johnson and even Nixon, and of Labour in Great Britain, had begun to lose their effectiveness. The Soviet Union responded with typical aggressiveness. With the U.S. economy suffering, with the memory of Vietnam still burning its way through the American psyche, Afghanistan was invaded; so was Poland, and martial law declared in 1981. But these aggressions were to be met with a strong response on the world stage by both Thatcher and Reagan, and ultimately, combined with other factors, led to the demise of Communism.

Ronald Reagan granted the Pentagon almost every new weapons system it wanted. His deficit spending to finance rearmament made the U.S. the world's largest debtor. Reagan was intent on getting the Soviet economy to have to participate in an arms race. The "evil empire" is what Reagan called the Soviet Union. In the year after Yuri Andropov succeeded the ailing Brezhnev, Reagan proposed SDI, the Strategic Defense Initiative, an antimissile system based in space, which was quickly dubbed Star Wars. Reagan's actions and his stridently anti-Communist rhetoric frightened America's allies, even Britain, and brought the world to a dangerous precipice. During the fall of 1983, after Soviet air-defense forces shot down a Korean airliner, the Cold War was as hot as it had been since the Cuban missile crisis.

Although the Soviets thought that Reagan was ready to attack in light of the Korean airliner being downed over Sakhalin Island, it was only saber rattling, and the world breathed a sigh of relief. A few months later, Andropov would be dead, replaced by Konstantin Chernenko, the last of the old guard of Bolsheviks. He would die only 14 months later, in March 1985, to be succeeded by a member of the new guard, a democratic-minded reformer from the Politburo. His awareness of the growing discontent among the Soviet citizenry, and his moves to liberalize Soviet society and foreign policy, would lead to the end of Communism in Eastern Europe, and to the end of his reign as well.

The 54-year-old Gorbachev was a realist. He knew that the arms race was crippling the Soviet economy, and that reforms were needed up and down the length of Soviet policy. He moved quickly to end the arms race with the United States. He also eventually succeeded in disengaging the Soviet forces from their costly conflict against the Mujaheddin in Afghanistan.

Domestically, Gorbachev developed two major policies. The first was Glasnost, or "openness," which meant removing some of the secrecy under which the Soviet system had traditionally operated. The second was Perestroika—"restructuring." This took two forms—the first was to introduce some democracy gradually into the political system. Through multi-candidate elections and secret ballots, Gorbachev ultimately created a new parliament, the Congress of People's Deputies, some of whose members were elected directly by the people.

The second plank of Perestroika was to reform the economy by gradually introducing limited free-market mechanisms and encouraging foreign investment. His momentous speech at the Geneva summit in 1985 opened the door for not only reform but rebellion:

> Force or the threat of force neither can nor should be instruments of foreign policy. . . . The principle of the freedom of choice is mandatory. Refusal to recognize this

principle will have serious consequences for world peace. To deny a nation the freedom of choice, regardless of the pretext or the verbal guise in which it is cloaked, is to upset the unstable balance that has been achieved. . . . Freedom of choice is a universal principle. It knows no exception.

Cold War rhetoric? Or something new? The truth is in the eye of the beholder, but such sentiments met with great approval among Soviet citizens, and the Eastern bloc countries gradually rallied to the promise of "freedom of choice." First Hungary declared that there would be a multi-party system with free elections; then various Soviet republics declared that their own laws superseded those of the Soviet Union; the dismantling of the Berlin wall on November 10, 1989, was the most fitting symbol of the end of an era. Czechoslovakia followed, announcing free elections.

The reform message from Gorbachev had been heard loud and clear. Emboldened by the possibility that Gorbachev would be true to his word and therefore feeling no fear of reprisal, Eastern Europe democratized and opened up. They had made their choice. Unfortunately for Gorbachev, the granting of this freedom led to the unraveling of the Soviet project in Europe and, eventually, at home.

Indeed, the problems within the Soviet Union were making him increasingly unpopular in some quarters. There was civil unrest in a number of the republics of the USSR. The Red Army had to be deployed to quell them. Part of this was aggravated by the 1990 congress elections within each republic. Glasnost encouraged nationalism, and this was further fueled in the same year when Article 6 of the Soviet Constitution, which gave the Communist Party the monopoly of power, was repealed. In the Baltic states especially the demand for national sovereignty was strong. Lithuania even went so far as to declare its independence.

In June 1990, an event took place that put a question mark on the future of the Soviet Union. The Russian Republic, which was led by Boris Yeltsin, declared itself a sovereign state, claiming that its own laws took precedence over those of the Soviet Union. Indeed, Yeltsin became the leading spokesman for the reformist movement.

But Gorbachev was well aware of increasing resentment among the traditional hard-line Communists, who were witnessing not only the erosion of their own power, but the increasing danger of a breakup of the Soviet Union. He also recognized that they still controlled many of the key organs of state—the army, internal security forces, and the KGB.

In order to secure his power base, Gorbachev therefore increasingly tried to steer a course that would both satisfy the reformers and placate the hard-liners. He even made hard-liner Gennady Yanaev his deputy, a move that he would later have cause to regret.

In January 1991, sensing that Gorbachev was leaning their way, the hard-liners attempted to reinstate pro-Soviet governments in the Baltic states. This culminated in bloodshed in Vilnius, the Lithuanian capital, after internal security troops occupied the television tower. There was further violence in the Latvian capital, Riga, and in Moscow, too, where thousands of people took to the streets, defying a ban on public demonstrations.

On March 17, 1991, a referendum was held among the 15 republics that made up the USSR about preserving the Union. But only nine of the republics held referenda, the remainder boycotting the exercise. While the majority of people voted for Gorbachev, it was noticeable that cities like Moscow and Leningrad within the Russian Republic voted against him.

Gorbachev therefore had to deal with Yeltsin in order to hold the Union together. Yeltsin, however, was enjoying growing support within the Russian Republic. The Communists within the Russian parliament tried to impeach him. The miners within the republic went on strike and marched on Moscow to demonstrate their support for Yeltsin. When the impeachment vote was taken on March 29, it lost. This consolidated Yeltsin's position, and June 12 he was elected President of the Russian Republic.

Yeltsin quickly took his revenge on the Communists, banning all Party activity within the Republic. Fearful that Yeltsin was about to instigate the final breakup of the Soviet Union, Gorbachev amended the text of the new Union treaty. The aim was for the fifteen republics to sign it on August 20.

It was at this point that the hard-liners decided that they must act against Gorbachev to prevent the complete dismemberment of the Soviet Union and the destruction of the Communist Party. But they were about to take a step which would have totally the opposite result of what they intended.

On the evening of August 18, 1990, KGB troops surrounded Gorbachev's dacha in the Crimea, where he had retired for a short holiday before the new Union treaty was signed. They cut all the telephone lines, therefore isolating Gorbachev from the outside world.

A delegation from the plotters then entered the house and demanded that Gorbachev either join them or hand over to his deputy, Gennady Yanaev. When he refused to do either, he was placed under house arrest.

The following morning the plotters made announcements in the state media that they were taking over control of the Soviet Union. Power was to be vested in the hands of an eight-man emergency council. This was made up of Yanaev as its head, Soviet defense minister Dimitri Yasov, KGB chairman Vladimir Kryuch-kov, Soviet prime minister Valentin Pavlov, interior minister Boris Pugo, and first deputy chairman of the Soviet defense council Oleg Baklanov.

With all the key organs of state under their control, these men appeared to be in total command of the situation and would now be able to rebuild the crumbling edifice that was the Soviet Union. But they had not reckoned with Boris Yeltsin and the mood of the majority of Muscovites.

Yeltsin was warned that the plotters intended to arrest him and went immediately to the Russian parliament building—the White House. Troops surrounded it. The other republics waited to see what would happen next.

Later that morning Yeltsin appeared outside the White House, climbed onto an armored car, and announced to Western TV news teams that Russia was resisting the coup and that he was calling a general strike against Yanaev and his committee. Within hours people were swarming the streets of Moscow and Leningrad. More troops were deployed, and the situation appeared increasingly fraught with danger.

But the generals in charge were split over how to deal with the situation, and their men were loath to fire on fellow Russians. Soldiers and civilians began to intermingle and declared that they would together defend the White House. It became clear that the Army was not going to obey the orders of the committee. It tried to institute a curfew in Moscow, but no notice was taken of it.

The plotters, realizing that the coup had unraveled, looked for ways to save their own skins. On August 21, Boris Yeltsin announced that Yanaev's committee had agreed to allow a Russian government delegation to meet Gorbachev at his Crimean holiday home. Yeltsin then ordered the arrest of Yanaev and his cronies.

The following day a haggard Gorbachev returned to Moscow by air. He was welcomed by Yeltsin and resumed his office as Soviet president. It was, however, only too obvious that the main power had switched to his rescuer, Boris Yeltsin, who was the hero of the hour.

Events now passed out of Gorbachev's hands. The Baltic republics of Estonia, Latvia, and Lithuania immediately declared their independence, which was quickly recognized by Western countries. They were followed by the Ukraine on August 24, Belorussia the following day, and Moldavia on the twenty-seventh.

The Russian parliament gave Yeltsin sweeping powers to reform the economy of the republic and to ban its Communist Party.

Gorbachev tried to salvage some form of union, but it was a lost cause. On December 8, Yeltsin and the newly elected presidents of Ukraine and Belarus, as Belorussia had become known, declared the end of the Soviet Union, forming the Commonwealth of Independent States (CIS) in its place.

Gorbachev finally resigned on Christmas Day, and the white, blue, and red flag of Russia replaced the hammer and sickle over the Kremlin. The Soviet Union was no more.

As for those who engineered the failed coup of August 1991, they were arrested in its immediate aftermath. The one exception was Boris Pugo, who committed suicide on the day after Gorbachev returned to Moscow.

The plotters were arraigned in front of the Russian Supreme Court in April 1992 on charges of high treason against the Soviet Union, which, of course, no longer existed. Their trial, however, came to nothing, with much of the blame being placed on Mikhail Gorbachev for creating the conditions that made a coup feasible.

As for the man that had thwarted the coup—Boris Yeltsin—he, too, faced increasing opposition within Russia. His hard-line monetary policy put the Russian people under increasing economic strain. The Russian parliament turned against him, and matters reached such a pitch that in September 1993 Yeltsin ordered it to be dissolved.

The parliament refused to dissolve itself, and after some violence in Moscow, the deputies locked themselves into the White House. Communists and others then broke through the police cordon to join the deputies. Others seized the main television studios.

On the morning of October 4, Russian military forces surrounded the White House. The deputies and their supporters refused to come out, and the troops opened fire. That evening the defenders of the White House were forced to surrender, and their leaders were arrested. Unlike the 1991 coup, which cost the lives of just three young Russians, there were over 1,000 casualties before the revolt was put down.

In February 1994 Yeltsin, in an attempt to heal political rifts, pardoned not only the Russian parliament leaders, but also the plotters who had tried to overthrow Gorbachev in August 1991.

These men had believed that they could save the Soviet Union and maintain the primacy of the Communist Party. They blundered by failing to recognize that Gorbachev's policies had changed the mood of the majority of the Soviet people. The result was the precipitous breakup of the Union and fall from grace of the Party.

With the dissolution of the Soviet Union came the disintegration of its economy, and attempts to implant monetarist policies on its ruins have led to severe hardship for the peoples of the former Soviet Union. This situation stems in significant part from the failure of that August 1991 coup.

Disaster in the Desert:
Operation Eagle Claw

THERE WERE NOT ONLY QUAKINGS and new vibrations in the Soviet Union and the Eastern bloc. In the Middle East, alliances with East or West became grounds for revolt and upheaval. In Iran, the West-friendly Mohammed Riza Shah Pahlavi, who lived lavishly and controlled a repressive private police force, was growing increasingly unpopular in the face of a rising tide of Islamic fundamentalism. In January 1979, there was a revolution in his country, and he was overthrown by a group of fundamentalists. Ten months later, Iranian students stormed the U.S. Embassy in Tehran and took its employees hostage. Negotiations for the release of the hostages dragged on with no diplomatic solution in sight. Washington therefore conceived a daring plan for their rescue.

Called Operation Eagle Claw, it was put into effect in April 1980, and was to prove disastrous and probably cost Jimmy Carter a second presidential term. The plan was a blunder largely because it was overambitious and much too complicated, and the risk of failure too high.

By the mid-1970s Iran was on course to become the most powerful country in the Middle East. This was the ambition of the Shah, the Iranian head of state. The Shah took advantage of his country's extensive oil revenues to develop its industries. He also used the oil revenues to equip his armed forces with modern Western weapons. Western leaders like President Jimmy Carter and British Prime Minister James Callaghan courted him as both a valuable ally in the Middle East and a means of bolstering their national economies.

But the opulence of the Shah's so-called Peacock Throne did not percolate down to the mass of the Iranian people. While the upper classes enjoyed a lavish lifestyle, the majority of the population struggled to make ends meet. They increasingly resented this and the growing Westernization of their country. Overt opposition was stifled, however, by the Shah's hated secret police—the Savak.

In exile in France was Islamic cleric Ayatollah Khomeini. He wanted to rid Iran of corrupting Western influences and became the focus of agitation against the Shah. Eventually, in January 1979, the country erupted.

The security forces were unable to subdue the ever more violent demonstrations against the regime by fundamentalists, students, and an increasing number of ordinary people. Realizing that he had lost control, the Shah fled the country and took sanctuary in Egypt. On February 1, 1979, Ayatollah Khomeini returned to Iran in triumph.

There was a final three-day street battle against government troops before Khomeini found himself in total control of the country. He moved quickly to establish a fundamentalist regime, making it clear that he intended to reverse Iran's Westernization.

An indication that the previously good relations between the United States and Iran had changed for the worse came on February 14. Iranian students attacked the U.S. Embassy in Tehran but were, however, evicted by the police.

The new Islamic regime demanded the return of the Shah so that he could be put on trial for crimes against the Iranian people. He himself eventually moved to Mexico, suffering from cancer. After some deliberation, President Carter allowed him to visit the U.S. for medical treatment. On October 22, 1979, the Shah flew to New York, where he entered a hospital. This enraged the Iranians, who demanded his extradition. But the United States refused. Subsequent anti-U.S. demonstrations in Tehran culminated on November 4, 1979, when students again attacked the U.S. Embassy. This time the police merely stood by.

All those inside the Embassy were seized as hostages. They would be released only if the United States handed over the Shah. After a two-week impasse, the students released the female and African-American hostages. U.S. hopes rose that the Iranian administration would step in and free the remainder.

But Khomeini himself then appeared at the Embassy and publicly announced his support for the students. He threatened to put the remaining 53 American hostages on trial for espionage. The United States retaliated by freezing all Iranian assets held in America. In addition, an embargo was placed on the import of Iranian oil. None of this had any effect on the regime in Iran, and the result was a deadlock.

Christmas 1979 was a sad time in America. The plight of the hostages was remembered at church services throughout the country. President Carter was conscious, however, that 1980 was a presidential election year. Republican front-runner Ronald Reagan pledged to make America great again. Carter's seeming inability to resolve the hostage crisis was playing into Reagan's hands, and his growing desperation drove him to adopt a military solution to the problem.

• • •

The East African airport of Entebbe in Uganda was the scene of a 1976 operation that provided the inspiration for solving the Iran hostage crisis. Israeli commandos had flown in and carried out a daring rescue of the passengers and crew of an airliner that had been hijacked by German and Palestinian terrorists. It was thought that the same principle could be applied to the U.S. hostages in Tehran.

America had a unit capable of performing this type of mission, called Delta Force, headed up by Colonel Charlie A. Beckwith. Beckwith was a Vietnam Special Forces veteran who had previously served an attachment to the British SAS. He was convinced that Delta Force could rescue the Iranian hostages.

The main problem facing the planners was that America had no military bases within thousands of miles of Tehran. Furthermore, the Iranian capital lies some 400 miles from the nearest approachable sea, the head of the Persian Gulf.

Although the American Sixth Fleet was off the Persian Gulf, to send U.S. ships into it would be seen as an act of extreme provocation by the Iranians. This would put the lives of the hostages at even greater risk.

President Sadat of Egypt provided a partial solution to the problem. America enjoyed good relations with his country. It would therefore be the forward mounting base for Operation Eagle Claw. The troops to be used were Beckwith's Delta Force and a company from the 75th Ranger Regiment based at Fort Benning, Georgia. The Rangers had long specialized in operations behind enemy lines.

The force would deploy to Egypt. While the bulk of the Rangers stayed in Egypt, the remainder were to be flown on by C-141, their destination the island of Masirah off the coast of Oman. From here Lockheed C-130 transports would fly them to a landing site in the desert 200 miles southeast of Tehran. This was code-named Desert One.

Once Desert One had been secured by the small Ranger team, eight CH-53 Sea Stallion helicopters would be flown off the carrier USS *Nimitz* with the Sixth Fleet off the Persian Gulf. The helicopters would fly to Desert One, be refueled, and take Delta Force to a holding point just outside the city of Tehran. Trucks, hired by CIA agents already in the city, would arrive at the holding point and take Delta Force into Tehran, while the helicopters remained at the hideout.

Delta Force would storm the Embassy and the Iranian Foreign Ministry, where three of the hostages were being held, and rescue them. The Sea Stallions would then extract Delta Force and the hostages. While this was taking place the remainder of Ranger company would fly in C-141s from Egypt and seize and secure the airfield at Manzarieh, 40 miles south of Tehran. If possible, the aircraft would actually land, but if there was resistance on the ground the Rangers would parachute in. The helicopters would then fly hostages and Delta Force to this airfield, and the whole lot, including the Rangers, would be extracted by C-141 and flown back to Egypt.

The one proviso made was that unless there was a minimum of six helicopters to fly on from Desert One, the operation had to be aborted.

On April 6, 1980, President Carter was briefed on the plan. He and his advisers appreciated that it was complicated and that the risk of things going wrong was high. But there seemed to be no other feasible option, and Carter's popularity was waning. So he reluctantly agreed that Eagle Claw should be put into effect. Overall supervision of the operation was to be in the hands of General David Jones, Chairman of the Joint Chiefs of Staff. He would report to Secretary of Defense Harold Brown and the President.

The Eagle Claw force arrived in Egypt from America under

a cloak of secrecy on April 21, 1980. After deploying to Masirah Island, Delta Force flew on to Desert One on the evening of the twenty-fourth. The plan now began to unravel.

Once the Iranian hostage rescue force arrived at Desert One, the Rangers set up a block on a nearby road and detained a busload of very shocked Iranians. A fuel tanker arrived. Its driver tried to speed away. The Rangers opened fire and the vehicle burst into flames. This lit up the desert like a beacon. Worse was to follow.

Well to the south, off the Persian Gulf, the carrier *Nimitz* had been a hive of activity. The eight Sea Stallion helicopters duly took off. One had problems with its navigation aids and returned to the carrier, while another developed a mechanical fault and force-landed in the desert. The remaining six helicopters ran into a sandstorm and were 90 minutes late arriving at Desert One.

Colonel Beckwith, who was in charge there, was told that one of the helicopters had leaking hydraulics and could not be used in the operation. He informed Washington and stated that he would have to abort the operation because he now had less than the stipulated minimum of six helicopters. He was told to carry on with the remaining five, but refused. President Carter then approved a withdrawal, but during the evacuation, in the dead of night, a helicopter collided with a C-130 transport plane loaded with fuel. A fiery explosion ensued and eight Americans were killed.

The disaster at Desert One meant that the Rangers detailed to secure the airfield near Tehran never left Egypt. The Iranians were quickly on the scene at Desert One. At dawn on the following day they arrived in force to inspect and film the site. The wreckage of the C-130 and the Sea Stallion especially demonstrated the degree of the American blunder.

The Iranians were jubilant at the American failure, and

quick to extract maximum propaganda value from it, publicly displaying items found at Desert One. A deeply humiliated President Carter tried to explain the operation away, but there was little he could say to save face. The operation had been an unmitigated disaster. An overly complicated and ambitious plan, and a lack of coordination, were blunders that made the prospects of success slim from the outset. Eagle Claw should never have been allowed to go ahead. The hostages remained in Tehran, and Jimmy Carter's approval rating with Americans continued to slip.

Despite the failure of Eagle Claw, a new plan was drawn up involving a C-130 fitted with rockets to enable it to land and take off almost like a helicopter. The idea was that Delta Force would be flown in to a sports stadium in Tehran. After the hostages had been rescued, the C-130 would lift off for freedom. But during trials the C-130 crashed. A second was modified in the same way, but was never deployed because the hostage crisis was finally about to end.

On July 27, 1980, the Shah of Iran died in Cairo. It had been demands for his return to Iran that had precipitated the hostage crisis. Now that he was dead, there were hopes in Washington that a solution could be found. Desert Claw, however, had made the Iranians even more intransigent. The Iranian stance impacted on the presidential election that November. Ronald Reagan emerged as the clear winner.

Carter still hoped to get the hostages released before he finally left office in January. He agreed to unfreeze Iranian assets in the USA and lift the oil embargo. The Iranians became more conciliatory, but the hostages remained in Tehran. On January 20, 1981, Ronald Reagan was officially inaugurated as the fortieth president of the United States. Literally minutes after he had been sworn in, news came through that the hostages had been put on a plane bound for Algeria. They were then flown to a U.S. base in Germany.

Finally, on January 31, 1981, 445 days after they had first been seized, the 53 hostages arrived back in America to a tumultuous welcome. They were taken in a motor cavalcade to the White House, where the newly installed President Ronald Reagan was there to greet them. It was an auspicious start to his administration.

As for Jimmy Carter, his failure to achieve a second term at the White House was largely due to his failure to solve the Iranian hostage crisis. Eagle Claw exacerbated the situation. And yet the ascension of the conservative, hawkish Reagan to the presidency seemed in other ways inevitable, and proved crucial to the eventual ending of the Cold War. Still, Eagle Claw, by any measure, was a dreadful and humiliating moment in American military history.

The Invasion of Kuwait

UNTIL THE END OF THE Cold War, the post-1945 international community found it difficult to act against naked aggression. The U.N. was too often a battleground between the rival camps, and exercise of the veto in the Security Council meant that little positive action could be taken, except to condemn. When the Cold War ended in 1989–90, there was a new determination to reduce conflict. One who did not realize this was Saddam Hussein of Iraq when he invaded Kuwait in August 1991. His miscalculation over the reaction of the international community was a grave blunder, and one that resulted in much suffering for the Iraqi people. Old Cold War alliances might have protected him from this. But those days were over.

Saddam himself had spent time in both prison and exile as a young man because of his revolutionary activities. In 1968 he helped lead a successful coup that established the Baathist Party in control of Iraq. In 1979 he became head of state and quickly exerted an iron grip on the country. He displayed his ruthlessness in using poison gas to put down a Kurdish rebellion and executing those whom he believed stood in his way. In 1980 he took his country to war against neighboring Iran. This was both to secure his position and prevent the import of Islamic fundamentalism. It was a costly and largely inconclusive conflict that lasted for eight years.

At the end of the war he renewed his persecution of the Kurds, using his oil revenues to buy arms from both East and West. But he was also turning his eyes to his small southern and oil-rich neighbor, Kuwait. He had three demands—control of two islands to give him better access to the Persian Gulf, concessions on loans made by Kuwait during the Iran-Iraq war, and higher oil prices so that he could make good the costs of this war. Since Kuwait was supported by the West, and there was general disillusion in the Middle East with this influence, Saddam thought that he would be supported by much of the Arab world.

Kuwait refused to concede to Saddam's demands, and President Mubarak of Egypt offered to mediate. No sooner had the offer been rejected than, on August 2, 1991, Iraqi forces invaded Kuwait and occupied it. If Saddam thought that the world would sit idly by, he was mistaken. Not only was there a series of forceful United Nations resolutions, but Saudi Arabia, fearing invasion by Iraq, agreed to allow Western forces to deploy on her territory. Furthermore, Arab nations, including Egypt and Syria, joined the U.S.-led coalition forces.

Throughout the next few months, during the massive military buildup in Saudi Arabia, Saddam tried numerous ploys to weaken the Coalition's resolve. This included the holding of Western citizens as a human shield, and attempts to split the Coalition. They all failed, and on January 17, 1991, Desert Shield became Desert Storm. The six-week air campaign that followed destroyed much of Iraq's communications. The subsequent four-day ground campaign destroyed the Iraqi forces in Kuwait, and restrictions imposed on Iraq after the cease-fire caused much suffering among his people. This was especially true in the extreme south of the country, where Shi'ites rose against the regime, and in the north, where Kurds did the same. Both were crushed. Saddam, however, paid little penalty for the blunders that had brought his country to the brink of total ruin. But understanding why Saddam Hussein made his move for Kuwait and how he was opposed involves a look back at his path to power, and a view, too, of how complicated are the shifting alliances of the twentieth century.

Until the late 1950s Iraq had been a friend of the West, especially of Britain, which had administered the country as a League of Nations mandate after World War I. However, in July 1958 there was a sudden and bloody coup d'état led by General Karim Kassem in which King Faisal and the Crown Prince of Iraq were killed. The country became a republic.

The previous year Kassem had survived an attempt on his life by a group of young Iraqis who were members of the Ba'ath Party, which advocated the formation of a single secular Arab nation in the Middle East. Among them was a student, Saddam Hussein, who was wounded. He managed, however, to escape to Syria and then Egypt.

In 1963 Kassem was overthrown, the Ba'athists took power in Iraq, and Saddam returned to Baghdad University to study law. But the president, Colonel Abdul Salam Arif, did not like the extremism of the Ba'athist government and, with help from the Army, removed it from power. The following year he arrested some party members, including Saddam Hussein, who later escaped and helped to reform the Ba'athist Party.

The military ruled Iraq for the next five years, refusing to hold elections. The Ba'ath Party used this to gain popular support, and allied itself to other political parties. In July 1968 they overthrew the president, now Arif's brother. The Ba'athists quickly gained total control and set up the Revolutionary Command Council to run the country.

While General Ahmed Hassan al-Bakr headed the Council, increasingly the real power fell into the hands of Saddam Hussein. It was he who directed the nationalization of Iraq's oil industry in the early 1970s, as well as directing Iraq's foreign policy. By 1979 Saddam controlled the country, and when al-Bakr resigned that year he took over as both chairman of the Revolutionary Command Council and prime minister.

Saddam Hussein's ambition was for Iraq to supplant Egypt as the leading country in the Arab world and to dominate the oil-rich Persian Gulf. To ward off threats against his position he set up an extensive secret police network. Furthermore, he projected himself to the Iraqi people to such an extent that he quickly became a national hero.

Saddam Hussein was, however, about to embroil his country in a long and costly war. For the past few years Iraq had been involved in border disputes with neighboring Iran. Tensions were aggravated by Ayatollah Khomeini's fundamentalist revolution, which had overthrown the Shah. Khomeini vowed to export his brand of extreme Islamism, and Iraq, with its largely secular regime, was a target.

To preempt this Saddam's forces invaded Iran, believing that the recent revolution had totally disorganized its armed forces. They enjoyed initial success, but the Iranians mounted a counter-offensive and drove them back. A bloody stalemate ensued.

The Iranians later cooperated with the Kurds in northern Iraq, who had long been agitating for independence. Saddam re-taliated with great ruthlessness, employing chemical weapons against the Kurds. Yet, in spite of this, he had the support of both the Soviet Union and Western countries, which supplied him with weapons, considering him a lesser evil to the fundamentalist regime in Iran. The war, however, dragged on until 1988, with no gain to either side. Not until 1990, after two U.N.-sponsored conferences, did both sides settle their differences. But Saddam's ambition to make his country the leading state in the Middle East was by no means diminished, and he was about to commit an even worse blunder than the eventually pointless eight years of war with Iran.

Although Iraq's economy had suffered grievously from the conflict with Iran, Saddam continued to build up his armed forces, which were equipped with sophisticated Soviet and Western weaponry. He had been lent enormous sums of money by other Arab countries—notably Saudi Arabia and Kuwait—to fight his war against Iranian fundamentalism. He did not expect to have to pay it back. But they insisted.

Saddam also had his eye on two islands close to the head of the Persian Gulf which were owned by Kuwait. He wanted to possess these to give him better access to the Gulf. Furthermore, he wanted higher oil prices to help defray the costs of the war with Iran, and he believed that Kuwait was a major instigator in keeping them low. Kuwait itself was a friend of the West, and Saddam believed that much of the Arab world resented this and would back him in his demands.

Kuwait refused to concede any of Saddam's demands. Toward the end of July 1990 President Mubarak of Egypt offered to mediate. Talks took place at Jidda, Saudi Arabia, on July 31. Saddam had, however, already made up his mind. The following day his delegation walked out of the talks.

On August 2, 1990, Iraqi forces invaded Kuwait and occupied it. But If Saddam thought that the world would stand idly by and allow him to annex his small next-door neighbor, he was to be gravely mistaken.

The first international reaction to Saddam Hussein's seizure of Kuwait was a series of forceful U.N. resolutions condemning his action and imposing a strict trade embargo. Saddam probably expected this, but the next step certainly took him by surprise. Saudi Arabia, fearing invasion by Iraq, quickly agreed to allow Western forces to deploy on her territory. Bearing in mind the strict Islamic law which prevailed in the country, this was an unexpected step in Saddam's eyes.

Other Arab nations also joined the U.S.-led Coalition that was forming. It was not surprising that Egypt, which also enjoyed good relations with the West, should do so. But Syria, which had long been suspicious of the West, also chose to join.

The Iraqi people soon began to feel the effects of the economic embargo, which was soon enforced by a strict naval blockade in the Persian Gulf. Only strictly humanitarian items were allowed through, and Iraq was unable to export any oil.

Saddam tried numerous ploys to weaken the Coalition's resolve. One tactic was the holding of Western hostages and displaying them on television. This ploy merely led to even greater international condemnation, and Saddam eventually realized that it would be expedient to release them.

He also played for time by indicating that he might be prepared to withdraw from Kuwait. He also tried to split the former Soviet Union from the Western powers. He could not, however, stop the military buildup in Saudi Arabia from continuing, and the Coalition's strategy turned from defense to preparing for an attack on the Iraqi forces in Kuwait.

In the very early hours of January 17, 1991, the Coalition unleashed Operation Desert Storm. The ensuing five-week air campaign that followed destroyed much of Iraq's communications, including bridges and telephone links. The lot of the Iraqi people became even harder. For the Iraqi conscripts in Kuwait the situation was even worse.

Saddam now performed a new trick. He launched Scud missile attacks against Israel, hoping that this would provoke Israeli retaliation and make the Arab members of the Coalition withdraw from it. Luckily, the Americans had a new, highly efficient air-defense missile system—Patriot. Batteries of these weapons were hastily deployed to Israel, which was persuaded to stay out of the conflict.

Realizing that he was cornered, Saddam now set the Kuwaiti oil fields alight. He also released oil into the Persian Gulf. These measures caused a potentially grave ecological crisis and blackened Saddam's international reputation still further. The ground assault into Kuwait was launched on Sunday, February 24, 1991. In the space of just four days the already shaken Iraqi forces were driven out of Kuwait. Saddam's generals were forced to accept defeat.

In the immediate aftermath of the war it seemed as though Saddam Hussein's regime might be toppled. The Shi'ites in southern Iraq rose in rebellion. In the north of the country the Kurds, too, took advantage of the Iraqi defeat in Kuwait. But the Coalition forces had only the limited mandate to liberate Kuwait and quickly withdrew those forces which had reached Iraqi territory at the end of the hostilities. In any event, if they had embarked on operations inside Iraq, it is likely that the Arab members of the Coalition would have withdrawn from it.

Consequently, Saddam was able to put down the revolt in the south. He also turned on the Kurds, driving them out of many of their villages. All the Coalition could do was to police laid-down Iraqi "no fly" zones in the north and south of the country. It also established so-called "safe havens" for the Kurdish refugees.

Since 1991 the United Nations has concentrated on removing Saddam's nuclear, chemical, and biological warfare capability through the deployment of inspection teams. While these had some success, they were often thwarted by Iraqi officials and were withdrawn at the end of 1998.

Cruise missile strikes have also been launched from time to time in an attempt to bring Saddam to heel. The "no fly" zones have been maintained, but from late 1998 the Iraqis increasingly challenged them, especially through locking on to Allied aircraft with their radar. Throughout this time the economic sanctions were maintained, with Iraq only being allowed to export oil in return for humanitarian goods.

Saddam Hussein blundered badly when he invaded Kuwait in August 1990 by failing to recognize the new international climate in the immediate aftermath of the end of the Cold War. Yet such was his grip over Iraq that he remained in power. It is not he but his people who have suffered as a result. It is often the way, and as we go to press, the Serbian strongman Slobodan Milosevic is testing the resolve of post-Cold War alliances. Again, there is suffering, blundering, and yet these things work toward new understandings. As always, the world hopes that new understandings will bring lasting peace.

Index